Mary Green

Food products of the world

Sixth Edition

Mary Green

Food products of the world
Sixth Edition

ISBN/EAN: 9783337201364

Printed in Europe, USA, Canada, Australia, Japan

Cover: Foto ©Andreas Hilbeck / pixelio.de

More available books at **www.hansebooks.com**

FOOD PRODUCTS

OF

THE WORLD

BY MARY E. GREEN, M. D.

MEMBER OF THE AMERICAN MEDICAL ASSOCIATION.
MEMBER OF THE JURY OF AWARDS ON FOOD
PRODUCTS, WORLD'S COLUMBIAN
EXPOSITION.

SIXTH EDITION

CHICAGO
THE HOTEL WORLD

To my friend and teacher,

MISS JULIET CORSON,

THE FIRST WOMAN IN AMERICA TO ELEVATE COOKERY TO THE
DIGNITY OF A SCIENCE AND THE BEAUTY OF AN ART,
THIS BOOK IS DEDICATED
BY THE AUTHOR.

INTRODUCTION.

There is no more important factor in the successful conduct of the household than a knowledge of the composition of foods and their dietetic value, and no greater aid to the housewife in this direction has ever before been published.

The working housekeeper is unconsciously a practical chemist, for unless she has some knowledge of the substances which she combines in various dishes she may produce some poor results from excellent materials. There is quite a goodly aggregate of information floating through the culinary air; this cook knows a little, that one, a bit more; and the better a cook is the less she is likely to know about the chemistry of foods. She may know that a little sugar or vinegar added to a soup or sauce that is too salt will modify the taste, but she probably does not know the reason why. She never has time to learn why things result as they do, but must learn from her more intelligent compeers or from her mistress just such facts as are stated in this book concerning the properties of foods and their nutritive value. In this respect this book may become a mine of knowledge to the cook and an incentive to better work.

To the average half-trained cooking teacher it will indeed be useful, supplying her with the practical knowledge not found in other text books, for I do not know of one which covers the ground so thoroughly as this. Written by a woman who possesses a medical and chemical knowledge of foods, their properties and their relation to health, and who is also a skilled housewife, the value of the book is self evident.

Dr. Green has a professional record that many men might envy. She has conducted a successful practice ever since her graduation from the Woman's Medical College in Philadelphia in 1868, has long been a member of the American Medical Association, and was unanimously chosen to serve upon the Jury of Awards on Food Products at the World's Columbian Exposition. I am glad that I had the advantage of being associated with her in the work of judging food products at the World's Fair. Dr. Green's scientific record, her practical experience in the art of alimentation, her professional application of the science of dietetics to the emergencies of every day life, have wonderfully fitted her for the work she has undertaken in this book.

No public library is complete without this book; no housekeeper can afford to be without it; no cook capable of comprehending what she reads can fail to receive great benefit from its study. It should be indispensable to the great army of club women, scattered all over this broad land, who are just now beginning to study housekeeping and the science of foods.

Juliet Corson.

PREFACE.

The subject matter in this book was originally published in a series of magazine articles begun just after the close of the World's Columbian Exposition. The fact that at the Exposition was gathered the most complete and cosmopolitan array of food products ever displayed is sufficient apology for the frequent allusions made to these exhibits throughout the book.

In some instances seemingly undue importance has been given to the consideration of certain foods, namely, condiments, vegetable oils, and mushrooms. In regard to condiments the literature extant is both scanty and inaccessible, notwithstanding the fact that they are deemed a necessity in every household and have been, owing to their antiseptic and aromatic properities, valuable articles of culinary use since the earliest of historic periods. In no country are vegetable oils superior to those of the United States produced, and Americans are but slowly learning their value for culinary and table use; while mushrooms, because of their high nutritive value and the ease with which they may be cultivated, deserve to rank among our staple foods.

Effort has been made to so demonstrate the hygienic and nutritive values of foods that the book may meet the needs of that large body of housekeeping women who have neither time nor sufficient energy to delve into purely scientific works on this subject and yet who feel that a knowledge of food values is indispensable in the preparation of dietaries for their families. The housekeeper who understands nothing of the chemical processes that occur in the sanctuary called a kitchen is simply a slave to her receipt book. The housekeeper who does, while giving due honor to the writers of recipes, may in emergencies become wholly independent of them.

For valuable aid in the preparation of this work I wish to acknowledge my indebtedness to the writings of Dr. Edward Smith, Pavy, Sir Henry Thompson, Whitehead, Goodfellow, Dr. Doran, Theodore Childs, Johnston, Youmans, and W. O. Atwater.

M. E. G.

CONTENTS.

CHAPTER XIII.

CHAPTER XIV.

CHAPTER XV.

CHAPTER XVI.

CHAPTER XVII.

CHAPTER XVIII.

CHAPTER XIX.

CHAPTER XX.

CHAPTER XXI.

CHAPTER XXII.

CHAPTER XXIII.

CHAPTER XXIV.

CONTENTS.

CHAPTER XXV.

FOOD PRODUCTS OF THE WORLD.

CHAPTER I.

THE IMPORTANCE OF AGRICULTURE AND FOOD PRODUCTION.

HE great achievement of the minds who conceived, builded and gave to the people the World's Columbian Exposition was both the magnitude of the whole project and its perfection. In scope it was limit-defying and yet of wonderful completeness. The large things were perfect and right. As in the sphinxes and portrait-statues of Egypt, the only sacrifices made were those of detail, never those of proportion. The artists and builders of the nineteenth century learned well these principles, dim though they appear in the shadowy perspective of the past, and if detail has been subordinated to mass or here and there lost sight of, the value of the whole has been but slightly reduced. This exposition will remain as the most perfect lesson ever written for the learning of man prior to the dawn of the twentieth century. Books are made and being made; the press of this whole land has been and still is enlisted in the service of the thought awakened. The Art Gallery has been the free lance of scores of writers; the Liberal Arts building the mine and treasure-house of a universe of artisans; woman has been discovered, re-discovered and then discovered again; Izaak Walton, revivified, has been set up as the deity of the Fisheries building; the oil of sentiment, full measure, has been poured upon the stormy waters of far-away La Rabida; the sea, earth and air have verily given up their secrets and their deities of trident and thunder-bolt are with us again.

On account of this immensity and completeness certain exhibits at the great fair were more popular than others, while even a casual visitor could not fail to observe that some received less attention than their absolute merit warranted. This was, usually, because the importance of these exhibits was too lightly estimated, or because their place, with its meed of honor, was not fully established in our world of industry. Perhaps on this latter account one building received somewhat less than its share of appreciation, although its exhibits have been pronounced by authorities as relatively more complete than any on the grounds. I refer to the Agricultural building. Common-place? Perhaps, perhaps not. The majority of exposition visitors, limited in point of time and matter of money, rushed headlong through exhibits, pell-mell, helter-skelter, attracted chiefly by whatever savored of sentimentalism, amusement and excitement. What could not be described by one of these terms was quite likely to be set down as common-place, and for this reason we heard comparatively little of our agricultural and food exhibition. Though a legion of visitors, interested and amazed, passed through the aisles of the Agricultural building during the summer of 1893 and examined the exhibits, food or food production unfortunately is not a fad and its champions are strangely silent. The faddists dwell now-a-days in the realms of religion, art and reform, unmindful of the necessity of agricultural interest and thankless for the labor of those who, through the production, preservation and scientific preparation of food, have made possible our wealth of science, literature and art. As the Agricultural building stood, during those months of enchantment, immense, strong, un-compromising, facing the inlet waters of beautiful Lake Michigan and the statue of the Republic, bridging the distance between the promise of higher science and artisanship as seen in the Liberal Arts building, and the relics of aboriginal agriculture and cookery in the Anthropological building on the south, so stands the fact of agriculture to-day in our national economy. As the building stood

there, continuing with its columned walls the colonnade over the
gateway of the lake, it formed part of the peristyle, and we remember that now no less than in the days of the Greeks did the peristyle enshrine a deity; theirs a god of power, ours a deity of liberty,
whose being is progress and whose spirit, law. As we saw the walls
of this building encircled by figures, bearing in their outstretched
arms the signs of the zodiac, we thought again of our agricultural
interests, encircled by the heavens and dependent upon their
moods and seasons for prosperity. As this building stood, proud,
ornamented with groups of sculpture, garlanded with flowers and
decorated with pastoral scenes that recall the husbandry of Virgil,
so from our food production spring the beauty and grace of our
present civilization. Without the productiveness of agriculture
our arts and industries could not exist. Without this, perfected by
science and re-
fined by method,
the highest intel-
lectual achieve-
ments were impos-
sible. Agriculture,
the science of
food - production,
is the broad head-
land upon which
the possibilities and successes
of the world to-day are an-
chored, a headland rocky and
stubbornly assertive, perhaps,
but overgrown with flowers
and from which are springing
the forests and giant oaks of
the ages to come.

In walking through the
corridors of this Agricultural
building, the earth and its
nations seem drawn up for
martial review. They chal-
lenge us and each other, throwing down the gauntlet with as
sturdy a pride as if it would not be taken up sooner or later in our
own versatile America. The history of the older nations, the cus-

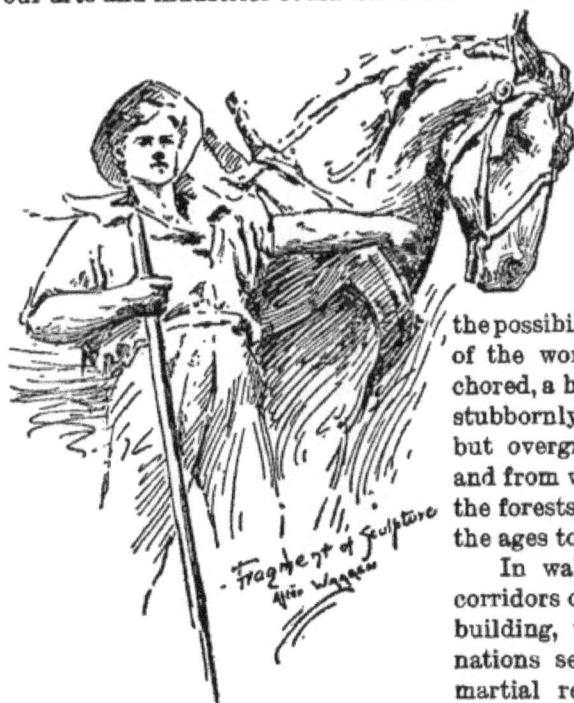

- Fragment of Sculpture
Attic Waggon

2

toms of the new, the social status of all, are revealed as satisfactorily by exhibited food products as by any other means. How do we know that Greece is fallen, that the days of Roman glory are past and that Egypt is to-day only a nation of donkey-boys? By the nature of their food exhibits. Sardines and sausages were sent from the land of the Capitoline, tobacco from Thessaly and classic Thermopolæ; from Egypt, from the land of the Ptolemies and Osiris, nothing but silence. Thus the tales are told.

Spain, the land of Isabella and Columbus, we see to-day as the great exporting bureau of choicest olive oil and sardines. France, the haven of domestic thrift, comes into view as the home of the mushroom and truffle. England and Scotland contribute superior canned meats and fish, preserves and condiments. Switzerland, the Netherlands and the Scandinavian countries become better known to us and each other by their dairy products. Russia sends grains, sugars and liquors; Italy cereals, sugars, macaroni and pastes. The countries of the far East and the tropics are no less well represented, for here we see the coffee of Arabia, Java and Liberia, the latter exceptionally fine. There is exhibited tea of all grades from Japan and Ceylon, mate from Brazil and Paraguay, chocolate—ah, such chocolate!—from the Isle of Trinidad, and liquors from lands galore. Siam, the country of bamboo, rice and bananas, sends preserved fruits, superior in some respects to any others on exhibition. India, Persia, Johore, Porto Rico, Jamaica with its sugars and rum, Orange Free State with its display of fruits, ostrich feathers and diamonds, British Guiana with its sugars, preserves and famous Demarara bitters, Trinidad, the land of asphalt and the cocoa-bean, Curaçoa, famous for its native *liqueur*,—all jostle each other in the democratic medley of an exhibition building. The malt and sausages of Frankfurt, the mineral waters of Carlsbad, stand in friendly proximity to the limes, dates and olives of Tunis; the bonbons and preserves of Uruguay hobnob with the wool and canned mutton of Australia, and at each turn we come upon some of our own American products, so varied, interesting and profuse.

Nothing equaling the agricultural displays of our states and territories was ever seen before. The wheat lands of Canada and our own great west sent their contribution in cereals of superior quality and statistics of immense production. Corn was there in all its glory of waving leaf and tassel as decoration upon the booths and, in its richness of yellow and white, as the exhibit proper. The fruit belts of California, of our middle states, of the south and east, were represented by such displays as would have graced the banquet board of an Epicurus. Apples, pears, plums of royal purple and gold were there, grapes worthy to crown the temples of a Bacchus, and oranges from the west and south, the golden apples of our own Hesperides. The forests of New York, the New England states, Kansas, Michigan, Ohio and Canada, sent their product in the form of golden maple syrup and sugar, the extensive sugar-beet industry of Nebraska contributed its share of sweetness, there were vegetables of all kinds and notably excellent specimens of canned fruits, pickles, jellies and preserves.

The great packing houses sent their quota of meat—the astonishment of foreign nations and a stimulus to an industry already far-reaching and immense. We are reminded of our great Texas pastures, of the sheep ranches of Montana and the west, of the game, big and little, from the Rockies, of our prolific lakes and rivers from the "Big Sea Water" to the tiny mountain trout stream which may be spanned with a step. All these pass before the mind of a thinking visitor and he feels that it is a matter of time rather than climate when in this immense country of the west the best of the agricultural products of all lands will be gathered. No other country possesses so great a variety of climate, and when our arid land is reclaimed by irrigation and our wealth and multitude of resources cease to be wasted, it is not too much to promise that all our lands instead of a tiny park will merit the title, "Garden of the Gods." For America picks up the gauntlet that the other nations throw down and assimilates their products to a wonderful degree, as it does their people.

No opportunity for so complete and perfect a study of the food products of the world has ever been given to the people before. Agriculture and food production, preparation and serving are arriving at last to a vantage ground of their own. They are coming to be recognized as the broad foundation upon which the social and intellectual superstructure of our civilization is based and upon which the quality of our arts and higher industries largely depend.

CHAPTER II.

THE first and chief demand made by aboriginal man upon the earth and the elements about him was for food; the first, last and most particular requirement of his civilized brother to-day still is that food be supplied him. This is the great common ground on which stand both savage and philosopher. The primitive man, we will suppose, for he left neither legend nor written records to tell us, ate his food at all hours and on all occasions when it was to be procured, when he was hungry, and as there was no positive assurance of a next meal, when satiated as well. To him this food was shelter, companionship and warmth. The starches, sugars and fats which it contained supplied fuel to the machinery of his body, giving him warmth and making possible great activity. The flesh-forming elements of his food furnished him with strength and restored the wastes of an active vitality. He ate, it is probable, whatever of meat he could procure and was guided in the selection of non-poisonous herbs and vegetables by the preferences of the animals which he observed.

The great difference at this stage between man and the animal, for in selection and appropriation their food was much the same, lay in the fact of man's cookery. One author has defined man as a cooking animal, and the comparison is apt. Primitive man, though at first he ate his food raw, very soon came to improve its flavor by the application of heat, and the next step, after fashioning a weapon with which to kill his game, was the moulding of a piece of mud or clay into a vessel for the cooking of it. At first his food may have been cooked by roasting it directly over the flame, by burying it beneath the coals, or later by boiling it in a pot. He then added herbs and aromatic berries for flavoring and, putting succulent roots into the pot, made a savory stew. Again, by the addition of more liquid and longer cooking a soup, excellent, I have no doubt, was the result. And all the invention of modern cookery has been unable to improve in point of healthfulness, nutrition and economy, upon t h e method used by aboriginal man, the slow boiling of meat in a clay pot over a fire. The whole science of cookery is coming back at last to something like that one simple process, excepting in cases where nutritious and economical diet is not the thing demanded. People in

Cliff-dwellers' Cooking Pots.

this age require composite cookery and among certain classes the demands of a cloyed sense and a satiated appetite have created most elaborate and useless dishes.

Now for health's sake we are awakening to the value of primitive methods again. We are suddenly discovering that a pot of clay, the outer surface of which is roughened, requires less heat and retains it more easily than if of smooth surface. This fact we publish as of special benefit to dwellers in high altitudes. But we presently learn that archæologists are bringing to light similar pots used three, perhaps five thousand years ago by the cliff-dwellers of Colorado, and our self-complacency silently steals away. The Boston baked bean pot is almost duplicated by those found in the mummy pits of Ancon, Peru, and, if their ghastly proximity to lower maxillary bones, femurs and skulls could be forgotten, it is easy to imagine that beans cooked in them would have a flavor superior to those cooked in the well-cured pots of antipodal Boston. The same simple and perfect methods of cookery are used by all primitive peoples, whether of past ages or of to-day, as the excavated burial mounds of America, of England and of other countries go to prove by means of the cooking utensils found in them. The uncivilized nations of to-day can teach us many a needed lesson wherever they may be visited, be they the Indians of North or South America, the savages of the South Sea Islands, or the Savannah and Arrawac tribes of British Guiana. The cooking vessels of aboriginal nations are of no small value to the archæologist in determining the plane of civilization upon which these peoples rested, and are important links in the chain of development whose last link compasses the modern science, or better, the modern art of cookery. The elaboration of dishes, often to a senseless and unhealthful degree, is peculiar to what we term civilized man. Food, and, usually, whether it can be afforded or not, elaborate food is to-day our main requirement. Our cooks, despots that many of them often are, receive as great salaries as our statesmen, and the mysteries of certain combinations of foods are guarded as carefully by the chefs who possess them as ever were the secrets of an imperial regime.

Food, to arrive at a definition, is that substance which is capable of sustaining an organism in a state of health and is that which makes possible the continuing existence of all forms of life, both animal and vegetable. In its relation to the human body, food is the means by which the waste of the system is restored, its energies made effective and a healthy condition maintained. Neither one food nor a small number, merely, is sufficient to preserve health for any length of time. As many elements are demanded by the system, more than a limited number of foods are required. Some foods contain a large proportion of the flesh-forming elements, others a greater proportion of elements which are starchy or heat-producing.

One of the most valuable contributions of science to the non-scientific world has been the analyses made of our food products. The results of such investigation are continually changing their vantage ground and the last score of years has recognized principles and proven theories that were formerly discredited or

From Mummy Pits of Peru.

unknown. The object of these analyses has been to determine the proportion of nutrient and non-nutrient elements in all foods, and by the aid of this knowledge to better our systems of diet.

· Foods are considered in these articles in a purely objective sense and are treated in much the same unpretentious way in which they were exhibited at the Fair. Not their properties but the foods themselves are classified; as simply, perhaps unscientifically, as they were shown by the exhibitors, ranged in rows upon shelves, placed in show cases, hung on hooks or stuffed into bags and boxes. These foods are most naturally classified, therefore, as follows: meats (fresh and preserved), poultry and game, fish and sea-foods, butter, butterine and cheese, vegetables, cereals (natural and prepared forms), sugars, fruits, condiments, and beverages. However, a discussion of these foods to be of any value must rest upon a scientific classification, one considering their properties. In this way their value to the human economy will be more easily considered and the treatment of them will be of more practical use than otherwise. By such means alone may the relative nutrition of certain foods be established and their value determined.

Just at this point it may be of interest to compare two or three of these classifications of food properties, all valuable, though established on widely differing bases. Dunglison, an accepted medical authority, classifies foods, in regard to their properties, as follows: (1) Feculaceous or starchy (potato, cereals, legumes); (2) mucilaginous (carrot, beet, etc.); (3) saccharine (sugar, raisin, etc.); (4) acidulous (orange, currant, etc.); (5) oleaginous and fatty (cocoa, olive and almond oils, animal fat, butter, etc.); (6) caseous (milk, cheese); (7) gelatinous (tendon, skin, cellular texture, etc.); (8) albuminous (brain, nerve, eggs, etc.); (9) fibrinous (flesh and blood). Dr. Prout simplified this lengthy analysis into four divisions: the aqueous or watery, saccharine or sweet, oleaginous or oily, and albuminous, as white of egg. Liebig still further simplified and changed this, dividing foods into two great classes: the nitrogenized or plastic elements of nutrition, comprising vegetable fibrin, vegetable albumin, vegetable casein, flesh and blood; and the non-nitrogenized elements, or those of respiration, comprising fat, starch, gum, cane sugar, grape sugar, sugar of milk, pectin (vegetable jelly), bassorin (a starchy substance), wine, beer and spirits. The former class furnish nutrition to organized tissue, while the latter, Liebig considered, are burnt in respiration, furnishing heat.

The chief point of difference between these and that classification which has finally come to be considered authoritative is the recognition of a substance called protein. The existence of this

substance was for many years disputed. Webster's dictionary of
1877 says of it: "The theory of Mulder is doubted and denied by
many chemists, and also the existence of protein as a distinct substance;" and a quotation from Gregory, following the definition,
reads, "The theory of protein cannot be maintained." However, it
is now recognized as the basic element of animal and vegetable
fibrin, albumin, casein and gluten. The word itself is derived from
the Greek verb, meaning "I take first rank;" and is found in the
lean or muscular part of meat, the white of egg, in cheese, and in
wheat, in the latter being the gluten which is developed in the
kneading of dough and which is specially valuable in the manufacture of macaroni. Protein is also contained in the "stock" used for
soups, being the gelatinous substance extracted from bone and
tendon by boiling them. The sugars and starches together, which are
closely allied in chemical composition, are designated by latest
authority carbohydrates, so called because they are composed of
carbon atoms, mingled with a variable proportion of hydrogen and
oxygen atoms. The most common of these are the granulated sugar
(seen upon our tables) and the starch used in the kitchen for cookery
and in the laundry. The granulated sugar belongs to a large group
called cane-sugars, comprising the products of the sugar-cane, the
sugar-beet, the sugar-maple, honey, the sugar of milk and a crystalline sugar, obtained from starch, called malt. The sugar of the
grape and other fruits and that called dextrose, obtained from
starch (usually corn-starch) by the action of warmth and acids, are
members of the glucose group of carbohydrates. Starch is the
principal member of the cellulose group, so called because the
starch granules are contained in a cellular structure (also starchy
in composition) called cellulose. Gum, a vegetable substance, is
another of the carbohydrates as is also dextrine, a substance
obtained from starch by means of dilute acids and which forms the
basis of an excellent mucilage, "the only kind fit for an editor's
desk." The oils and fats form another group and the properties
remaining are water and mineral matters. Of the latter, phosphate
of lime and chloride of sodium, as our common salt is known chemically, are the most important.

The following table is in a convenient form for reference and
may be considered authoritative until modified, as all former ones
have been, by subsequent discoveries. It is based upon the latest
investigations of science, notably those made at various experi-

mental stations, located in the United States under the auspices of the government:

I. **PROTEIN**
- Albuminoids
  - Myosin (lean) of meat.
  - Albumin of egg, blood, etc.
  - Casein of cheese.
  - Gluten of wheat, peas, beans, etc.
- Gelatinoids
  - Ossein (tissue) of bone.
  - Collagen (glutinous basis) of tendon.
- Meat extractives.

II. **CARBOHYDRATES**
- Cane-sugar group
  - *Sucrose* or cane-sugar
    - Sugar beet,
    - Sugar maple,
    - Date-palm,
    - Sorghum,
    - Honey, etc.
  - *Lactose* or milk-sugar, containing galactose.
  - *Maltose* or malt-sugar.
- Glucose group
  - *Dextrose* or grape sugar.
  - *Levulose* or fruit sugar.
  - *Galactose* or milk sugar.
- Cellulose group
  - Starch.
  - Dextrine (obtained from starch).
  - Gum.
  - Cellulose or woody fibre of plants.

III. **FATS**
- Fats of meat.
- Oils of milk, butter, olive, nuts, vegetables (wheat, cotton seed, etc.).

IV. **MINERALS**
- Chloride of sodium (salt).
- Calcium phosphate (phosphate of lime) and others.

V. **WATER.**

The analysis given is self-explanatory and indicates at a glance the properties of all those food substances which make for the health and activity of the human system. Those possessing protein as a basic element are useful in restoring the wastes of the system and forming the basis of muscular and skin tissue. The fats and carbohydrates (sugars and starches) furnish heat and a certain amount of energy, and if more are taken into the system than are daily consumed, the surplus passes off as waste material, or may be stored up in the body for future use. This takes the form of fatty tissue, also of a starchy substance called glycogen, stored up in the liver.

While both water and mineral matters, particularly salt and phosphate of lime, are necessary to insure a healthy condition of the system, they are not, strictly speaking, nutritious.

During the last score of years there has been a widespread and growing interest in the production and proper using of foods. This has come in some degree from the fact that science, in ascertaining the properties of food, has demonstrated its aggravated misuse and waste by the average community of people. The question of better facilities for food production was a serious one at the time of the creation of the Department of Agriculture at Washington in 1862. Later, experimental stations have been established in various states, the inspection of milk and certain kinds of meat has been in many states compelled by law, and special legislation is being made from year to year in reference to imitations and adulterations. Our supplies of fish and game, which were in danger of being exterminated, are now protected at certain seasons by law and in many ways legislation, a very great assistance to any line of reform, has proved a most efficient stimulus to agricultural interest. An understanding of the proper use of food materials is coming to be considered an educational branch of no small importance, and, in fact, if matters continue as they have begun, the study of food is in danger of becoming a fad. What was accomplished in Germany at the beginning of this century by Benjamin Thompson (Count Rumford) in securing a better diet at no greater cost for the men of the Bavarian army, is now being accomplished in America for our army of poor, and in the way of lunches for our army of shop-girls, clerks and students. The soup-kitchens established in all our great cities, the cooking classes for the instruction of both rich and poor, indicate a slow gravitation toward more hygienic methods of living. All these influences are proving to an extravagant nation that hygienic and palatable food is usually far from costly, and that fifteen cents, reinforced by brains, may provide a better meal than ten times that amount otherwise.

No lesson should be more quickly learned by American people than economy in the use of agricultural products and no time was more appropriate for the learning of it than the period of the World's Columbian Exposition. In our United States food products are so profuse and cheap that wastefulness is a temptation. Most foreign nations consider our food waste greatly to our discredit and their chief message to us is one of thrift. We have taught them better methods in the production and cultivation of foods, and it is hard to tell which lesson was more needed. As one remembers the wooden plows, the clumsy and immense tools of iron exhibited at the Fair from Siam, Johore, even from many European countries and our own Mexico, then considers the wretched social condition about us, the reckless waste of a cheap and bountiful food supply by the ignorant classes and their corresponding periods of suffering, it seems as if the best cure for both conditions were a world-comparison of agricultural products and methods. Just such a comparison was made possible by the exhibits gathered under the roof of the Agricultural building during the Columbian Exposition. Not until deductions are made, not until their lessons are learned by all nations, may the triumphal arch of universal brotherhood be reared upon other than an infirm foundation.

CHAPTER III.

N ANCIENT ballad of Merrie England declares to us that all Britons
are infallible as long as fed on beef.
Whether the ballad was made to fit
a still more ancient custom, as with
many of the Roman legends, or
whether the practice of beef-eating gave rise to
the ballad, there is no means of ascertaining; but
it is no more true of England than of most other
nations that their feast songs were always of meat
and their drinking songs of wine. Wine flowed
freely at the tables in historic days, and vegetables, now so important a part of a meal, were then but a few, poor notes in the song of
a classic feast. The boar's head was decked with holly, never the
potato, and the sirloin of beef is still regarded in England with all
the homage due to a thing of noble lineage. Even the pumpkin of
to-day, glorious in the richness and molten gold of its surface,
gathered from summer skies as it lay like Danae beneath them;
even that takes rank inferior to our strutting, gobbling, national
bird, the turkey. One author says: "There is a peerage of meats.
It includes the princely venison, the cardinal ham, the baron of

beef, and the knightly sirloin. Every canvas-back duck is a duke, and each saddle of mutton a marquis."

Here is Dean Swift's description of what constituted an aristocratic mid-day dinner of Old England: "Oysters, a Sir Lyon of beef, a shoulder of veal, then fish which were to be dressed with claret, tongue, pigeons, cowcumbers, fritters, almond pudding and soup. After the soup was removed, venison, pasty black pudding, hare and goose." Small wonder that viands in those days had to be "spiced to the brink" that they might tempt a satiated appetite; small wonder that gout and apoplexy were common disorders among the well-to-do classes, for it was accounted nothing strange that even good Queen Anne should die of the latter disease.

During the epoch of the Roman republic, peacocks occupied the place of the modern sirloin, and in the middle ages the coarse meat of this bird, far from agreeable to the modern epicure, was considered a luxury and served with great pomp. The costliness of these birds sufficed to immortalize the extravagance of both Vitellius and Heliogabalus, who served dishes composed of their tongues and brains.

Certain it is that from the time primitive man pulled his first mollusk from the water and ate it raw—from that later time when he captured the cave bear and boiled its shoulders in a clay pot of his own making—down to the gastronomic luxuries of a Careme or a Francatelli, the important article of diet has been meat. Whether the fish and larvæ of the native Australians, the horse-flesh of the Pampas Indians, the reindeer meat of the Laps, the buffalo meat of the North American Indians, or the juicy cut of beef served in a Delmonico restaurant, man's meal-time enjoyment, be he civilized or uncivilized, wise or unwise, largely depends upon meat. It is eaten by the people of tropical countries as well as by the Siberians and Icelanders, and, generally speaking, those classes which do not consume meat are prevented from so doing either by its scarcity or because of religious or moral belief. There has been an attempt made, I believe, to demonstrate the theory that only those nations whose diet is a mixed one, including meats, ever do valuable service in science or invention. However that may be, it is certainly true that the best physical condition is maintained on a mixed diet of which about one-fourth per cent consists of meat.

There is a large class of people to-day who, under the banner of vegetarianism, discard the use of flesh foods. But, with the exception of the absolutely strict vegetarians, they consume large quantities of very concentrated forms of animal food, namely, milk, cheese and eggs, so characterized by the nitrogenous elements or protein which they contain in abundance. That the theories advocated by the vegetarians are worthy of consideration was proven by the general interest in the Vegetarian Congress held in Chicago during the summer of 1893. But their position seems to be rather a protest against the inhumanity of our slaughter pens than against meat per se. The latest investigations of dietetic science demonstrate that the human system cannot be maintained in a state of perfect health on a purely vegetable diet. A glance at the preceding tabulation of the properties of food shows that the tissue-building substance or protein is confined almost wholly to animal foods. There is a variable but small proportion found in vegetables, especially in the cereals and legumes, but the amount is so small in these, in proportion to the amount of fats and carbohydrates (sugars and starches) as to be inadequate. Another fact has been demonstrated, both by Professor Atwater and certain German scientists, which is that the tissue-building substance or protein of meat is more digestible than that of vegetables. It has been proven by a careful experiments that, of the protein contained in beef and other meats, the entire amount taken into the system is assimilated by it; while in the case of vegetables, even considering those richest in protein, beans, peas, oat-meal and cracked wheat, one-third and often more remains undigested. On account of this variation, any classification of foods in regard to the amount of nutriment which they actually contain without considering the ability of the system to assimilate them is faulty. For, in a diet composed of even those vegetables richest in tissue-building material, the system is put to great waste of energy in eliminating the undigested protein as well as the unassimilated surplus of fats and carbohydrates. H. Newell Martin, professor of biology in Johns Hopkins University, says: "The strict vegetarians who do not employ even such substances as eggs, cheese and milk, but confine themselves to a purely vegetable diet (such as is always poor in proteids), daily take far more carbon than they require, and are to be congratulated on their excellent digestions which are able to stand the strain. Those who use eggs, cheese, etc., can, of course, get on very well, since such substances are extremely rich in proteids, and supply the nitrogen needed without the necessity of swallowing the vast bulk of food which must be eaten in order to get it from the plant directly." On the other hand, it is true that too much meat is consumed, generally speaking, by the well-to-do classes, and the vegetarian doctrine is doing valuable service in favor of a more hygienic system of diet. The happy medium between the two extremes is reached as yet by only a small proportion of people.

Animal foods may be divided into three classes: meats, eggs, and milk in its various forms, such as butter and cheese. Meats are the flesh products of various domestic animals, giving us beef, veal, mutton and pork; of poultry, of wild game and fowl, of fish, shell-fish, turtle and other sea-foods. The meats which we consume most largely come from our own domestic animals; they, the most consistent vegetarians of all. The sustenance they derive from the vegetable kingdom has many elements in common with the elements of their own composition for we recognize both animal and vegetable protein, though widely differing in its proportion to the other elements. At one time it was believed that each element of animal flesh came to it in the same form directly from the vegetable kingdom. Liebig, however, determined that the animal world had ability to transform one kind of organic substance into another and that this was done in the conversion of vegetable substance into animal tissue. It is unnecessary to pursue this reasoning further than to state that the organic matter of the animal world has its source in the organic matter of the vegetable world, and that vegetable food is converted by the animal's processes of digestion into the complex tissue known as meat. For the reason, therefore, that the animal saves mankind a large amount of the labor of converting vegetable into animal tissue, meat is a highly digestible food. When waste of human energy and of undigested portions are considered in the case of man, meat is an economical portion of diet as well. The principal meat both in England and our own country is beef, and the fresh meat exhibited at the World's Columbian Expo-

sition, though limited in quantity, illustrated all the characteristics of the best.

Beef is in best condition when the animal is from four to five years of age, preferably grass-fattened. Stall-fed animals contain a surplus of fat which, as has already been noticed, is not agreeable nor useful as a food beyond a certain limit. While the prize fat oxen and prime Christmas beeves are very good to look upon they are usually far from becoming an economical food, so much of the fat being unused, or, if eaten, unassimilated. Beef should be firm and dry, presenting some resistance to the touch. A juicy or flabby condition of raw meat indicates unhealthiness of the animal. The color should be a bright red, neither pale nor of a purplish hue, the latter condition indicating that the meat was bruised, not well bled or that the animal was diseased. There should be no odor excepting a pleasant one. The best meat is marbled, with firm light streaks of fat running through the muscular tissue. Deep yellow fat generally indicates age, or the use of a certain kind of food given for the purpose of fattening.

Veal is younger beef, but a more expensive and less nutritious meat. The calf is usually slaughtered when from six weeks to nine months old. Dr. Edward Smith is authority for the statement that in England calves are killed when under one month old, being considered very choice eating. This was prohibited in Boston in 1855 and is not done now in America unless stealthily. Veal, like the meat of all young animals, such as lamb and sucking pig, is not digested easily on account of the tenacity of its fibres, rendering it difficult of mastication. It is highly gelatinous containing, however, not a large proportion of protein.

Mutton, by most persons, is considered of agreeable flavor and requires but mention as it is almost uniformly good in all markets. The best is grain and grass-fattened and is less liable to disease than either beef or pork. However, it is less suitable for persons of very active life than beef.

Pork is the one condemned meat and has received more abuse, just and unjust, than has ever been heaped upon any other one food, partly due to the religious prejudice by the Jews and Mohammedans against the use of it. Certain foreign countries have legislated against the importation of it, particularly that exported from America, and this has had a salutary effect upon the industry. However, it is probable that it was often condemned unjustly, and our American pork is, in general, quite as free from disease as the product of any other country. Inspection of it before exportation is now compelled by law in the large cities of America, both pork and other meat being subjected to examination by microscopists. Swine that are kept about slaughter-houses and fed upon offal, as is done in many of the small towns, are wholly unfit for food, and pork from such sources ought to be condemned; but the meat of corn-fed hogs from the western prairies is probably as untainted as beef.

Pork is not health-giving when eaten exclusively or in large quantities, as it is not as nutritious as other meat. It contains but a small proportion of protein—less than one per cent in very fat pork (Atwater), and a far larger proportion of fats than the system can relish or digest. However, it excels all other meats in the facility with which it can be preserved by salting or drying and the finely cured portions are considered quite delicious when properly cooked. Swinton tells us that a favorite meat of the old Romans was young pork. Bacon is coming to be advocated by dietetists as a valuable food for young children and for invalids. It is both appetizing and easy of digestion and can be taken when such foods as veal, pork in other forms or even new potatoes, could not be digested.

These meats were exhibited at the exposition, but, owing to the difficulty and great expense of shipping a long distance, they were exhibited in a fresh state only by the American packing-houses. It was a source of regret that foreign countries were unrepresented in this respect, but there is no reason to suppose that America would have suffered by any comparison. The exhibit was not large and was contained in one immense refrigerator car, through the glass sides of which could be seen splendid prime beef, hung in quarters; also veal, pork and mutton. Pipes within the car, covered thickly with hoar frost, showed the air to be cold, untainted and dry. The meat was thus kept through the hot summer months almost as fresh as when first placed on exhibition.

The method of taking care of meats so that, when prepared, they may be put on the market in their most attractive, cleanly and healthful form, has been scientifically studied by the great packing-houses of America, notably those of Armour, Swift, Cudahy, Libby, McNeill and Libby, North Packing company, Nelson Morris and a few others.

It is universally conceded that such meat is far more healthful, in general, than that prepared in small cities and towns. Such an industry naturally is and rightfully should be carried on in large headquarters, and it were far better, so far as health is concerned, did the dwellers in country districts depend more largely upon them for their meat supply. Every operation in a large packing-house is based upon some scientific reason and is conducted with great cleanliness and perfection of system. Meat slaughtered after the Jewish custom, the requirements for which date back to the Mosaic law, is regarded by many as superior to that of the ordinary markets. Though the great packing-houses adopt a method far more humane, their care, system and cleanliness are even greater. Such system, reinforced by the microscopic inspection regularly carried on in every such house, renders their products thoroughly excellent. More than any other institution they are responding to the demands of the people for wholesome food in a way in which Americans may justly take pride.

CHAPTER IV.

THERE is a quality inherent in all food which under natural conditions renders it changeable and perishable. The properties of all alimentary substances are susceptible of change. The atmosphere which surrounds us comes in contact with every substance; unless removed or excluded, as when in a vacuum, through the agency of unnatural means. It contains germs which are always active, paying "with eternal vigilance" the price of their victories, and whose mission is the destruction of all organic substances. These are the active causes of the change known as decomposition. To prevent such change, various means have been devised for keeping food from putrefaction and in a wholesome condition. These methods are known as drying, salting, chilling, heating, canning, coating with gelatine or fat for the exclusion of air, and the use of chemicals.

Drying was undoubtedly the first method used for keeping meat in a wholesome state, and was practiced in pre-historic times by the earliest races of mankind. After returning from the chase and partaking of a feast, precursor of the modern "game dinner," satiated man pondered while he digested. Without a doubt he earnestly desired to preserve the unused game from decay that he might have sufficient for periods of famine, inclement weather or when on the long marches customary with nomadic peoples. His perceptive faculties were at that time sufficiently acute to perceive that meat, cooked, was longer preserved than meat in a raw state. Thus the earliest method of preserving meat is known to have been by slowly drying it over a fire, either upon sticks or upon frames made from the twigs of trees. By this slow method of heating and drying, the non-nutrient juices of the meat were evaporated. The product of such a method is to-day called "jerked meat." If this meat, after being dried, is pounded until dessicated it is called pemican or pemmican. In some of the South American states it is called *charqui* and in Uruguay and Nicaragua, *tasajo*. Meat still continues to be dried in this primitive way in nearly all countries; not, however, by the most progressive classes. In America, drying is effected chiefly by heat alone, though often aided by the sunshine and air. Drying wholly by the action of the air is a tedious process and in most places cannot be satisfactorily done, owing to the moisture of the atmosphere. When heat is used, great care must be exercised or the flavor of the meat will be destroyed.

Meat dried is in its most nutritious form for preservation. Only the water is evaporated, all of the nutriment being retained. It is estimated that one pound of dried meat contains as much nutriment as about four times that weight of fresh meat, so greatly has drying reduced its weight and bulk. This method is the one chiefly used in warm climates, because no other simple process ensures safe preservation, and because both nutritive value and flavor of the meat are retained.

Thus far the only scientific objection made to the use of meat preserved in this way is that it is not sufficiently cooked to destroy larvæ or germs of disease which may exist. The flesh of wild animals is much less liable to be infected with these discoveries of civilization than that of the domesticated species. A lower caste Buddhist, it is said, once broke in pieces the microscope which revealed to him living organisms in the water and vegetables of his daily food because his religion forbade the destruction of even the lowest forms of life. Through the same ignorance, before the days of chemistry and the microscope, all meat was considered healthful by English speaking people, but though our laboratories have discovered germs to us, we cannot believe that they could be annihilated by the destruction of our microscopes. In that respect, the East Indian has the advantage of us.

The native races of America brought many specimens of dried meat to the World's Columbian Exposition. One specially interesting exhibit was placed in the Anthropological building and consisted of a complete collection of Indian foods, gathered by the chief of the Nez Perce tribe. Miss Alice Fletcher, a recognized authority, told me that this collection was undoubtedly the most complete and interesting ever made by the native, uncivilized American. There were exhibited wild vegetables, fruits and berries, part of them dessicated and combined with wild potato meal into cakes. The meat was their favorite kind from the elk and bison, and was prepared in the usual way, pemican. Longfellow, in his poem of Hiawatha, describes a typical Indian feast in the following words, the *mondamin* referred to being Indian corn:

> " Then on pemican they feasted,
> Pemican and buffalo marrow,
> Haunch of deer and hump of bison,
> Yellow cakes of the Mondamin
> And the wild rice of the river."

Catlin, whose large collection of portraits of the North American Indians comprised part of the Smithsonian exhibit at the exposition, frequently refers, in his "History of the North American Indians," to their pemican or dried and pounded buffalo meat. This they mix with equal parts of fat and pack in bladders which are usually dried and then buried in the ground, the primitive store-room and treasure-house for preserving meat from hostile tribes.

Mexico, Siam and Uruguay exhibited dried meats. That from Mexico, known as jerked meat, showed a very crude method of drying; but it is a food article of great value to the people and, owing to their warm climate, is a satisfactory way of preserving it. The largest exhibit of dried meat came from Uruguay, the direct product of the *saladeros* or killing grounds. These are situated along the coasts and rivers of that country and correspond to our packing houses. The vast herds of cattle, which range over the plains of South America, were formerly considered valuable only for their hides. More recently, their meat has been dried and the product is

called *tasajo*. In preparing the meat for drying, the great sides of
the carcasses are entirely divested of bones and fat, and the meat is
placed upon frames in the sun. It is frequently turned and, owing
to a dry atmosphere, it is possible to complete the process without
the use of salt. This *tasajo* is an unattractive food, as it is bleached
by the sun until colorless, somewhat resembling dried codfish.
Three grades of quality are made, one entirely without salt, which is
used at home; a second grade, slightly salted, which is sent into the
interior of South America; and a third, very salt, which is exported
to Jamaica and the West Indies. The *tasajo* exhibited at the exposition was put up in canvas-covered packages, about two feet square
and about fifty pounds in weight per package. When taken out the
meat was unfolded much as a hide of leather would be straightened,
but it was quite palatable and not unlike, in flavor, our own dried
beef. The commissioner, Senor Murgiondo, told me that this meat
was an important factor in the revenue of Uruguay. There were
also exhibited several kinds of *tasajo*, pulverized, of value as food
for invalids. This, combined with an equal quantity of chocolate,

"HAUNCH" OF DEER AND HUMP OF BISON"

is made into lozenges and bonbons, and was also displayed in the
form of a powder for use with hot water as a beverage. These preparations were all agreeable to the taste and, forming one of the
most concentrated and nutritious foods, merit special mention from
a dietetic standpoint.

Siam exhibited specimens of the dried meat commonly used in

that country, which was no less interesting than the South American product. This meat is dried wholly without salt, then pounded and shredded by hand with a knife to the finest possible degree. This shredding is all done by women, after the drying and bleaching process of the sun is completed. There were at the exposition about two dozen specimens of shredded meat and fish from Siam, put up in glass jars, all of it having much the appearance of fine excelsior. It was of good flavor and quite appetizing, though from its appearance it was impossible to distinguish fish from meat. I marvelled at the time and labor involved in such preparation and asked the commissioner if all meat were thus prepared in Siam. "O, yes," he replied, "the women prepare it all. They have plenty of time and nothing else to do." And so, in far away Siam, these patient little women sit day after day, knife in hand, shredding meat, happy, it may be, in a fashion all their own. These cans of shredded meat told volumes about the Siamese, and on every page was written patience, industry and care. The meats exhibited were beef, pork, chicken, veal and duck beside a large assortment of fish, cuttle-fish, squid and shrimp.

Nearly every packing house in America which was represented at the exposition displayed samples of dried beef, and it was fully as characteristic and interesting as that from other countries. It is not, however, as rich in nutriment, much having been lost in preparation by salting before drying. It is dark and of a red color, owing to the use of saltpetre in the brine, and also because it is dried in the shade. The salt and saltpetre, used in curing, add to its keeping qualities but detract from its nutritive value, as the entire juices of the meat are not retained. Our dried beef is far more marketable than any from other countries and represents an immense industry. This is because of its better appearance, although a method which does not retain the entire nutritive substance cannot be considered perfect. Chipped dried beef is deservedly popular and when put up in cans, as is done in many packing houses, may be preserved indefinitely.

Dried sausages, or as they are better known, "summer sausages," are the rock upon which epicureans and the common clan split. There is never a half heartedness in the way in which summer sausages are regarded. They are either liked desperately and with conviction of their innate piquancy and superiority or they are as unqualifiedly despised. I think a motto must have hung in every sau-

sage-maker's shop over three continents while the summer sausages
at the exposition were being made, and this was it: "Who peppers
the highest is sure to please." There were exhibited summer sausages from many foreign lands, rivals of our own in their fragrant
endeavor to win a coveted medal. These are great favorites with
many persons and, while they are not required for the proper serving of any meal, still they are the very particular *bonne bouche* for
a lunch, and disciples of the Fatherland can no more reverently enshrine them than upon the side-board, flanked with cheese and
beer. Just what becomes of the enormous quantities made and
marketed I doubt if any woman will ever discover. There are a few
things, good and bad, which men have from time immemorial appropriated to themselves, and among them are summer sausages.
Perhaps this is because, as an admirer said, they "leave a pleasant
taste in the mouth."

The making of summer sausages requires much skill, not only
in selecting and proportioning the meat but in the seasoning as
well. For there are spices of all sorts and savors, pepper, salt, garlic
and minced herbs. Each house seasons its summer sausages differently for they are made to suit the taste of the maker, or the demands of a particular locality. No meat at the exposition seemed
so capricious in flavor, quality and general appearance as the summer sausages. After being made and stuffed into casings, they are
hung for a few months until properly cured. As they are usually
made in winter they are dry and well cured by summer time and
hence their name. I learned that there is an art in sausage making and that there are secrets as well, guarded as sacredly as the
porcelain maker guards the secrets of his clay. There is real inspiration in the pride of a sausage maker over his products. Decked
in cap and white apron and armed with a long, sharp knife, he deftly
cuts the sausage in twain. He holds it before an admiring gaze,
then brings it nearer that we may catch its ripened fragrance.

At one of the American exhibits the artist in sausages was a
German, whose duty it was to display the goods at their best advantage. As he cut sausage after sausage a smile of satisfaction
passed over his countenance. Did he not come from the land of
sausages? Was he not confident that no product excelled his own?
Did he not know that every sausage was a masterpiece of its kind?
And he tempted us to taste again and again and just once more
until a score of varieties in all their mottled color and fragrance of

herbs and spices lay before us. No longer shall France, Germany, Italy and Spain appropriate the laurels of marjoram, thyme and garlic. America has taken a conspicuous place at their side, for the excellence of flavor, variety and attractiveness of her summer sausages. There were numerous varieties from Mexico, Argentine Republic, Brazil, Uruguay, Germany, England, France, Italy and Spain. Italy distinguished herself by having the largest sausage exhibited, weighing fifty pounds. On Italy's day at the great exposition there was feasting and rejoicing and this mammoth sausage, called "Mortedella," was both host and banquet on that occasion. Just one year before, that sausage was made across the water, intended to become a fatherland greeting to the sons and daughters of Italy planted upon American soil. A deft carver, appareled in whitest linen and armed with keenest of knives, sliced pieces for each of the crowd that on that day passed through Italy's pavilion. Each stopped long enough to wash down the morsel with wine from his native land of sunshine and little wonder that their cry was "Vive l'Italia!"

Uruguay preserved her exhibit of summer sausages with special care. They were large in size, well made, rolled in tin-foil and inclosed in individual tin tubes.

Spain was very proud of the giant sausage of her exhibit, nearly seven feet in length. Around it smaller ones were hanging, all suspended by the national colors of yellow and red. The exhibits made by all countries were interesting and paid something very like homage to this article called a summer sausage. Its forerunner was the pemican of the Indian and, such pranks have the extravagant flavorings of civilization played with it, soon it may be entitled to a place among condiments.

CHAPTER V.

PRESERVATION OF MEATS BY SALTING AND CURING.

ALT is the common name for chloride of sodium and occurs in nearly all forms of nature, in the vegetable and animal as well as in the mineral kingdoms. It is in most cases found deposited in the earth in the form of rock-salt and is procured by mining. Salt also exists in solution both in ocean waters and in saline springs, from which it is obtained by evaporation. It is held in suspension in the atmosphere and all animal and vegetable substances have it in varying proportions in their tissues. Salt is abundant in the secretions of the human body and in the blood, of which latter substance it is the natural antiseptic. It aids in the absorption of food and holds in solution the fibrin and albumin of the blood. In the material world its uses are manifold, it being the basis of all glass and soap manufacture and valued as an agent in the composition of certain disinfectants. The use of salt as a fertilizer dates back to the ancient customs of China and Hindostan, and throughout all ages its value to the human system has been known. One of the ancients called salt a substance "divine;" others declared it acceptable to the gods. History tells us that salt was first used as a flavoring for meat among the Phœnicians, and we also know that the Roman soldiers of a later time, who served their land for a small sum, received part of their wages in salt, so valuable was the substance at that time. From this custom is derived the word salary. Some idea of the esteem in which salt was held may be gained from the fact that it was once the custom to deprive prisoners of it; but when this deprivation was found detrimental to health it was discontinued.

The action of salt upon fresh, raw meat is to partially extract the water or juices. These juices hold the albumin and salts of the meat tissue in solution. Salt also absorbs heat and lowers the temperature of anything with which it comes in contact so that its general effect is to cause meat to become tough and to lessen its nutritive value. Liebig estimates that the nutritive value of meat so treated is diminished one-third, often one-half, both because of the juices extracted and because the toughening renders it difficult of digestion. A considerable portion of the nutriment is held in solution in the brine, from which it cannot be extracted for use as food; and it is a common saying among rural people that every pailful of old brine is worth a dollar. This is because old brine is so filled with the extracted juices of the meat first placed in it that any cured in it afterward loses a far smaller per cent of nutriment. For this reason brine is saved by farmers and those who salt their own meat and, after scalding, is used again and again. Salt prevents the development of germs in meat impregnated with it and may preserve it for an indefinite time.

The methods now used in preserving meats by salting are (1) immersion of the meat in a solution of salt, known as brine; (2) by packing in dry salt which, by the extraction of the juices of the meat, soon becomes dissolved and penetrates the tissues; (3) by rubbing dry salt into the meat, a method known as "dry curing;" (4) by using salt sparingly and completing the preservation by drying and smoking. Saltpetre, also a mineral product, is usually combined in small quantities with the salt and helps to retain the red color of the muscular tissue. It possesses antiseptic qualities as well but is chiefly used for keeping the meat in good color, this giving it greater commercial value. Soda is often used with salt and saltpetre, its tendency being to overcome the hardening and toughening which salt causes. The antiseptic properties of borax render it also valuable. The latter substances are detrimental to health if used for any length of time, even in minute quantities, and it is desirable that substances equally valuable as preservatives but without their injurious properties may be found. Sugar is also used to some extent, particularly in the milder method of curing, known as pickling.

Beef, when intended for home use and not for exportation, is usually preserved in a pickle containing salt, salt-petre, sugar and such spices as give it the most desirable flavor. Shoulders, hams, bacon and tongue are cured for the American markets with as little salt as is necessary to ensure their preservation. Each packing-house, whether of America or Europe, tries to out-do the other in placing its cured meats on the market in the most palatable and attractive form. Not infrequently the quality of a single kind of cured meat, such as ham or bacon, establishes the reputation of its house for excellent meats in general.

At the exposition, the display of salted, cured and pickled meats comprised hams, shoulders, bacon, and pork in all its cuts, known commercially as clear pork, mess pork, backs, lean ends, etc. All these from American houses were exhibited barreled as if ready for shipment, with the single difference of having glass heads upon the barrels through which the exhibits could be seen. The exhibit of cured beef was also placed in the regulation barrels, displaying all the marketable cuts, brisket, ribs, navels, plates, and a fat extra cut which is put up expressly for the markets of India. Tongues were shown by the barrel and half barrel, a wealth of that delicious lunch meat, and all, excellent in color, showed care and skill both in selection and cut. The dry-cured sides of pork were packed in salt in square boxes, ready for shipment. Each box contained one hundred pounds of pork. To what extent America is endeavoring to capture foreign trade was shown very plainly at the exposition by the names given to various cuts of meat. The dry cured pork was variously designated as Cumberland cut, Yorkshire sides, Birmingham sides, South Staffordshire sides and Wiltshire sides. In the hams there were Staffordshire, Manchester, Boston and New York cuts, while the California and Picnic hams were so nicely cut and trimmed that one would hardly have believed them to be only shoulders, after all. These cured shoulders are desirable for home use in the way of lunches as they contain but little fat, much of which is wasted in

British Guiana Cooking Vessels.

the ordinary ham. As nearly as can be ascertained, the honor of introducing this method of curing shoulders, providing an appetizing meat at a low cost, belongs to the packing-houses of the United States, the only country which exhibited them. Some comprehension of the importance of the American industry in salted and cured meats may be gained from the following official report for the fiscal year of 1892 to 1893. The American exports of bacon amounted to 397,000,000 pounds; ham, 82,000,000 pounds; salt pork, 53,000,000 pounds; and of salted beef, 58,000,000 pounds.

The salted and cured meats coming from other countries did not compare favorably with those exhibited by the American houses, and only dry-cured meats were sent. The foreign countries exhibiting these were Argentine Republic, Brazil, Mexico, Italy, Belgium, France, England and Canada. Much of the foreign meats of this class were injured by exposure on ship-board, through delay in reaching Chicago and in being placed in the buildings. The methods of curing and styles of cut differed somewhat from those used in America and, in awarding medals, both American and foreign judges considered all these differences of standard. The hams sent from abroad were in most cases cut square at the base instead of round, and the shanks were cut very long. They were not polished as hams are in America where competition forces the packing-houses to put goods on the market in an attractive form, and where hams and shoulders are as rich in color and texture of surface as light mahogany. Neither were they as closely trimmed, perhaps because that would mean waste, although in America such trimmings are used for potted meats.

Meat is preserved by salt in all countries and in many different ways. It is rendered particularly appetizing when smoked after being mildly cured or salted and such treatment renders it thoroughly wholesome. There is little more to be desired, excepting that some method may be found by which chemicals, injurious even in the slightest degree, will not be used, and a method, as well, whereby a greater proportion of nutriment may be retained.

CHAPTER VI.

PRESERVING OF MEAT BY CANNING, COOKING, FREEZING, USE OF
CHEMICALS AND OTHER METHODS.

IEBIG says: "The property of organic substances to pass into a state of ferment-ation and decay in contact with atmos-pheric air, and in consequence to trans-mit these states of change to other organic substances, is annihilated in all cases with-out exception by heating to the boiling point." As is well known, heat is a com-mon means of preserving alimentary sub-stances and is unfailing in its effects. Food undergoes but little change in being heated to the boiling point and, if afterwards protected from the atmosphere, may be preserved indefinitely. The advantage of using heat as a preservative was first made known by M. Appert of France, in 1809, although it is claimed that the same method of preserving must have been known to the inhabitants of Pompeii, as sealed jars containing figs in a perfect condition have been found in the exca-vated ruins. Appert succeeded in preserving in glass jars meats, vegetables and fruits and for this important discovery the govern-ment of France gave him 12,000 francs. One year later de Heine, then in England, patented a process by which he claimed that food could be preserved by completely exhausting the air with an air pump. All attempts, however, were unsuccessful until the process patented by Wertheimer in 1839 came to be used. This provided that the food to be preserved should be placed in tin or metal cans, the interstices being filled with water, juices or other fluid, and the lid to be securely soldered upon the can. The cans were to be then set in water and boiled, the air being expelled through small holes pierced in the lid. When the food was sufficiently cooked and the air entirely driven out, the holes were to be filled with solder, completing the process. Food thus treated would remain in a perfect state almost indefinitely and but little improvement, if any, has since been made upon that method. The theory of these men, however, differed from that accepted by modern science, although the same means were used and the same results obtained. It was originally believed that the oxygen contained in air was the destructive agency, and that the expulsion of air alone was sufficient to prevent decomposition. Professor Tyndall was the first, I believe, to demonstrate that the atmosphere contained living germs, destructive in a varying degree, to all substances. Meats, fruits and vegetables may thus be preserved by first being heated to the boiling point and then being kept from contact with the air.

This is the process used in all the large canning factories of America as well as the countries abroad and is practiced in every household in which fruit is preserved. Canneries are scattered all over the United States; those of the Atlantic coast preserving meats, fish and vegetables, those of Washington and Oregon furnishing our tables with choice salmon, while those of California send to us the delicious fruit of that state at a nominal cost. Tons of meat are daily preserved by this method in the large packing-houses of Chicago and the eastern cities, as well-cooked as that of the most careful housekeeper. In these canneries one is first impressed with the appetizing odor of the cooked meat and then with the cleanliness, rapidity and system with which the whole process is carried on. Said a friend recently—a housekeeper of more than average ability— "I never tasted canned meat. I insist upon cleanliness in the handling of my food and prefer to know where the meat comes from."

Let us see. This lady lives in a small city, the cattle and other meat being slaughtered in the suburbs. The quarters are brought into market in the same wagon which carries calves, lambs and poultry. The handling and cutting of the meat is done by men not over neat and often far from skillful; and from the shop it is carried home to my lady's kitchen. Here again, neither utensils nor help are cleaner than in the packing rooms, in fact, not as much so, for in the latter place steam, the great purifier, the universal germ destroyer, makes everything cleanly and odorless. Everything possible is handled by machinery. The animal, after being dressed, hangs for forty-eight hours in the chill-room and the meat is cooked, for canning, entirely by steam in large cedar vats. The boning of pigs' feet, the selecting of pieces for pot- ted meats, the examining of. tongues that no blemish may be found, the pack- ing into cans, the weighing; the en- tire process, if viewed impartial- ly, would more quickly remove the prejudice against canned meats than any argument. Certainly those who know eat it with far less mental discomfort than meat from an ordinary market; first, because prime cattle are always selected for use and, secondly, because of the cleanliness with which the meat is handled. So extensive is the in- dustry in canned goods that they are marketed in nearly every country on the globe, exports of canned beef alone, during 1892, from the United States amounting to 79,000,000 pounds.

The exhibit of canned meats from America was far larger than that from other countries, doubtless owing to the proximity of the canning houses, several of which are located in Chicago. The ex- hibits from various houses were much the same and comprised the following cuts of meat: brisket of corned beef, plain corned beef, brawn, pigs' feet, boar's head, boneless pigs' feet, dried beef (in cans), beef tongues, lunch (pigs') tongues, lambs' tongues, roast mutton, roast and boiled beef, minced steak, compressed ham, stewed kidneys, sweetbreads (sub-lingual and thyroid glands), Ger- man rare-bits (of pigs' head), English lunch meat, tripe, Oxford sausages, *oxen-maul salat* (salad of beef's palate), beef collops, strips of breakfast bacon and *chili con carne* (pepper with beef). The last named dish is made from small pieces of meat to which is added a varying amount of chili (pepper) according to the different receipts for making. It is a popular article of food, chiefly exported to the markets of Mexico and California, and whoever has visited the former country must remember with pleasure the national dish, *chili con carne.*

The canned meat industry of Australia is immense and rapidly growing and that country ranked next to the United States in the size of its exhibit at the World's Fair. The export trade in canned goods between Australia and England is an important source of revenue to the former country, comprising the meats exhibited at the exposition: corned beef, beef brawn, roast beef, boiled beef, rump steak, ox lips, ox cheeks, beef palate, ox tails, corned mutton, stewed kidneys and sheep's trotters. To the memory of Charles Dickens these latter pay classic and savory tribute, and visions of England with its "old ale, ripe wine, much sack and a pen'o'worth of bread" cluster appetizingly about the memory of him who wrote of sheep's trotters. One of the judges at the exposition,—is it treason to tell of it?—became half indignant when urged to taste of sheep's trotters. Never could he taste a morsel so plebeian! True, he was uncommonly fond of pigs' feet, "dainty morsels," said he, "easily digested, appetizing, and—every one eats them, you know." So he wrapped himself in the recollection of pigs' feet, which are never out of mud until securely cooked and canned, while I ate, alone, a delicate tidbit called "sheep's trotter," far superior to a pigs' foot, well cooked, well flavored and nicely canned. Perhaps the time is coming when the extravagant American will no longer consign to the garbage heap so good a thing as a sheep's foot. The Australian corned mutton was as good as corned beef, excepting to those persons found in every community to whom mutton in any form is distasteful. The sheep used are the large Cotswold variety, and so cheap are they in Australia that a fine animal sells for fifty cents and its mutton retails at four cents a pound.

The meat sent from Canada, Belgium, France, Argentine Republic, Uruguay and Japan was chiefly beef and beef tongue. Spain exhibited roast beef, sirloin steak, tongue and *cabrita.* The cans, when opened for inspection, all showed choice meats, and with a bottle of crisp, round olives the tasting and judging was more pleasurable than usual. "What is *cabrita?*" we questioned. "Kid," was the reply. Visions of theatre bills, oyster cans and garbage, the natural food of the American kid, assailed us and the very atmosphere grew livid. But in spite of all prejudice, the fact remains that *cabrita* is a tender, delicious meat, far less assertive in flavor than the mildest of mutton.

Great Britain sent, preserved in the regulation tin cans, Irish stew, lamb with green peas, roast mutton, mutton chops, ham, tripe with onions, Oxford sausage, truffled sausages, chicken sausages and Scotch "haggis." The latter is well-nigh the Scottish national dish, highly prized across the water but seen in America rarely, except at the feasts of the bonnie Scots. Here is the recipe for making it, copied from an old English cook-book:

The heart, tongue and part of the liver of the sheep is minced fine with half its weight of bacon. Now add a cup of bread crumbs, the rind of one lemon, two eggs, a glass of wine, two anchovies, pepper and salt. Mince all thoroughly together, place in a well buttered mold and boil for two hours.

Whether served hot or cold this is a more than agreeable dish. Referring to Scotch "haggis," one of our best known American cooks, a writer upon cookery, says: "We need some mild laws to make people like such elaborate compounds as the foregoing, which are considered very fine across the sea and are encased in jelly and ornamented; at least to make people eat them after the trouble of their making." He then refers to a certain banquet given in Chicago, for which an expert French chef prepared the dish, and says: "Yet the way the Phillistines, after tasting with their knife points, pushed it away and took to plain beef and ham was sad for the artist to see." The same author adds that haggis may be modified by the use of truffles, particularly when used for luncheons, and after being made, may be kept for some time.

Germany had certain canned meats put up after a fashion and combination of her own. There were, among others, ham with chestnuts and goose with beans, the latter dish rather a heavy one to the American taste. From Strasburg, the city of goose livers, there were sent quantities of meat for goose-liver pies, although the Germans still place the French name upon the labels, "Pâté de foie gras, aux truffes, du Perigord." There was also ham, Burgundy style, ham with champagne sauce, fricandeau of veal with puree of green peas, and sausages, best of all, from "Frankfurt-am-Main." Said one of the judges, as he stood before the rows of opened cans, "Frankfurter" in hand: "Many a time in Frankfurt, have I seen them make these sausages. A man stands at one end of a tank grinding away at sausages which fall into the boiling water with which the tank is filled. At the other end the people stand eating them." Very few Americans ever taste the genuine Frankfurt sausage, but must be contented with those made here, rarely so skillfully seasoned or so delicately made.

Days ran into weeks before the immense displays of canned goods at the exposition were all examined and the special points which determined their excellence were the following: (1) That the meat be well-selected, free from fat and tendons, and of good color; (2) that the seasoning be delicate; (3) that the cans be well filled. Meat put up in cans must vary in nutritive value according to the amount of water used in cooking, this holding the albumin and extractive salts in solution. The entire juices should be retained as far as possible, both for their nutritive value and for flavoring.

Potted and deviled meats, preserved in cans and jars, are always in demand for lunches, picnics and camping parties, and are a relish as well as a food proper. No other preserved meats make such excellent sandwiches, and they are prepared usually from ham, chicken, turkey, beef and tongue. The meat is minced to extreme fineness, so that it resembles paste in consistency, and is seasoned delicately to retain the natural flavor. The deviled meats, of which there are various kinds, are minced also, but differ from potted meats in being made very hot with peppers and spices. The seasoning varies with each canning house or locality. Beside the meats mentioned, herring, anchovies, rabbit and quail were exhibited, potted and also deviled.

All the American packing-houses sent potted meats put up in tin cans. The only foreign countries which exhibited these were England and France, and these goods differed chiefly in being preserved in small earthen pots as well as in metal cans.

Pickled meats were exhibited to a limited extent. They are so called because, after being cooked, they are protected from the air by being put into plain or spiced vinegar; cloves, allspice, lemon and bay leaves, with or without the addition of red peppers, being the seasonings most commonly used. These meats are chiefly useful for lunches, picnics and in restaurants. Only the choicest parts of the animal are used for pickling, tongues of beef, pig and sheep, pigs' feet and tripe. They are usually pu up in small kegs or half barrels.

There are other methods of preserving meat which need mention although not largely used and not wholly satisfactory. One of the oldest and best known is the preservation of meat by cold. The Eskimo knows that if his whale or seal blubber be buried in the snow, it may be preserved indefinitely. As long as meat is kept frozen it remains perfectly fresh, although its flavor is somewhat altered; but it must not be allowed to thaw. Ice has been used for this purpose for many years, particularly in the transportation of fresh meat, but owing to its expense the cold storage method has superseded it. This allows the meat to be kept in a stationary temperature just above the freezing point, and owing to this system our American beef may be placed upon the London markets very cheaply and in a perfect condition. Said Lady Somerset recently, when comparing the products of the fresh young soil of America to those of the impoverished land of England: "Why, even now, Mr. Armour of Chicago is underselling the local butchers in the little town of Ledbury on the castle lands." Australia sends large quantities of meat to England in a fresh state by means of the cold storage system and the refrigerator car at the exposition kept meat in a fresh state during six, hot, long, summer months.

Meat is also preserved by means of a coating of fat, which serves to exclude the air. Such meats, however, must first be cooked, that the germs may be destroyed, then covered with melted fat or oil. This method of preserving, using a vegetable oil, was largely employed in preparing the exhibits of both Spain and Italy. The food thus preserved includes sardines, anchovies, squid, tunny-fish, and cuttle-fish, besides such vegetables as mushrooms, artichokes and truffles.

Creosote is another preservative, and also a powerful antiseptic. It is the active principle in smoke and the meats upon which it is used are called ham, bacon, and dried beef.

A method has been patented in England according to which freshly killed meat is dipped into a solution containing one per cent of carbolic acid and seventy-two per cent of alcohol. After the meat has been removed and dried it is placed in a concentrated alcoholic solution of sugar. It is then cut in pieces, and packed in casks, the interstices being filled with melted fat. Another method which is practical in preparing meat for far distant markets, provides that it be exposed to a current of refrigerated air until stiffened. It is then sprinkled with powdered borax and is transported in a refrigerator car. A method known as Kauffman's, which has been long in use in households, consists in fumigating the meat with sulphur. If this is done several times, meat may be kept in hot weather, without ice, for a considerable time. There is also a material, advertised under the name of "Preservaline," which consists of borax, boric acid, saltpetre and salt. This added to water makes a brine in which the meat is immersed.

While the use of chemicals keeps meat in a marketable condition, such meat, from a dietetic point of view, ought to be used with caution. As a general thing, any substance the antiseptic properties of which are sufficient to keep meat unchanged by atmospheric contact, renders such meat a questionable article of diet.

CHAPTER VII.

N THE foregoing chapters reference has been made chiefly to meat proper, those portions of the animal which lie about the bones and are known as muscle and fat. But there are other portions, termed offal, which are valuable as food, but which are often cast off as refuse in dressing an animal for market. In small cities this waste is invariably seen but in the large cities, particularly in the packing houses, not only is that part of the animal utilized but many of our table delicacies are portions of offal.

In broad terms, about one-third of the animal may be marketed as offal. In sheep the weight of it may equal the weight of the meat, while in hogs there is a smaller amount, compared to the weight of the body, than in any other animal. I was told by the representative of one of our largest packing houses that there is no profit on the meat proper, only upon the offal. The head of this house is a multi-millionaire. Meat is sent from his establishment into interior cities and towns and is sold at the price of country beef, though generally of a better quality because well matured, well fattened and more skillfully cut. The prices at which it is sold, eight, ten and twelve cents a pound, prove that there can be little, if any, profit on the meat directly, when the expense of handling and shipping is considered. That the profit upon offal which is utilized is not inconsiderable may be seen from the following report of animals slaughtered from this house during 1892: hogs, 1,750,000; cattle, 850,000; sheep, 600,000. The following table by Edward Smith states the relative proportion of the offal to the meat of various animals. It indicates how great would be the loss to those handling and consuming meat if these portions were not utilized:

	Carcass.	Offal.
Store oxen	59.3	38.9
Fat oxen	59.8	38.5
Fat heifers	55.6	41.3
Fat calves	63.1	33.5
Store sheep	53.4	45.6
Half fat sheep	59	40.5
Very fat sheep	64.1	35.8
Store pigs	79.3	18.8
Fat pigs	83.4	16.1

Those portions of offal used for food are hearts, livers, ox-tails which are used for soup; the kidneys and the kidney fat which is a constituent of a most cleanly and wholesome article of food, butterine; tongues of cattle, sheep and pigs, ox-lips, ox-palates and sweetbreads. The lungs, being rich in nitrogenous matter, are minced and combined with other meat, being greatly valued in some countries as food, and the blood is, to some extent, used for blood puddings and sausages, dishes in great favor with the Germans. The stomachs of cattle are cleansed and made into tripe, a dainty which the old Greeks regarded as fit for heroes; for in the palmy days tripe was often the principal dish seen upon the banquet tables of those men who met to celebrate the victory of gods and mortals over the sacrilegious Titans. Caen, France, is to-day celebrated for the manufacture of its tripe, the preparation of which is a general industry. All such portions of offal are more rich in protein or flesh-forming elements than meat; the percentage of salts is about the same while they contain relatively much less fat. A large proportion of offal is utilized commercially. The skin is sent to leather tanneries, the hair and specially the long ends of the tails of cattle are used in the making of mattresses; the trimmings of the hides are sent to gelatine factories from which they are returned in the form of delicate and transparent gelatine, the delight of every housewife. Parts of the hoofs, bones and horns are made into glue, the hoofs and horns themselves being converted into buttons, spoons and ornaments. The intestines are cleansed and salted for use as sausage casings, the undigested food in the stomachs is dried for fuel, the bladders are used for the packing of putty and all scraps are dried and used for fertilizers. The bones are dried and ground for fertilizers and for use in refining sugar. The blood, which is rich in albumin, is preserved, coagulated and dried, also used both for the refining of sugar and the manufacture of fertilizers. Even the stomachs of pigs are used for the manufacture of pepsin, while the refuse fats are sent to the soap factory which returns in exchange, soap and glycerine. Connected with the packing house already referred to is a laboratory in which a number of excellent preparations of pepsin are made, as well as a medicinal preparation from the thyroid glands of the sheep. It seems that the science of economy would "o'erleap itself" in its endeavor to reduce waste to a minimum amount, for it has been said that "every portion of the pig is utilized, even the squeal, which may be preserved by phonograph!"

Much of the poetry of the old times is lost in this practical utilization of offal, for, however deliciously cooked and flavored, there is nothing more prosaic than beef collops, sweetbreads, and boar's head turned out of an American tin can. There is little atmosphere of the oak forests of England or the valorous knight of the chase about a boar's head such as this; and we may well cling to the old rhymes and ballads. Dryden tells of "sweetbreads and collops which were with skewers pricked," and there is an old song of the boar's head which is still sung at the annual feast at Queen's College, Oxford, it having been first published in 1521. Wherever the boar's head was used, a custom dating back to the era of William the Norman, it was borne, profusely decorated with holly and bay at the head of a triumphal procession to the banqueting hall.

> " The boar's head in hand bear I,
> Bedecked with bays and rosemarye,
> And I pray you, masters, be merry,
> Quot estis in convivio.

> " The boar's head, as I understand,
> Is the bravest dish in all the land,
> When thus bedecked with a gay garland,
> Let us servire cantico!

> " Our steward hath provided this
> In honor of the King of Bliss
> Which on this day to be served is,
> In regimensi atrio!
> Caput apri defero
> Reddens laudes Domino."

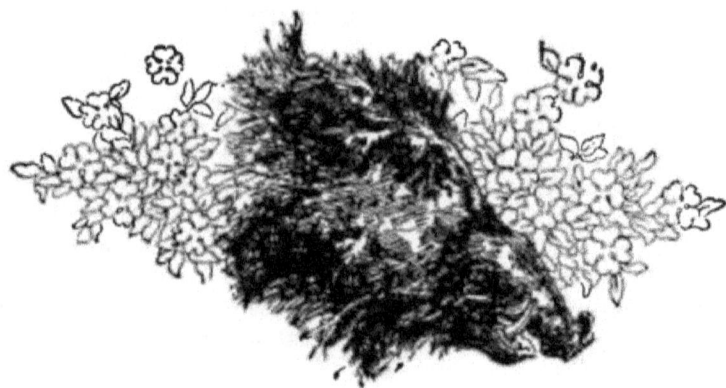

CHAPTER VIII.

OULTRY is wild fowl domesticated, although the origin of its domestication and its use as food is lost in tradition. There was an early period in which all birds, now called poultry and fowl, built their nests in the tangled leafage of a jungle and gathered berries, buds and slugs for food. To-day their descendents are fed and protected by their quondam enemy, man, that they may minister to his fondness for chicken-pie and pâté de foie gras. It is stated that wild fowl were first domesticated in Burmah, Darwin believes, from the jungle-fowl of Bankiva. There is also a Chinese tradition that poultry came to that land, originally, from the West, perhaps directly from India, while the records of ancient Babylonia indicate that poultry-raising was an industry with the Chaldeans as remotely as the ninth century, B. C. It is known that domesticated fowl were common among the Britons, prior to the Roman invasion in 55 B. C., and poultry-raising has been practiced in most European countries since earliest times. To-day, while wild birds or game are becoming gradually rarer and more expensive, the domesticated species is being still more largely used and the industry of poultry-raising is an important one in nearly all countries. While in hotels and at elaborate dinners the place of honor in the menu is still occupied by the sirloin of beef, the dinner is never complete without poultry in some form and game, the latter usually broiled, following the punch or sherbet. At any modern dinner, at all complete, a prominent place is given to some of the poultry family, a goose, a pair of ducks or better still a turkey, the most recently domesticated bird of all. While among meats the boar's head is assigned the "crown and semblance" of honor, among birds there is, as well, their proper and distinctive standard bearer, the peacock. As with the boar's head, the peacock served the double purpose of food and epicurean decoration, with the single difference that, while boar's head is still seen upon the holiday tables of England, the peacock, in such role, is a thing of the past. It was most highly esteemed as a food in the middle ages, and legends tell us that the bird was first obtained by Solomon from the spice islands of the Orient. The bird was not used as food later than the reign of Francis I., when it first came to be employed merely as ornament upon the tables. It was highly spiced and covered completely with its own gorgeous plumage, its tail outspread, the eyes in which, they tell us, symbolized eternity. Winter relates that "the same peacock was served again and again and on special occasions, such as weddings, his beak and throat were stuffed with cotton and camfire." This was lighted for the divertisement of the guests much as the brandy poured about a plum pudding is set a-fire just before being placed upon the table. From that time until this France has been called the greatest fowl-consuming nation in the world, and the statement was well borne out by the display of canned and truffled fowl which was sent by that country to the World's Columbian Exposition.

As a whole, fowls have a distinct dietetic value, although, in regard to nutritive properties, there is little difference between theirs and other meat. Their flesh is rich in nitrogenous matter, but contains little fat unless, as with poultry, they are specially fattened for killing. The meat of poultry is classified as light meat and dark, the latter considered more delicious in flavor, while that of wild fowl is always dark and savory. It is also considered more tender and digestible than the meat of tame fowl, as one author states, because of the violent exercise undergone by the bird prior to killing, and is greatly preferred by the gourmet. The flavor of certain wild fowl is distinctive and largely depends upon the food eaten by them. That of the highly prized canvas back duck is due to its feeding upon the wild celery, as the root of the *valisneria* is called. These beds of wild celery are located along Chesapeake Bay, and the flesh of the duck is in fine condition only when its diet is wholly vegetarian. This is not always the case, for at times the duck's food consists of fish, which causes its flesh to lose all that is valued in its flavor.

The flesh of the ptarmigan savors of the spruce leaves of its native mountains, the partridge owes its spicy flavor to the aromatic nuts and berries which it uses for food, while the Congo chickens of Africa are considered excellent because fed upon pine-apples. Even in the case of the turkey, a delicious flavor may be imparted to its meat by a diet of sweet potatoes and nuts continued for several weeks before killing. Such birds, however, demand extravagant prices and the story is told of an Italian restaurateur in New York who accomplishes the same thing by flavoring the meat, *post mortem*, as it were. He mixes a pint of vinegar and claret with a cupful of olive oil in which the bird, dressed, is partly immersed. It is turned daily for a week and then cooked, a dish fit for a king. But one surely ought to be satisfied with the skill of the average cook who makes his dressing of bread crumbs with oysters, mushrooms or Italian chestnuts, the daintiest of sweet marjoram and summer savory for seasoning, pepper and salt, plenty of butter and a suspicion of nutmeg. What matter whether the turkey be stuffed before death or after? It is the American dish typical, combining the intangible piquancy of the French, the heartiness of the English and the generous savoriness of the lands of the Danube and the Rhine.

It is essential that the flesh of both poultry and game be tender before cooking and in some countries it is the custom to give fowls vinegar for that purpose just before killing them. The most common method, especially with game, is to let it hang until tender or "ripened," by which time it has acquired a peculiar flavor, much liked by certain epicures and designated as "gamey." Such meats are in the incipient stages of decomposition and Chrysostom says of them: "The tendency of putrefaction to impart deleterious qualities to animal matter, originally wholesome, has long been known. To those unaccustomed to the use of tainted meat, the mere commencement of decay is sufficient to render the meat insupportable and noxious. Game, only enough decayed to please the palate of the epicure, has caused severe cholera in persons not accustomed to eating it in that state." The detrimental effects of such meat, which is always poisonous, are counteracted in a measure by the heat used in cooking it and also by the digestive fluids which are antiseptic in their nature. Then, too, its frequent use renders the system less liable to be affected by it. The liking for it is undoubt-edly a depraved and vitiated taste which may have descended to certain of us from uncivilized ancestors. The Indians of America are accustomed to bury meat for weeks, until it is putrid. Then it becomes more or less of a delicacy according to the degree of its putre-faction. Even the Greenlander buries his meat until half decayed, when it is used as a relish, called *mikiak*. The Chinese, Siamese and Burmese use putrefied fish as a basis of certain of their choicest condiments, while the epicures of cultured Europe and America disdain the barbarity of such tastes. But is this any more barbaric than the hanging of game until tender from decay before cooking? It half persuades one that the cycle of gastronomic tastes is being completed in this return to the customs of the savage, for when man feasts upon partially decomposed flesh his taste is not an iota in ad-vance of that of the rudest of his ancestors.

Chicken, the most common of domesticated fowls, is more largely used in Europe than here because it is possible to obtain it when other meat in good condition may not be procured. It is in-dispensable to mulligatawny soup, and to the curry of rice, so staple a food with the Siamese, Javanese, East Indians and many European nations. Siam exhibited dried and shredded chicken. The various canning houses of America sent displays of potted chicken, plain and seasoned; of boned chicken, plain and truffled; of deviled chicken, the same meat canned plain without seasoning, and curried chicken in abundance. France, a country which annually spends fifty-two millions of francs for different species of fowl, exhibited varieties of chicken, both whole and minced, dressed with truffles. Beside this there was a profusion of bottled *crete de coq* and *crete de rognons de coq*, portions of the fowl which are not as yet accepted articles of food in America but which are imported to a small extent for foreigners living here.

Probably there is no fowl more tortured than the goose, that the markets may be furnished with the enormous livers from which are made the pâté de foie gras. The goose is kept caged and in a warm place and is stuffed with fattening foods, until the liver, in which this unassimilated food takes refuge, becomes gorged with fat and enormously enlarged. The goose is then killed and the liver, when put up with truffles, is pronounced by all the world "the most delicious of morsels." At the exposition France and Germany met each other in friendly rivalry over their famous goose-liver pies. Strasburg and Paris had each a fine display though Germany still uses the French name, pâté de foie gras. In France, I am told, the food of these geese is seasoned until stimulating to quick growth, this producing the peculiar flavor so well liked in the livers when prepared as "pâtés." The story is told of a certain queen of France who spent fifteen thousand francs in the effort to have a certain flavor imparted to these goose-livers by the method of feeding. Goose livers are far from being healthful articles of food. It has been previously shown that the human system can assimilate only a limited amount of fat and should not be burdened with a quantity taken merely to please a perverted appetite, and which must be thrown off as effete matter.

Germany exhibited canned goose with beans. Goose, however, is not as much used in this country as abroad, our only exhibit being plain canned goose from the state of Maine, although there is a familiar ditty heralding its excellence when dressed with "sage and onions."

Duck was not largely exhibited at the exposition, only a few houses sending it. The largest display was from Siam, dried and shredded. The bird itself, when tame, is closely allied to the goose in habits and its meat is quite similar in flavor.

What the goose is to France the turkey is to America. It has long been known as our national bird and is quite generally appropriated to the celebration of our great national holiday, Thanksgiving Day. Its meat is superior in flavor to that of the goose, and we are already learning, as has been noticed, the French extravagance of improving this flavor by special feeding. There was plenty of turkey sent to the exposition, all canned, the finest being boned and put up with truffles. There was turkey meat potted in glass, the dark meat in the center and the white surrounding it which, when sliced, made a very ornamental dish. There was also deviled turkey of

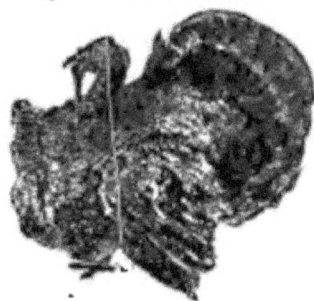

5

various kinds, most of which was seasoned with condiments to the disadvantage of its natural, delicate flavor.

The foreign countries, those which exhibited canned quail, partridge and other wild fowl, were far more largely represented than America. The finest display of partridge and quail at the exposition came from Argentine Republic. They were preserved whole in cans, the partridge in oval tins, each tin containing two birds. The commissioner told me that these tins of canned partridge could be sold in Argentine Republic for a sum equivalent to the American dime. Said he: "These birds are so plentiful that if a covey is started by a hunting-party they may be beaten down with clubs." The birds were well put up but with their flavor somewhat modified by the highly seasoned sauce in which they were preserved.

England presented a great variety of game, potted and canned. There were curried venison, rabbit and hare, pâtés of snipe, woodcook, plover and lark; and pheasant, delicious truffled pheasant from the preserve of a member of the peerage. These preserves, as the land owned by the peerage, and which are used only for hunting grounds, are called, furnish excellent game at every hunting season. Most of it finds its way into English markets, as it brings a good price and is largely in demand. The pheasant is popularly supposed to be best prepared for cookery if hung by the tail until it is sufficiently ripened to become detached from that appendage. It is probable that pheasant when intended for canning are not so treated, for I attributed the flavor of those at the exposition to the truffles, with which they were prepared. The partridge and woodcock vie with each other in regard to flavor and delicacy and epicures have never yet agreed upon which is best. An English rhyme tells us that—

> " If the partridge had the woodcock's thigh,
> 'Twould be the best bird that ever did fly;
> If the woodcock had but the partridge's breast,
> 'Twould be the best bird that ever was dressed."

But to taste of pâté of lark seemed sheer sacrilege, the bird of all birds, immortalized by Chaucer, Shelley, Wordsworth and William Shakespeare. Sentiment must be forgotten by the Englishman of to-day for the London markets are supplied from the country about Dunstable with not less than four thousand dozen of these dainty songsters annually.

Russia presented a large variety of wild fowl, nicely preserved, whole, in tin cans, put up without seasoning or sauce. Each bird could be lifted from its can entire and, though dry enough to be served upon a napkin, was tender, delicious and perfectly preserved. The list included hazel-hen, a bird similar to the American grouse; heath-hen, also a grouse; Scotch-hen, snow-hen, a species of pheasant; ptarmigan, called also the spruce grouse; and capercailzie, a grouse, native to the mountains of northern Europe.

Nearly all countries preserve fowl, each differently and some more skilfully than others. England and America, only, make a specialty of boned and potted meats and in these, no other country excels them.

CHAPTER IX

FISH.

HE fisheries exhibit at the Columbian Exposition was placed in a building of its own, located at the northern end of the grounds, upon the upper lagoon. The large exhibits of preserved fish, the miles of filmy netting spread and draped into place by rods, oars and tackle in the main building, indicated a vast amount of energetic research upon the part of our own as well as foreign nations. The aquaria of living fish in the structures on either side of the central part demonstrated, in most interesting fashion, the extent and dignity of the occupation of fishery.

The Fisheries building was fashioned after the old Spanish-Romanesque style of architecture, wholly unlike in motive and treatment anything else on the grounds. The very capitals of its columns forewarned one of the wetness of the exhibit within its walls for, as Ruskin tells us, capitals of such shape are peculiar to northern and rainy climes. Profusely decorated, they slanted abruptly inward from abacus to shaft as if for protection from inclement weather above. The decoration seemed to have been dredged from a sedgy pond or weedy sea-marsh and, by some modern Medusa, stiffened into the stone adornments of column, capital and arch. Frogs, lizards and crawfish, their legs indicating a furious scramble on their part to escape, were caught in a tangle of sagittaria and pickerel-grass. Lobsters and crabs disported themselves among the fingered masses of sea-weed; fish, lithe of body and grotesque of countenance, meandered over the columns, quite secure

from disturbance by their meshy protection of net; and also with
coquettishly clasped tails, adorned the handrails of the porches.

The living exhibit in the aquaria was not intended to be a food
display, but rather a natural science lesson. The aquaria were
placed in the end structures which were polygonal in shape, the
salt and fresh water displays being separated by the central building. Anemones, like gorgeous flowers, brightened the salt water
tanks and as the sea-horses and amiable little fiddler crabs floated
past them, one was reminded of nothing so much as the quaint con-
ceits which have made fame and fortune for the artist, F. S. Church.
The fresh water exhibit was far larger, containing specimens of
nearly every variety known to the waters of our lakes and rivers;
the mammoth sturgeon, *mishe-nahma* as our Indians call it, the
slender pickerel, the calico bass, and the tiny trout from our mountain streams, the daintiest fish of all. But nothing could be farther
removed from any suggestion of food than these fish of the aquaria,
demurely floating about in the radiance of electric light. Not a
suspicion of gaminess could be attached to them. The shark gazed
deprecatingly through the glass at what he may have thought to be
a human menagerie on parade, and the very sword-fish seemed to
breathe apologies for inability to sheathe his ugly weapon.

The main building, larger than the others, contained scientific
data of all forms of aquatic life, displayed by means of maps, preserved and stuffed specimens, casts and explanatory literature. All
classes contributed their share. There were, besides fish of all varieties, sponges, jelly-fish, polypi, star-fish, sea-urchins, leeches, crusta-
cea, reptiles, aquatic animals and even water-fowl. Fish culture
was illustrated by means of hatcheries exhibited in both the Government and Fisheries buildings. The science of fresh water ang-
ling was also demonstrated with all its death dealing apparatus;
traps, nets, rods, reels, lines, gaffs, spears, creels, artificial flies and
bait; all the intricate appliances with which man must reinforce his
own skill and acumen before he can cope with the wariness of one
timid little fish. The methods of sea-fishing were most completely
shown by Norway, Japan, Canada and those of the United States
bordering on the Atlantic ocean. The fishing gear of all nations
and many kinds was shown, illustrating trawl, herring, long-line and
other methods. Fish-hooks, knives, traps, wiers, nets, lobster and
eel-pots illustrated special fisheries such as herring, cod, mackerel
halibut, oyster, lobster and sponge.

But the most interesting feature, in many ways, was the food exhibit of preserved fish. There were salted fish, dried fish, smoked fish, and canned fish; fish flour, fish delicacies such as sardines, anchovies and caviare, and oils from the whale, cod, seal, shark and dolphin. Fish is an important article of diet among all nations, to say nothing of those communities depending almost wholly upon it. It is, of course, most largely used by those who follow fishing as an occupation, chief among whom are the Norwegians, the people on the coasts of Ireland, those of the Mediterranean coasts, the Eskimos of the Arctic regions, the poorer classes of Chinese and East Indians and a limited class on the Atlantic seaboard of America.

It is commonly believed that a fish-consuming people are not robust, becoming liable to leprosy and other scorbutic diseases, as these affections are common in China, in lower India and among the Eskimos. This is true, however, of only the most ignorant and destitute classes, and, it is more than likely, because of their inability to procure even a small quantity of vegetables, cereals or fruits than because they are deprived of all animal foods excepting fish. The people of our own coasts and those of Norway are as rugged, healthy and prolific as could be desired and the women of fish-eating communities are often remarkable for their robust and picturesque beauty. In neither case, however, do these people depend chiefly upon fish for sustenance. They cultivate and use vegetables and grains extensively and in the case of the Norwegians, one of their fish is salmon, the meat of which somewhat resembles beef. A diet, continuously adhered to throughout years and generations, consisting mainly of a certain animal food fosters a tendency to scorbutic or skin disease. It has been stated that the population of England was continually depleted in early times by scurvy, owing to the fact that vegetables had not then taken their place as a necessary article of diet and that the people were compelled to subsist chiefly upon meat. This is especially the case in tropical countries and is probably the reason that such tendencies among the fish-eating natives of lower Asia are attributed to their fish diet.

In regard to its nutritive value fish compares most favorably with meats, containing about the same proportion of protein, but, excepting the sturgeon and salmon, far less fat. Fish is considered to be a specially suitable food for brain-workers on account of the phosphorus contained. This belief is without scientific foundation,

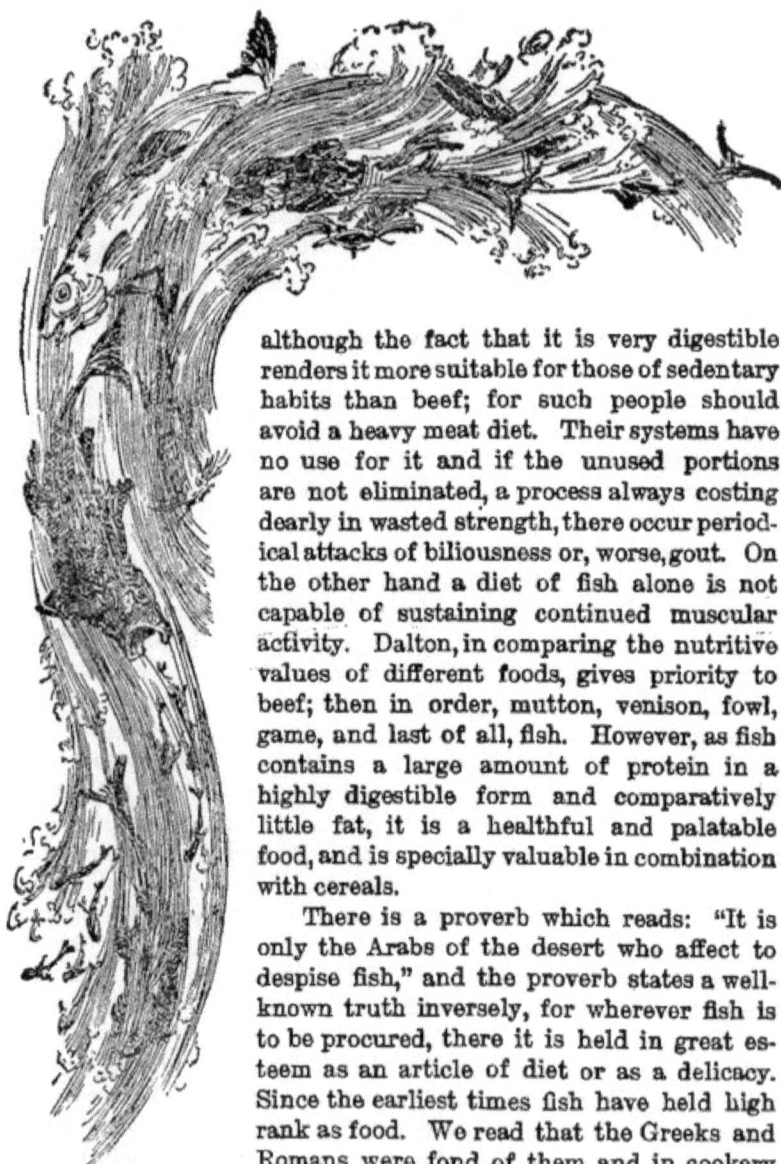

although the fact that it is very digestible
renders it more suitable for those of sedentary
habits than beef; for such people should
avoid a heavy meat diet. Their systems have
no use for it and if the unused portions
are not eliminated, a process always costing
dearly in wasted strength, there occur period-
ical attacks of biliousness or, worse, gout. On
the other hand a diet of fish alone is not
capable of sustaining continued muscular
activity. Dalton, in comparing the nutritive
values of different foods, gives priority to
beef; then in order, mutton, venison, fowl,
game, and last of all, fish. However, as fish
contains a large amount of protein in a
highly digestible form and comparatively
little fat, it is a healthful and palatable
food, and is specially valuable in combination
with cereals.

There is a proverb which reads: "It is
only the Arabs of the desert who affect to
despise fish," and the proverb states a well-
known truth inversely, for wherever fish is
to be procured, there it is held in great esteem as an article of diet or as a delicacy.
Since the earliest times fish have held high
rank as food. We read that the Greeks and
Romans were fond of them and in cookery
combined them with oil, wine, eggs, carrots, cheese and sweet herbs.

Modern tastes are simpler in this respect for we chiefly prize the natural flavor which heat develops, and a whitefish broiled, a shad "planked," or a dainty smelt, browned quickly in smoking oil, is quite to our taste without added flavorings. It is said that we are not as epicurean in regard to fish as were the ancients; and this is to some extent true, for it is not always possible to procure them in a perfectly fresh state. There is an art of fishmongery in our age, and by means of painting the gills and various other devices, stale fish are often relieved of the appearance of their condition. The Greeks very early enacted a law, which we might adopt with benefit, stipulating that the fisherman or fish vender must remain standing until all his fish were sold. America, surrounded by ocean and gulf, traversed by the greatest rivers of the world, and holding in her midst a chain of immense lakes, seems intended to supply the inhabitants with an abundance of fish for food. When supplies of any kind are plentiful, however, more or less lavish expenditure and waste are the result and the effects of such waste were early noticeable in our fresh water fisheries. More fish were taken, frequently, than were needed for food; they were unprotected during the spawning season; seines, traps and pounds were used and the smaller fish were wantonly destroyed.

The early fisheries' reports from time to time pointed out a noticeable decrease in the coast fisheries as well as those of the great lakes. It was seen that some protection to the fishing industry was a necessity and in February, 1871, laws were passed which had for their object the preservation of the food fish of the United States. By the next year the Fish Commission was in working order, its first appropriation being $15,000, and it became a separate governmental bureau in 1888. To-day the Department of Fisheries is working along the same line with the Department of Agriculture toward better methods of food preservation. The department specially investigates the geographical distribution of fish and endeavors to preserve the equalization of such distribution; it experiments for the purpose of learning the economical value of fish as food; and by experiments in other directions endeavors to determine the best methods of fish propagation and culture. The careful and efficient research of the Fish Commission has resulted in an awakened public sentiment which will no longer calmly submit to the useless destruction of fish by seines, traps and other means; and the exhibition in the Fisheries building, with that made by the Fisheries Department in the Government building at the exposition, was the crown and memorial set upon twenty years of philanthropic work.

The fish in the aquaria, intended merely as an educational exhibit at the exposition, far outnumbered in variety those used for food, although it is estimated that in the United States alone, including coast fisheries, there are about one hundred varieties used for the latter purpose.

Among edible fishes the white-meated variety is more easily digested than those possessing red flesh, as the former contain far less fat. If fat be contained to any extent it is usually deposited in the liver, as with the cod, while in red-meated fish such as salmon, it is distributed throughout the tissue. All fish are in best condition before spawning, just after the season has passed being far less valuable for food. Their flavor is influenced by the food consumed by them, no variety being more susceptible than the trout. It is the fish, *par excellence*, when caught in mountain rivulets, but of decidedly different flavor after being fed for even a short time in trout ponds. Someone has compared the flavor of smelt to that of cucumbers and grayling to that of thyme; and we all are familiar with the sedgy taste of pickerel and catfish caught from muddy, grass-grown ponds. It is related that the ancient Romans valued turbot as a food more highly if caught after the fish had feasted upon some disobedient slave, thrown into the pond; an incredibly horrible custom but finding almost a parallel in the brutality with which turtle, lobster, and other foods are sacrificed to the whims of so-called epicures.

The food exhibit proper showed many varieties of preserved fish, the different methods of preservation being dry salting, salting in brine or pickling, drying without salt, pulverizing to fish-flour, pounding and shredding, canning, and preserving in oil. Each of these methods depends either upon the demands of the country in which the fish are preserved or the requirements of an export trade.

The United States occupied first rank in respect to the magnitude of its display, although the exhibits of Canada, Norway and Russia were but little inferior in any respect. Large displays of dried, smoked and canned salmon were sent by the great canning companies of Washington and Oregon. The salmon attains an enormous size, as was seen by specimens sent from Portland, Oregon, frozen into cakes of ice, one fish weighing sixty-seven pounds. Sturgeon, dried and in "scraps," was sent from the Northwest, being a fat, coarse-meated fish and one difficult of digestion. In early times its flesh was considered a great delicacy, Henry I. of England having once proclaimed it to be a royal fish and one to be eaten at no table but his own. But its quondam reputation has long been forgotten by modern fish lovers. Fishermen attribute its rank flavor to its food, and it is variously known as "herring-sturgeon" and "mackerel-sturgeon," these smaller kinsmen furnishing it with food at different places or times.

The same canneries sent also canned sturgeon roe or eggs, known as *caviare*. This is considered a great delicacy and from its appetite and thirst-provoking qualities has been called the "savory preliminary" of a feast. That of Russia, where it is usually eaten in a fresh state, is described as being "grey, pearly, succulent and delicate, of which most of the caviare found in this country is but the shadow of the substance." The word *caviare* is of Turkish origin, and the delicacy was earliest used by the Moslem tribes inhabiting Russia. It was introduced into western Europe by the merchant traders of Constantinople and was well known in the Elizabethan age of England. At that time, however, it was esteemed only by the wealthy and was considered to be as far above the taste as it certainly was beyond the purse of ordinary people. Hamlet, in speaking of a play, makes the comparison: "It pleased not the million; 'twas caviare to the general; but it was an excellent play."

The exhibit of caviare at the exposition was contributed to not alone by foreign countries but by America. That from North Carolina was salted and dried. It is also largely produced from the roe of the New Jersey sturgeon. The roe is shipped to Europe, repacked, relabeled and then shipped back to America to be resold at an advanced price. It brings, originally, from five to seven dollars per keg, each keg being from 100 to 130 pounds in weight, and the last year's production of caviare, as shipped abroad at a low price, was valued at $140,000. Americans are rapidly developing a taste for this delicacy, which is useful in the making of sandwiches as well as in fish-dressing and sauces.

The Great Lakes were represented by whitefish and trout while the eastern states displayed mackerel, haddock, bluefish, salmon, halibut, and cod. The latter is especially valuable for food as its flesh contains, proportionately, far more nutriment and less fat than the majority of fish. When caught in season it is meaty and tender, in fishing districts becoming a staple article of diet; but when caught out of season its flesh is stringy, tough and flavorless. It is usually cured by salting and by exposure to sun and air until thoroughly dried. The cod furnishes two delicacies, highly prized by all fishermen, which were sent in cans to the exposition—cods' sounds and tongues. The sounds are the swimming bladders of the cod and are delicate and gelatinous when cooked. The tongues are tempting morsels, and neither these nor the sounds are often found in inland markets, owing to the great liking which people on the coasts have for them.

Halibut was displayed cured, as is usual, by salting and smoking. There was also a display of smelt, the silvery little tid-bit which is always delicious but never plentiful enough. Sardines, genuine American sardines (which are only little herring), put up in genuine cotton-seed oil, took their place with the others. There is no objection to these as an article of food, especially when put up in a pure, vegetable oil, but to be given the name of *sardines*, a French label and a high price, seems very unworthy the American nation. Call them herring in vegetable oil, make them so good that rich and poor want them and so cheap that all can buy, and another name may be added to our list of distinctively American productions.

Canada had a praiseworthy exhibit, not only of fish foods but also of boats and fishing appliances. There were exhibited salmon, canned and dried; dried, boneless cod, and cod shredded; hake and haddock, dried sturgeon, and cods' tongues in cans and half-barrels.

Norway's display was particularly large and full of interest. There were exhibited boats and fishing-gear of all kinds showing the people to be of unusual thrift and intelligence, as well as painstaking and scientific. There was exhibited complete analyses of different fish foods, so arranged that the most unlearned could at once see the relative nutriment and wastes. This exhibit was arranged in sets of glass jars, all the jars being plainly labeled. Jar number one contained two pounds of a certain fish. Jar number two contained the entire amount of nitrogenous or tissue-building elements found in a similar two pounds of the same kind of fish. The next jar contained the fat or oil, the next the water, extracted, and the last jar the ash or waste matter. If protein in its most digestible form were desired a glance indicated which fish was most suitable; if oil were necessarry, another was seen to be most valuable. Such experiments are forging along the right line, and, if carried on in all lands and with all foods, it were not long before people would be fed as intelligently as is live stock by the average farmer.

The Norwegian dried fish were haddock, coalfish, stockfish, ling, cod and boneless cod, shredded fish, and fish-flour. The haddock were cured without salt, dried until extremely hard, and tied into bundles weighing fifty pounds each. Fish flour was shown, prepared from various fish which, after being well dried, are pulverized. This fish flour is extensively used as food in Norway, chiefly for biscuits, puddings and soups. The following fish were well preserved in brine: stock-fish, herring, klip-fish, ling, cusk, cod, haddock, mackerel and anchovies. Among canned fish were sardines, anchovies, herring in oil and a large assortment labeled, "Delicatessen." The latter included fish-balls, fish-balls in jelly, fish-balls in wine sauce, cods' roe, fish pudding, fish *gratin* and fish-balls in fish bouillon.

Among all the nations of the far East, there were none which more genuinely won the respect of this hurrying, restless, western continent than did the Japanese. Whatever the food exhibited might be, every detail of its history, growth and manufacture, even to a chemical analysis, was given. The labels upon all their food articles contained full in-

Siamese Fish Broiler

formation, showing that the Japanese are unrivaled in patience, that they are absolutely honest in the manufacture of their goods, and that they endeavor, not to put upon the market the largest quantity, but to make each article perfect in workmanship. Their dried fish were nicely prepared and attractively put up; salmon, herring, sardines, skate, and sharks' fins, the latter a great delicacy. The salted fish were salmon, cod, mackerel, herring, tunny and tai. Herring and sardines were preserved in oil; various fish were canned, some of which were placed in the cans in layers separated by grape leaves.

Seaweed, so largely used in Japan as a food, was also exhibited.

It is prepared by being cleansed and then pressed into thin sheets, as delicate and transparent as mica. This seaweed has an agreeable taste and imparts its own flavor to other food which may be cooked with it. The entire exhibit of Japan, as well as that of Norway, was educational to a marked degree.

Russia exhibited largely. There were sturgeon steak, caviare, herring, smoked eels, sprats and anchovies. The exhibit impressed one with the fact that the most highly prized article of all was caviare. All were carefully preserved.

Great Britain exhibited dried fish from Dublin Bay, the celebrated "Finnan haddies," and herring, most excellent herring. Little wonder that herring-pies have been famous in England for nearly three centuries, for we learn that in 1629, twenty-four herring-pies, each containing five herring, were carried to court, a custom not yet forgotten. This is the recipe for making: Five herring, to be seasoned with half a pound of ginger, half a pound of pepper, a quarter of a pound of cinnamon, one ounce of cloves, one ounce of long pepper, half an ounce of grains of paradise (a something very peppery and which, we are told, was then much used in beer). These pies were to be washed down with good ale.

Herring are essentially modern fish, for neither the Greeks nor Romans knew of them. The Dutch first brought them from the Scots and pickled them so excellently, it is said, that they derived great profit from the sale. But the herring of Great Britain, such as were seen at the exposition, kippered, pickled, and put up in cream of tomatoes, are unequaled. There were also tunny fish, cod, pilchards, white-bait, turbot, soles and sprats, Yarmouth bloaters, eels and anchovies, herring milt and herring roes. One firm made a special exhibit of silvoceas, a fish resembling the herring and possessing a delicate flavor. They were served to the public daily, and became very popular, put up in cans with tomato sauce and kippered.

The fish exhibits of both New South Wales and Mexico were largely educational.

The Mediterranean countries sent chiefly sardines put up in olive oil, the firm meated little fish whose popularity is so great that all sorts of imitations follow in its wake. Italy and Spain both sent tunny in oil, also cuttle-fish and squid. Both the latter fish have much the flavor and texture of shrimp. The cuttle-fish was also preserved in oil, sections of its arms resembling huge pipes of macaroni and the eating of one of these fearful disc-like suckers by one unaccustomed to it brought to mind in all its horrid vividness, the cuttle-fish described by Victor Hugo. Still, the flesh much resembles the meat of the lobster claw and was considered as great a luxury by the ancient Romans as it is to-day by their descendants. Squid is put up in its own inky fluid and is far from attractive in appearance. It consists simply of an elongated sac with tentacles at one extremity, being largely eaten in Portugal and other countries of southern Europe.

Siam exhibited several varieties of fish, all dried, some whole and some pounded and shredded. There were cuttle-fish, squid, shrimp, prawn, and bass, including very many varieties with untranslatable names. The skate was also exhibited dried, a cartilaginous fish, in flavor somewhat like Japanese seaweed.

As a food, fish are absolutely free to those who wish to procure them from the waters and should be one of our lowest-priced articles of diet. Fish do not require care as to protection, propagation or feeding and were it not for the reckless waste of this product by nets and traps the occupation would not be governed by the element of chance or "luck" which renders it a precarious one, and its product higher in price than ordinary meats.

CHAPTER X.

HELL-FISH may be generally classified as crustaceans and mollusks, the former possessing an articulated body which is protected by a coat or shell-like covering. The latter are invertebrate and inarticulate animals whose shells enlarge yearly to accommodate their growth. The former class includes lobster, crabs, crawfish, shrimp and prawn, described by Dr. Edward Smith as fibrinous, because composed of actual muscular fibre. Mollusks may be subdivided into bivalves, comprising the oyster, scallop, clam and mussel; and univalves, including the periwinkle, cockle, limpet, whelk, etc.

Nearly all species of shell-fish were known to the Greeks and Romans, the universal favorite being the oyster. Crustaceans were usually eaten raw, and Pliny tells of a crawfish (which was probably a lobster), measuring four cubits or nearly six feet in length. It is said that the Romans were better connoisseurs of fish and shell-fish than are the moderns and the deviled crab of to-day may have had for its prototype the crab and mussel minced meats of two thousand years ago. In the sixteenth century the lobster was largely used as food, being roasted in an oven and served with vinegar, its meat, until a recent date, being considered very nutritious. But the flesh of all crustaceans is difficult of digestion, owing to the peculiar toughness of its texture, and is likely to cause the ambitious gourmet serious discomfort. An attack of indigestion may follow the

8

eating of shell-fish and frequently a disturbance of the skin, producing an eruption. Notwithstanding these peculiarities, shell-
fish are considered the very *delicatessen* of foods, preference being
given to the lobster. It is served with condiments and, were the
gastric juices not spurred to an unusual extent by these excitants,
it is probable that the chances of indigestion after a midnight
supper would be greatly increased. But so delicious is considered
the flavor of its white, tenacious flesh that many are those who will
continue to enjoy it in spite of risks. A certain physician, who is
widely known as a lecturer upon hygiene and foods, declares the
flesh of all shell-fish unfit to be eaten owing to the dubious character of the food consumed by them. He terms them "scavengers
of the sea." They are usually found, it is true, in the estuaries and
shallows where the rivers empty into the sea, waters none too clean
at any time and often foul. Still, it is possible that they purify the
refuse in assimilation, to some extent, as does the rhubarb plant or
mushroom, which gathers nourishment from a heap of compost.

In structure the lobster resembles the common crawfish of our
inland creeks and consists of a thorax, terminating in a head, and an
abdomen, called the tail. It is protected by an external shell, which
it sheds yearly, the covering of the thoracic organs being split while
that of the tail is cast off whole. The meat is found chiefly in the
tail and claws, the latter more delicate in flavor. The lobster
breathes through branchiæ or gills, portions rarely if ever eaten. The
contents of the thorax consist mainly of liver, commonly called
brain, which is too fatty to be digestible. Lobster catching by parties who go out in boats is considered to be as rare a sport as is
"crabbing," the catching, when hooks are used to dislodge the quar-
relsome creatures, being highly exciting to any unwary fisherman
whose fingers come in contact with the treacherous claws. The
female or hen-lobster is in greatest demand because of the eggs or
"berries" which are found attached beneath the tail. The eggs on
boiling change in color from black to bright red, and with the "coral"
or ovary are valued by the *chef de cuisine* for garnishes and for ingredients of his sauces.

Crabs resemble lobsters in possessing an external skeleton covering both the thorax and an insignificant tail. They are also possessed of ten legs, the first pair of which terminate in vicious looking claws. Few of the many varieties of crab are used for food, the
commonest being the blue or edible crab (*callinectes hastatus*). This

crab inhabits the shallow waters throughout the entire extent of the Atlantic, Gulf and Pacific coasts and is always to be found in seaboard markets. In the South and East the blue crab is chiefly valued at that period of the year when it has cast off its old shell and is in a "soft-shelled" condition. It is then broiled whole for eating while, when hard-shelled, it may be deviled, baked and served upon its own dainty skeleton. The edible crab of the Pacific coast, from San Francisco to Puget Sound, is used only when hard-shelled on account of its immense size, the shell alone being as large as a breakfast plate. The meat of these crabs is delicious and they are marketed, boiled, ready for salad or other preparation. They are used only when caught from the deeper waters and are so plentiful that the finest retail for ten cents apiece.

Crawfish, aside from minor differences, might be lobsters in miniature. They inhabit secluded places in both fresh and marine waters, appropriating for food whatever of mollusks, larvæ or insects, living or dead, come in their way. Owing to their voracious appetites Audubon has termed them "little aquatic vultures." Crawfish, particularly those of the fresh waters, are but little larger than shrimp or prawn, although those of the rivers of Russia attain considerable size.

Shrimp and prawn are tiny creatures found along the coasts of the United States, of Europe (specially the southern countries) and of Great Britain. Even upon the sea-coast, they are usually boiled before being marketed, the heat changing their color to a tint known as "shrimp pink." Prawn resemble crawfish in appearance and habits and are larger than shrimps. Both are considered a luxurious and delicate food, and, although their flesh is tenacious to the verge of elasticity, they

Lobster.

are more digestible than lobster. The tails of these tiny fish are the only portions eaten, although the rest of the body is often used for flavoring soups and sauces. Like the lobster and crab they are prepared with condiments.

At the Columbian Exposition the shell-fish industry was extensively represented. Numbers of lobster-pots were exhibited, quantities of cans containing lobster meat and, to crown all, a mammoth lobster shell, relict of a recently defunct decapod which weighed twenty-three and one-half pounds. Canned lobster was sent from the northeastern portion of the United States, from Canada and from Japan; from England, lobster canned plain and with curry. Japan sent canned crabs; and shrimp, both canned and dried. Shrimp and prawn were sent from the southern of the United States; shrimp, dried and pickled, were sent from Mexico, pickled shrimp from New South Wales. The process of preparing shrimp and prawn by drying might to advantage be more largely employed in America. By such means they could be obtained at inland markets at a more reasonable price than now prevails.

Of the bivalves the oyster is the most extensively used and by far the most highly esteemed. With a delicate and perfect flavor it has the advantage of a lineage antedating the descendants of the Tarquins and immortalized by the poets of all ages. One of the Greek writers calls it "the truffle of the sea," and the poets of ancient Rome vied with each other as have those of the modern world in attempts to picture its seductiveness and·charm. There may be persons, William Matthews suggests, who do not like oysters but, "like ghosts and anthropophagi, they have never appeared to us." The eloquence and grandeur of the old world were nourished upon the oyster. It was the first, intermediate, and last course at the Roman banquet tables and many a master of eloquence, among others Martial, Horace, Pliny, Seneca and Cicero, paid unto it inspired and poetic tribute. The Romans were the first to establish oyster beds extensively and theirs became widely famous, the oysters being as immense as those of Louisiana and Alabama.

After a few centuries of neglect the oyster was put permanently into fashion by the foppish old Louis Quatorze. It became universally liked throughout all Europe and oyster culture has since then been carried on more extensively each year.

The status of oyster culture in Europe has been most thoroughly investigated by Bashford Dean of Columbia College, New York. According to his investigations the countries which now most extensively cultivate the oyster are England, France, Germany, Spain, Portugal, Italy and the Netherlands. Italy is the home of oyster culture, it having been accomplished in Rome as early as the time of Crassus. The most noted of these culturists, of whom there were many, was Sergius Orator, a wealthy patrician. Oysters were also cultivated at Tarente, a prosperous and ancient city, at which place the most extensive beds in all Italy are located to-day. The system used is known as vertical or "rope-culture," ropes being used upon which the oysters lodge and grow to maturity.

The oysters of England were known to the ancient world. The largest natural beds lie in the estuary of the Thames but there are also cultivated areas, the greater part of which are controlled directly by parliament. Lessees of these beds are compelled by law either to cultivate them or forfeit the lease. The process of culture consists in planting the "brood" oysters over areas, smooth, hard and clean of bottom and in no danger of being overwhelmed by mud or sand. When the tiny oysters become of sufficient size they are removed to deeper waters to fatten for market.

To quote from Mr. Dean: "The Dutch have come to be looked upon in Europe generally as the most successful administrators of the oyster industry . . . . an industry which not only gives employment to the poorer coast population, but pays into the national treasury, in rental of state lands hitherto absolutely profitless, an annual income of nearly a half million of dollars." The importance of oyster culture to so small a country as Holland is appreciated when we learn that the entire cultural area of that country is not half as great as that of Long Island alone. The principal beds are those of the Zuyder Zee and of the Schelde estuary. The Dutch breed their oysters upon tiles, ranged sidewise in rows along the shore, and from these remove them to deeper waters from which they are dredged for market. The oysters of Holland and Ostend, Belgium, are considered valuable and of fine flavor in all European markets. Those known as Ostend oysters are those which are simply fattened at Ostend, having been originally obtained from the cultural beds of other countries.

The oysters of both Spain and Portugal are peculiar in shape, flavor and color. This is thought to be due to the physical conditions of their locality, as they have not been successfully bred in any other place. There are few, if any, cultural areas, the extended coast line making it possible to always depend upon the natural beds from which they are dredged and sold to fishermen to be planted in rented areas of their own. Oysters are there considered a cheap, and in some respects, an inferior food.

The oyster beds of Germany are located only on the shores of the North Sea bordering Denmark. These beds were described as early as 1652 in the Danish chronicle and are, by tradition, the property of the crown. Oyster culture has been practically a failure in Germany, owing to the sediment and mud in the waters, lack of food for their growth, and the coldness of winter (Moebius). The oyster supply depends, therefore, upon the products of natural beds.

The natural oyster beds along the coast of France were for many years considered inexhaustible and not until the last fifty years has oyster culture been practiced. Now the seed oysters are attached to roofing tile until sufficiently large to be removed to deeper waters to fatten for dredging. The French have encountered many obstacles in the culture of oysters owing to the physical conditions of their coasts and coast waters. The two principal species are known as the "flat" and the "Portuguese" oyster, the former round, the latter long and deeply ridged. The oyster grounds of France have long been under absolute control of the government.

The oyster industry in America is carried on chiefly in the celebrated regions of Chesapeake and Long Island, along Connecticut, in the southern gulf waters and along the western coasts. The oysters are cultivated upon shells spread carefully over smooth, hard bottom; in parts of Connecticut on twigs and branches, and in California upon frames made of bamboo.

The chief enemies with which the young oyster has to contend

Starfish Destroying an Oyster.

are mud and sediment, too low temperature of the water during winter, freshets, certain species of periwinkle, and starfish. Beyond dredging no remedy for these latter destructive agencies has been used in the East, though in the West the starfish are kept out of the beds by fences of bamboo, closely staked.

The nutritive value of the oyster is low, though its digestibility renders it of great value to the invalid. After the "fattening" process they bring a higher price than before, although, as the oyster does little more than absorb the fresh water, it is no more nutritious. Many still prefer the flavor of the smaller variety dredged from the natural bed. They contain only from twelve to fourteen per cent of nutriment, slightly more than mussels, this accounting for the fact that a quantity may be eaten at the beginning of a meal without ruining the appetite for the heavier foods which follow. One author relates that Vitellius once ate a thousand oysters for a meal; but one is inclined to take the statement with at least as much salt as the gluttonous old emperor must have taken with the oysters.

Oysters are eaten only when "in season," from September to May, although this custom is not arbitrary. In May the spawning season begins and for a few months they are poor and unfit for food, giving rise to the popular saying that they should be eaten only during those months the names of which contain R. There are over sixty varieties in existence and in general the small oyster is confined to temperate climates while the large varieties abound only in warmer waters. They have been found in lower Asia a foot in length and proportionately broad, and I assisted a few years ago in the eating of one fresh from the Gulf waters near Mobile the shell of which measured ten and one-half inches by four. It was as delicious as the daintiest of blue-points and as fine in flavor as any of the dozen little oysters clinging to its shell. The oysters found in the warm tides of the Pacific coast are, on the other hand, extremely small though excellent of flavor.

It is considered by many that the flavor of an oyster is not improved by cooking while its digestibility is diminished. For these reasons it is very generally eaten raw, with or without condiments, a custom which may have inspired the reminiscent lines written by Gay:

> "The man had sure a palate covered o'er
> With brass or steel, that on the rocky shore
> First broke the oozy oyster's pearly coat,
> And risked the living morsel down his throat."

Dr. Roberts states that the greatest benefit and most enjoyment can be obtained from the oyster only when it is eaten raw. The dark colored mass or liver of the oyster is, says he, "simply a mass of glycogen or animal starch. Associated with the glycogen, but withheld from actual contact with it during life, is its appropriate digestive ferment, the hepatic diastase. The mere crushing of the oyster between the teeth brings these two bodies together, and the glycogen is at once digested without any other help than the diastase. The raw, or merely warmed oyster, is thus self-digestive." He further says that a cooked oyster has to be digested by the gastric juice of the consumer, like any other food, the heat having destroyed the associated ferment, while long cooking may render it almost indigestible.

Owing to the inland location of the exposition, no raw oysters were exhibited, though there were canned, dried and spice-pickled oysters in abundance.

Clams, as food, are nearly as important as the oyster, although chiefly used by the classes living along the coasts upon which they are found. They are readily marketable, are abundant and are easily procurable from the sandy beaches at low tide. Like the oyster the clam consists of a tough, fibrinous portion and a soft mass, the latter part more digestible. It is not highly nutritious, but of desirable flavor. The "little-neck" clam, peculiar to the New England coast, is sacred to the clam broth and that most epicurean feast of all, the "clam-bake." Webster used to prepare clam chowder for his friends at Marshfield, and the dish is as typical of that region as is the "Boston baked bean." Clams have been used by the New Englanders for centuries and several times during the early struggles of the Plymouth colony they were the only food remaining between the people and starvation.

The early settlers of Seattle and the region about Puget sound are still called "clam diggers" because clams have been since the first a principal article of food. The round clam or "quahaug," though an indigestible morsel, possesses a flavor sufficiently delicate to render it valuable in the making of clam broth. The long-neck clam is of small size when found on the eastern coasts of America, but those from Washington and Vancouver are extremely large, bearing about the same relation to their eastern cousins as the gigantic California pear to one grown upon a stony New England hillside.

At the exposition there were specimens of clam broth or bouillon from Maine, and, in a building called the New England Clam Bake, clam chowder was daily served to hundreds of visitors. Dried and preserved clams were sent from the far Northwest, the largest specimens coming from the Vancouver Indians. The Japanese sent clams which were preserved by being pierced through the neck, hung in rows of one or two dozen upon a stick of bamboo, and in that way dried.

The scallop is in greater favor in America than in Europe. It is procured during the summer months by dredging boats, chiefly in the Long Island and Cape Cod regions. The powerful *adductor* muscle, which serves to close the shell, is the only portion eaten.

The mussel is a small salt water mollusk, about two inches in length, and best liked for food when about two years old. Its flesh is of a yellow color when cooked, being tough and somewhat indigestible. In America it is used chiefly for bait and as a fertilizer of land but in the European countries it has wide favor as food. Off the coasts of England thousands of tons are collected and marketed annually and it is estimated that the mussel fishery alone of France has been worth $175,000. There they are cultivated in enclosures of sea water. In China, the mussel industry is extensive, large quantities being dried for food. The mussel is eaten by only a limited class in America. Along the Pacific coast, particularly about San Francisco, mussels are abundant, those only being eaten which are taken from the deeper and outlying waters. Mussels found near the shore are poisonous, owing to their feeding upon the sewerage of the cities which is there emptied.

The cockle is found along the shores of America as well as off France, England, Ireland and Holland. Immense quantities are consumed in the latter countries, both fresh and pickled, and as they cost in the market about twenty-five dollars a ton they are specially valuable to the poorer classes of people.

The limpet, as well as the cockle, periwinkle and whelk, is eaten chiefly by the lower classes of Europe, being considered in America indigestible and of none too good a flavor. It is always marine, and is found in America adhering to the rocks along the coasts. The whelk is an active little gourmand, whose food consists of dead fish, crabs and other mollusks. Periwinkles are found upon the rocky shores of both Europe and America at low tide, being largely consumed for food in the former continent. The sea-ear, or Abalone oyster, belongs to the limpet family. It is found in large numbers along the California coast. It is eaten fresh, though it is also dried, and often weighs a pound. It is specially valued by the Chinese, and is always found in their markets at San Francisco. Some idea of the commercial value of this mollusk as a food may be seen in the fact that a few years since the Abalone trade was worth $250,000 annually. The owl-limpet is another and smaller variety, so called from the figure of an owl impressed upon the pearly inside coating. It is greatly valued as food by the Chinese, being eaten raw, cooked and dried.

Many a person has laughed over the assurance of a certain naturalist of earlier days who, in classifying animals according to their outward appearance, placed the turtle in the category of insects. For a reptile it is and must remain according to later dictum, the only one of its class, except the edible iguana from the Isle of Trinidad, which had the honor of being exhibited in the rank and file of food products at the World's Columbian Exposition. The turtle has existed since the mesozoic period of the world's history and more species have been discovered in fossilized formations than are now in existence. It was known to the ancients, and Pliny, among other writers, states that boats were made of its shell. He probably referred to the trunk turtle, an immense animal which reaches a length of seven or eight feet and a weight of nearly a ton. It is still found in the Mediterranean but its flesh is wholly unfit for food.

There is a story extant that Antony at one time gave his cook a city for so skilfully preparing a certain dish that it won praises from Cleopatra. This dish is believed to have been turtle, a meat largely used by the wealthier Romans.

Turtle is not a hygienic food, though its praises have been sung from time immemorial by epicures and poets. It is said that any meat, from pork to chicken, may be counterfeited by its various portions, such different flavors are possessed by its flesh. It is tender and palatable but extremely fat, rendering quantities of it cloying to the appetite and difficult of digestion. Doubtless its reputation as a luxury depends upon its comparative rarity and upon the wine, oil and condiments used in cooking it. The turtle seen upon our tables is a food too highly spiced and far too fat to be of any great value to the human system and is far more likely to promote disease than to maintain health. Sailors and people living along the shores off which turtle may be easily obtained soon cease to eat it and return to a diet of dried codfish or even humbler fare with grateful relish.

Mr. Bates, naturalist and author, who spent two years upon the Amazon where turtle is found in great abundance, states that he became so nauseated with the taste and odor of turtle meat that he suffered from hunger on several occasions when there was scarcity of everything else rather than eat of it. The native women cooked it for him in a variety of ways. A soup was made from the chopped entrails; the tender flesh from the breast was minced, mixed with farina and roasted, and steaks from it were cooked in fat. Sausages were made from the stomach filled with minced meat and boiled and, on other occasions, a piece of the meat roasted and dipped in vinegar made an agreeable change. The flesh attached to the shell of the back is called "calipash" while that attached to the lower shell is known as "calipee."

Turtle soups were largely exhibited at the exposition, the only soup exhibits not containing them being those sent by the western packing houses of America. Turtle in any form is a luxury, unobtainable by those of limited means who live inland, and whoever eats largely of it is quite sure to demoralize his liver and bring on indigestion.

There are about forty species of turtle and tortoise inhabiting the oceans adjacent to America, only a few of which are used for food. The green turtle is the most valuable, being famous for the soup made from its flesh. It attains a large size, sometimes weighing a thousand pounds, and is caught in the deeper waters, usually by means of nets.

Terrapin, a smaller species of the tortoise family, is found in both fresh and salt waters. The salt water variety is the "diamondbacked" luxury of epicures and is marketed at enormous prices. Its color is a dull brown. It is slow of growth, reaching a marketable size in not less than six years. It is then from six to seven inches long and three inches in height. The flesh is most prized during hibernation, when the terrapin is found buried in the mud of the salt marshes. There are two terrapin farms in the United States, one, the oldest and most famous, in Maryland, the other near Mobile, Alabama. A farm consists of alternate canals of sea water, cut in from the coast, and ridges of land, the whole enclosed by a high fence. Every terrapin caught in the ocean is taken there and, as they breed rapidly in the farm, the industry is profitable in spite of the years that elapse before they reach a marketable size. They retail at from forty to sixty dollars a dozen.

CHAPTER XI.

SOUPS AND MEAT EXTRACTS.

T IS written that the chefs of France in the time of Louis, le Grand Monarque, devised "bouillon" and "consommé" because mastication was considered to be vulgar. The vast display of soups at the Columbian Exposition half persuaded one that the rest of the world had reached the same conclusion and lived upon nothing else. For so indispensable is a soup considered to even an ordinary dinner that the canning houses both at home and abroad find ready market for their goods. One reason that prepared soups are so largely bought is that the average housewife cannot prepare one in the limited time she is willing or able to give. She will inevitably omit the one indispensable consideration, time; for without consecrating the better part of a day to its making, one's soup is a failure. The making of a good soup is an art, and requires not only skill but tact and sympathy. Slow cooking is a chemical necessity, and any hastening of the process means ruin.

Soup gives a great amount of nourishment while it requires of the system a minimum of exertion in assimilation. It soothes an impatient stomach into gentlest of humor and may serve as the major part of a meal or only as a dainty appetizer. Count Rumford, after five years of experiment in feeding the poor of Munich, found that the most savory, most nourishing and least expensive food was soup, generally made from pearl barley, potatoes, bread, and seasonings. But among the better classes soup is simply the first course of a more or less elaborate dinner. Says an author, "A soup is to a dinner what a portico is to a mansion; it is not merely the first thing to which you come but it also serves to give an idea of what the architect intends to do afterward." Brillat-Savarin says, "it rejoices the stomach and disposes it to receive and digest other food," and to many, a dinner without soup would be far from relishable. The true gourmet prefers a light soup, served hot and in small quantity, the heavy soups, such as the pureés, creams, mullagatawny, and turtle soups being ruinous to the appetite and all too traitorous to the courses which follow.

The lighter varieties are either extract or gelatine soups. Bouillon, the best known of the former kind, is made from chopped lean beef and, like beef tea, must be entirely free from fat. It is clarified with egg, strained, and may be served either hot or ice cold. Bouillon is a stimulant, containing very little nutriment.

Consommé has no English word-equivalent. It is a gelatine soup, richer and more nutritious than bouillon. It may or may not be brown, but should always be clear, various articles being added to the liquor at times to give it variety. It is then known by various names, such as consommé au riz, when rice is added; consommé julienne, vegetables being used; consommé aux petits pois, consommé with green peas; or consommé d'Italie, consommé to which small fancy or alphabetical pastes are added. Each cook may vary ingredients or flavor, providing that the jelly-like consistency is retained. Consommé and bouillon are the bases of all good meat soups, delicacy of flavor and aroma being their prime qualities.

Purées are composed of meat-stock and vegetables, the latter being reduced through a sieve until the whole soup is of a thick, creamy consistency. Cream soups differ little from purées except in the addition of cream. Velvet soups are made of tapioca, perfectly cooked and strained into the stock. These soups require the perfect suspension of all ingredients in the stock. Bisques are purée soups seasoned with crayfish and are always delicate in flavor. Potage is a creamy soup, resembling a purée.

Bouill-abaisse is peculiarly a French dish, said to be nowhere found of greater excellence than at Marseilles. As the name indicates, it is a broth reduced to some consistency by evaporation, being usually a fish broth. Thackeray has immortalized it in the following lines:

> " This Bouillabaisse a noble dish is,
>   A sort of soup or broth or brew
> Or hotch pot of all sorts of fishes,
>   That Greenwich never could out do;
> Green herbs, red peppers, mussels, saffern,
>   Soles, onions, garlic, roach and dace;
> All these you eat at Terre's tavern
>   In that one dish of Bouillabaisse."

The French have another soup called "Potage a la jambe du bois," or "soup of the wooden leg." It is made from a shin of beef and is served with the shin bone (the wooden leg) "emerging like the bowsprit of a wreck from the sea of vegetables."

Mullagatawny soup is of East Indian origin, the name being derived from two Tamil words meaning pepper-water. Its chief ingredients are chicken, rice and curry; plenty of the latter by all means.

Turtle soups are perhaps the most highly seasoned and most epicurean of all soups known to us, but as has been stated, they are far from being hygienic articles of diet.

The superiority of good soups over bad lies largely in the flavorings. "Bay-leaf," it has been said, "is to soups what vanilla is to sweets;" and the *bouquet garni* of the French consists of parsley, thyme, laurel, bay and cloves, with or without a small onion.

The different varieties of soups exhibited at the Columbian Exposition were green turtle, mock turtle, terrapin, consommé, bouillon, Julienne, ox-tail, chicken broth, chicken with rice, with curry, with gumbo and with tomato; purées of peas, green peas, corn and game; creams of asparagus and celery; mullagatawny, beef with barley, mutton broth, and soups of oyster, hare, game, kidney and venison.

The Australian soups differed from the others in being concentrated until quite solid and gelatinous. Both the French and English sent "dessicated soups," consisting of dessicated meat and vegetables which require cooking for some time in a quantity of water before being used. Both of these preparations are eminently valuable in army or navy or for the use of travelers who are compelled to carry their own food supplies.

Meat extracts are a perpetual monument to the fallibility of popular as well as scientific opinion. When Baron Liebig first gave to the world his fluid extract of beef he believed it to contain all the nutriment necessary for the maintainance of health and vigor in any person using it. The world in general and doctors in particular accepted this new gospel because of the prestige of Baron Liebig's name. Physicians of a generation ago have much to answer for, as it is now believed that many a patient may have been actually starved to death on Liebig's *extractum carnis.*

Thirty-four pounds of lean beef are required to make one pound of extract. Fat, gelatine and albumin are excluded, leaving only the salts and extractive flavors, principles which are of little nutritive value. The extract contains the *creatine* of the beef which is to meat what *theine* is to tea or *caffeine* to coffee; and it also contains the *ozmazone* which gives to meat extracts their peculiarly aromatic flavor. Beef extract is therefore not nutritious, although valuable in any exhausted condition of the system because of its stimulating and restorative properties. By promoting organic activity in systems which are debilitated it is far more valuable than alcoholic stimulants, because of the absence of depressing secondary effects.

Beef extract is a valuable adjunct in every household because of its appetizing qualities and for the flavor it may impart to various kinds of soups. Its use as a refreshment produces such tonic and stimulating effects that it is now served hot in nearly every drug store or restaurant in America. The best American beef extracts are in every respect equal to those of Liebig.

Meat extracts are both fluid and solid, though it is not always wise to decide in favor of the latter. There are a few solid extracts on the market consisting moro largely of gelatine than of extractive principle. One beef tonic, consisting of pulverized beef and beef extract, is valuable because a greater amount of nutrition is contained than in the simple extract.

CHAPTER XII.

MAXIM as ancient as the time of Democritus of Abdera reads: "Whatever pleases the palate nourishes." Modern science has proven the truth of this maxim and has given us acceptable reason why condiments are no more necessary in palace of connoisseur than in hut of barbarian, why they are as eagerly used by the native of Labrador as by the swarthy son of the tropics; why they are the property of Mohammedan, Confucian, Buddhist, Gentile and Jew, of all castes, races and civilizations. Acting principally upon the nervous system through the sense of smell, condiments stimulate the flow of both the saliva and the gastric juices. They materially aid digestion, and the familiar phrase, "to make the mouth water," states a physiological fact. From this standpoint the fragrant aroma of steaming coffee and the savory odor of a stew are as truly condiments as pepper and salt; for condiments are the magic wand which transform most commonplace of foods into essences, subtle and delicious. They are equally appropriate to the steaming *potage* of the French peasant and the sacrificial altars of Palestine and Greece. Nothing more closely tests the skill of the cook than his use of these appetizing flavors. Like genii of the fairy tale, they are willing, versatile and obedient as slaves; when master their pathway is likely to be strewn with sorrowful though most aromatic wrecks of soups and *hors d'œuvres*. They should permeate foods as incense does the atmosphere, delicate, impalpable and as indescribable as they are requisite. The too abundant use of a certain condiment or spice, the lack of another or the injudicious mingling of certain others will ruin the finest pudding, sauce or soup over compounded.

7

Condiments and spices are as ancient as civilization. The oldest books of the scriptures, notably Exodus, Leviticus, Job and the Canticles, make frequent reference to salt and spices, substances which were costly and chiefly dedicated to royalty and the uses of temple and altar. The Greeks followed the Semitic customs to some extent in their disposition of spices, not using them as largely in their food as have later races. They were fond of aromatic flavorings and it is said that the laurels of Greece, of which the cinnamon is a species, possessed that quality to a greater extent than those of any other country, although all laurels have aromatic leaves.

Homer in the Iliad refers with naive surprise to those people unaccustomed to the use of salt, and in the ninth book pictures Patroclus as

> "He strows a bed of glowing embers wide,
> Above the coals the smoking fragments turns,
> And sprinkles sacred salt upon the urns."

By the mediæval Romans condiments were well liked. They made, according to one author, a pickle from the tunny fish, just as their languorous descendants are doing to-day, and also prepared a condiment from the intestines of the mackerel. "Liver of the capon, steeped in milk and beccaficoes, and dressed with pepper" was another of their highly seasoned dishes.

In the thirteenth century Dante, in the description of the alchemists and forgers of the tenth gulf of the Inferno, refers to one Niccolo of Siena "who first the spice's luxury discovered." Contemporary with him in England, Wm. Langland, in his "Vision of Piers the Plowman," inquires if thou "hast in thy purse any hot spices?"

Frequent reference by the writers of that day indicates that these substances were expensive and used mainly by the luxurious. Venice had for many years controlled the trade in spices, which were brought overland from the Orient in immense caravans, and not until Diaz and Vasco de Gama, in the fifteenth century, rounded the Cape of Good Hope did their costliness diminish. After that event spices and condiments ceased to be regarded merely as luxuries and became as necessary to the plainest of soups as to the *Purce de volaille a la Bearnise* of the French chef.

All classes of people use condiments in some form, from the wealthy epicure who flavors his terrapin with mace, salt, pepper and sherry to the negro who sifts okra through his fingers into his gumbo soup or the Indian, stirring the contents of a steaming kettle with twigs of sassafras.

Condiments have been defined as those substances eaten with meat and combined with salt while spices are chiefly added to articles containing sugar. They may be classified as follows:

VEGETABLE
- AROMATICS: Clove, cinnamon, cassia-bud, pimento or allspice, nutmeg, mace, cardamon, pepper, cumin, coriander, fenugreek, grains of Paradise, anise, dill, caraway, basil, chervil, celery, fennel, bay-leaves, summer savory, parsley, thyme, sage, sweet marjoram, mint, tarragon, onion, leek, garlic, saffron, capers, turmeric and curry powder.
- PUNGENT AROMATICS: Mustard, horse-radish, chillies, ginger.

MINERAL: Salt.

ANIMAL: Pastes and essences of shrimp, lobster, bloater, anchovy, etc.

SAUCES: Chutney, Tabasco, lime juice, Worcestershire, ketchup, carachi, cassareep and soy.

PICKLES: Various vegetables and fruits, such as cucumber, olive, sanphire, etc.

FLAVORS: Vanilla, tonka bean, almond, chocolate, orange and various fruits.

ACIDS: Vinegar, lime juice, lemon juice, verjuice.

CORDIALS: Curaçoa, Noyau, Ratafia, anisette, kuemmel, absinthe, Chartreuse, Maraschino, etc.

Salt is even more valuable as a condiment than as a preservative. It is used in every staple article of cookery and, as has been said, 'Plutarch was right when he styled salt the condiment of condiments." Cereals and vegetables are tasteless without the addition of that mysterious quantity, "a pinch of salt," bread is insipid without a dash of it, as also are cakes and puddings. Meats, when so cooked that their own salts are not extracted, as when roasted, are more palatable without additional salt than any other food so prepared.

Though salt is unused because unattainable by certain barbaric peoples, such as the Bedouins, it is considered to be a necessity by all others. Aristotle relates that in Greece a salt spring was believed to be a direct gift of the gods, salt always comprising part of the religious offerings. Salt is referred to in the Scriptures more than a score of times. In Leviticus we find the command that "every oblation of thy meat offering shall be seasoned with salt." In Job occurs the question "can that which is unsavory be eaten without salt?" The Biblical comparison to salt which has lost its savor refers to the custom still retained in Oriental countries of adulterating with earth the salt which finds its way to the extremely poor who can not pay the original high price. So costly was salt in the ancient world that the old caravan routes were first formed for traffic in this article. The "Salarian Way" of Rome was so named because of its immense commerce in salt and to this day the trade route across the Sahara is by this means mainly supported. Recently the salt beds of Europe and the salt mines and wells of the western hemisphere have made this article so abundant that its cheapness effectually protects it from adulteration.

Cloves are the unexpanded flowers of an evergreen tree found in the East Indies and indigenous to the Molucca Islands. They are called by the Chinese "fragrant nails" owing to the peculiar shape of the dried clove buds, and the English word is derived from the Latin *clavus*, and French *clou*, also meaning nail. It is doubtful if cloves were known to the Greeks or Romans, the Venetians having first obtained them from the Arabians, while the clove trade was later monopolized by the Portuguese. Then it was owned by the Dutch who expelled the Portuguese from the Spice Islands in 1605. The Dutch made great effort to control the entire spice trade of these islands, which was a source of abundant wealth, and were even known to furnish the market with the adulterated article, the oil of clove being extracted by pressure and the buds being given a fresh appearance by a glaze of olive oil. They also preserved the mother clove, or fully developed fruit. This resembles an olive in appearance and, being less pungent in flavor than the bud, makes a dainty sweetmeat. The clove tree is not hardy and grows best when planted in loamy soil, sheltered from the winds by the hills. It has

Clove.

been introduced into the West Indies and Guiana. Cloves from the Moluccas and Ceylon are more valuable, being richer in oil, darker in color and far more aromatic.

Cinnamon is the inner bark of a tree allied to the laurels. It is indigenous to Ceylon and the Penang Islands although believed by some authorities to have originally come from China, where it has flourished since the remotest times. As it is mentioned in the Old Testament it is conjectured that the Hebrews obtained it from the Arabians who in turn procured it from India. Later it was mentioned by Herodotus. It is known that Hippocrates used cinnamon

Cassia Buds.

medicinally and the modern medical world has but recently made cassia. In shape and size they resemble cloves, in aroma, cinnamon, and are usually preserved whole for sweetmeats or spices. Cassia is mentioned by Moses as an ingredient of the holy oil, in Psalms as a perfume and in Ezekiel as a spice.

Allspice, sometimes called Jamaica pepper and properly, *pimento*, is native to the Island of Jamaica and has not been successfully cultivated outside of the West Indies. The pimento tree is an evergreen of the myrtlebloom family, all of which are exotic the discovery that oil of cinnamon is a valuable antiseptic and germicide. Not until 1506 was cinnamon discovered wild in Ceylon and not until 1770 was it improved by cultivation. The tree grows to a height of twenty and occasionally thirty feet, although, as the bark from the young shoots is of finer flavor, that only is used. Cinnamon shrubs are cultivated in fields, the finest being located in the region of Colombo, Ceylon. The shoots, which grow in clusters of from four to ten, are cut to the roots twice a year, after the rains. The epidermis is peeled off, the bark is put up in bundles about forty inches long and thus dried and marketed. Three grades are exported, the finest, thin, of a brownish yellow color, fragrant and sweet of odor and correspondingly high of price. It is also adulterated with cassia bark, a cheaper production.

Cassia is the inner bark of a species of cinnamon called Chinese cinnamon or *cassia lignea*. The greater part of it is exported from China. The bark is put up in bundles about half the length of cinnamon bark and is more pungent and less sweet of flavor. Cassia buds are the unripened fruits of the tree which produces Chinese trees, and reaches a height of thirty feet. The allspice of commerce consists of the berries of this tree, exported whole after being dried, and so called because their aroma resembles that of cloves, cinnamon, juniper and nutmeg. The berries are gathered when green, being left on the twigs until dried by the sun, by which means all the essential oil is retained.

Nutmeg is the kernel of the fruit of an exotic evergreen tree native to the Banda and other of the East Indian islands. In appearance it resembles the orange, yielding fruit when eight or nine years of age and bearing for fifty or sixty years. It requires a light soil, moisture and shade, and cannot be propagated in regions in which these conditions are not present. The tree bears fruit during most of the year, in the Molucca and other islands three crops a year being gathered. The fruit, which requires nine months in which to mature, is carefully dried before the pericarp is removed

Nutmeg.

and the kernel taken out. There are three varieties, the male or barren, the royal and the queen, the last, a small, round nutmeg, considered most valuable. The inferior nutmegs are used for the extraction of nutmeg butter or oil, known as "oil of mace." About six per cent of volatile oil is contained. It is stated that more nutmegs are exported to the United States than to all Europe. The Dutch formerly preserved the entire fruit, kernel and pericarp, in a syrup of sweet vinegar for a sweetmeat. This nation when in control of the spice trade of certain of the East Indian islands made strenuous efforts to confine the nutmeg tree to the Bandas. But the "nutmeg bird," a species of blue pigeon, frustrated their designs by scattering the nuts all over the islands after feeding upon their pulpy covering. So determined at one time were the Dutch to keep the price of nutmegs high that, if an unusually large harvest occurred, part of it was burned by them.

Mace is the reticulated aril covering the kernel. When fresh, it is of a crimson color, reaching the golden tint only when dried and after some months. In its properties it is similar to the nutmeg. The leaves of the nutmeg tree as well as the fruit are highly aromatic.

The cardamon is a member of the ginger family and is native to Malabar, Madagascar and Ceylon. That from the latter country is of quite large size. It consists of a rhizome or root stock from which rise tall, flag-like leaves. The flower stem springs directly from the root and is much shorter, bearing racemiform clusters of small white flowers. The fruit consists of greenish pods half an inch in length, each pod being three capsuled and containing numerous seeds. These seeds are pungent in flavor and constitute the valuable part of the plant. The pods are dried slowly as rapid drying causes them to split, thereby losing the seeds. Cardamon seeds were used by the ancient Greeks both as a spice and as medicine.

Round Pepper.

Pepper, with cinnamon, salt and incense, was one of the staple commodities which anciently passed over the caravan routes between Venice and India. At that time its price was extremely high and, according to E. M. Holmes, rents were frequently paid in this article as late as the middle ages. After the sack of Rome by the barbarians one of the articles of tribute demanded by Alaric was a thousand pounds of pepper. As late as the eighteenth century the pepper trade was confined to the Portugese. In recent years it has become one of the cheapest of our spices.

The pepper plant is a vine, of the order *piperaceæ*, which grows wild in China, is also indigenous to Malabar and other islands of the East Indies, and has been introduced into the West Indies. The plants require a rich moist soil, bearing after the fourth year and continuing fruitful for from eight to fourteen years. The most famous of the pepper islands are the Penang, which furnish more than half the amount produced by the entire East Indies. Only the berries of the pepper plant are valuable and those, being gathered before fully developed, have a wrinkled appearance when dried. The berries used for white pepper are decorticated either in the islands or in London and reach the United States ready for grinding. The finest grade passes through more than twenty different operations before it is considered marketable.

Black pepper differs from the white in the leaving on of the hull, which is black and contains the acrid principles of the flavor. Hence, white pepper is less pungent and fully as fine in flavor as the black. Shot pepper consists of the finest berries, those richest in oil. It is selected by throwing a quantity of the berries in water. Those which sink are collected, labeled, and sold as shot pepper.

Long pepper, referred to by the Greeks as *piperi macron*, is the unripe fruit of a species of pepper, an inch or more in length and and shaped like a spike. The flavor is similar to that of ordinary black pepper. African pepper is another variety. Those best known to the western markets are Penang, Tellicherry and Malabar.

Cumin or cummin is a small herbaceous plant, native to Egypt and very early cultivated in the Mediterranean countries. It is now grown in India, Sicily and Malta, the seeds only being valuable. These contain a large proportion of essential oil which gives them an aromatic but acrid flavor. They are not now used in cookery though receipts are still extant which prove them to have once been considered a valuable culinary spice. The Latin poets relate that the ancients used cumin seeds medicinally, their effect being to produce languor. They are referred to in Isaiah as being "beaten out with a rod" and also in the Mosaic law regarding tithes.

Coriander.

Coriander is a small umbelliferous plant native to the eastern of the Mediterranean countries but now cultivated quite generally in both Europe and America. The fruits, erroneously called the seeds, are nearly always mentioned in the earlier recipes for meats and puddings and to this day many a country housewife considers them indispensable to the flavoring of dried apple pies. The plant grows wild in all parts of Palestine, especially in the Jordan valley.

Fenugreek is an herbaceous plant allied to the clover. It is native to the Asiatic countries and is still cultivated in France and Germany. The seeds were formerly used as a spice, but now only as an ingredient of curry powder, owing to their strong, bitter and unpleasant flavor.

Grains of Paradise are the dried seeds of a reed-like plant allied to the ginger family and indigenous to western Africa. The fruit which contains the seeds is four or five inches in length and of a bright red color. The seed are now never used, excepting occasionally by brewers. Formerly they were esteemed as a spice for cookery and were one of the ingredients of the famous Norwich herring pies of old England. In flavor they are extremely hot and pungent.

Anise is a little annual of the order umbelliferæ and scarcely more than a foot in height. It is indigenous to Europe, although cultivated in many of the northern Mediterranean countries. The seeds are powerful aromatics, used both medicinally and in the preparation of a *liqueur* called "anisette," which is to the Italians what kuemmel is to the Germans. The star anise is a tree allied to the magnolias, the seeds of which are stronger and less pleasant of flavor than those of the common anise. They are called star aniseed from the star-like shape of the fruit. The anise mentioned in the New Testament as part of the tithes is a different plant, believed to be dill.

Dill is a small herb, native to Spain, which produces umbelliferous stalks of yellow flowers. It is still cultivated in portions of temperate Europe. An aromatic oil is extracted from the tiny seeds which are also used, whole, for flavoring pickles.

Caraway is also an umbelliferous plant growing wild in the meadows and pastures of both Europe and Asia. It is cultivated for its mildly aromatic seeds, although in the northern countries of Europe the root, which resembles the

Caraway.

parsnip, is also eaten. No aromatic of temperate climates is more common than the dainty, white-blooming plant growing in the kitchen gardens of both hemispheres. Its seeds are used for the spicing of cheese, cakes and candies, and in Germany in the rye bread called "kümmel-brod," which is universally eaten. The seeds are also used in the making of an aromatic cordial called "kümmel."

Basil is not now used as extensively in cooking as formerly. Its native haunts are India and Persia, although since it yields gracefully to culture, it is to be found in many old-fashioned kitchen gardens. Its aromatic properties are similar to those of other garden herbs.

Chervil is an umbelliferous annual possessing aromatic leaves and somewhat resembling parsley in flavor. It is used in Europe as a pot-herb for soups and stews, but is chiefly known in America as one of the obsolete delicacies which deserve to be still popular. The root, which is fleshy and fusiform in shape, is cooked and eaten by the people of southern Europe.

Celery is a veritable plebeian, originally growing wild in the ditches and fens of Europe, a coarse, offensive and poisonous vegetable. Few plants are so susceptible to the influences of cultivation and it is difficult to recognize its unaristocratic prototype in the tender, white and aromatic stalks of the garden product. It belongs to the parsley family and every portion is useful to the cook, from the daintily curled tops which may be used for both flavor and garnish, the stalks which may be eaten plain, dressed raw in salad or cooked, to the seeds, the flavor of which makes even the poorest of soups relishable. The seeds are now commonly ground for the making of "celery salt" or "celery pepper," as the same product is variously called. A variety of celery, called *celeriac*, is cultivated in certain European countries, notably Germany, the root only, which is large and fleshy, being eaten. The famous "wild celery" of Chesapeake Bay is simply "eel-grass," an aquatic plant which bears no relationship whatever to the umbelliferæ, of which order celery is a species.

Basil.

Fennel is an umbelliferous plant, native to portions of temperate Europe and Asia, especially Portugal. The fruits possess an aromatic flavor while the tender shoots are used for salad. The plant and its culinary value was well known to the Romans, and it is to-day cultivated in both Europe and America. The fruits of the European fennel are used in the making of an aromatic drink, while in America the plant is chiefly cultivated for its leaves. It has been said that fennel is to fish what mint is to lamb, and in certain of the southern states mackerel is considered of too strong a flavor to be eaten unless cooked with fennel. The fennel thus used grows wild, the green leaves being tied in bunches and boiled with the fish.

Bay Leaves.

Bay leaves are the leaves of a shrub belonging to the laurel tribe, which grows wild in the Mediterranean countries. Among the Greeks the bay leaf was consecrated to the uses of poetry, heroism and religion. Not until later times was it used as a flavoring for foods and for the decoration of various dishes. It grows wild in certain of the the southern states but the leaves are usually exported from Europe, dried. The leaves are used in soups, stews and pickles and, although the average housewife finds it next to impossible to procure them, scarcely a recipe for these articles of food but includes bay leaves among its flavorings.

Summer savory is a hardy little annual which has long grown wild in southern Europe and is now largely cultivated for culinary use. Both the summer and winter savories are fragrant and are valuable in the seasoning of sausages and gravies.

Parsley is a native of the island of Sardinia and, having been improved in both fragrance and appearance by culture, is more valuable than any other herb for the garnishing of dishes. Its curled, crisp, green leaves give the poorest salad or meat a tempting appearance, well sustained by the fineness of flavor it imparts. Its flavor somewhat resembles that of celery. The little herb may be seen in nearly every garden during the summer months and often in a pot, or kitchen window-box during the winter, from which it may be plucked fresh daily. The experienced cook would part with any other half dozen condiments more willingly than with parsley. The plant belongs to the *umbelliferæ*, which order includes the carrot, parsnip and celery. It is said to have come originally from Egypt and mythology represents Hercules as adorning his head with its curled leaves.

Thyme.

Thyme, a little under shrub native to the Mediterranean countries, is allied botanically to sage, summer savory and sweet basil. It possesses very small leaves and whorls of tiny, lilac-colored flowers, from which thymol or oil of thyme, a valuable germicide, is distilled. In flavor it is fragrant and aromatic and it may be readily cultivated in gardens. The wild thyme of our banks "where ox-lips and the nodding violet grows," is a different variety of the same order. Its name is derived from the Greek word *thumos*, meaning incense or perfume.

Sage is a small plant of the order *labiatæ*, and is native to southern Europe. It has been so greatly changed by cultivation that little semblance of the original plant now remains in the sage of our gardens excepting the flavor. It was known to the ancients and to-day its fragrant, grayish green leaves constitute one of our commonest flavorings.

It was an Englishman who once said that "mint made lamb out of an old sheep"! Perhaps he loved it also because of the legend that it once existed in the form of a beautiful maiden, transformed by Persephone into the modest aromatic of our gardens. The mint designated is that member of the labiate family known as spear-

mint, native to Europe but grown in all portions of the United
States and largely marketed. It is a small, green herb, the leaves

Mint.

being highly aromatic and, when bruised, yielding a valuable essential oil. It is equally liked in the mint sauce so indispensable to
mutton and the mint-julep—

> " This cordial julep here,
> That flames and dances in his crystal bounds."

Sweet marjoram grows wild in Spain and Portugal and, in a
cultivated state, throughout Europe and the United States. It is a
member of the mint family and, like spear mint, possesses aromatic
leaves.

Tarragon is a small, aromatic herb, native to
Liberia. It is cultivated in Europe and is the
estragon of the French, who use the young
plants largely for salads. It is hardy, and is
grown extensively in America, being used for
flavoring vinegar, mustard and pickles. Tarragon vinegar, from the excellence of its flavor,
should have a place in every household.

The onion is believed to have originated in
Egypt although it was known in very early times
in India. In the former country it was wor-

Tarragon.

shiped as a deity. "Cucumbers, and the melons,
and the leeks, and the onions, and the garlick" formed the daily

food of the Israelites in Egypt. Italy and Spain are now noted for the immense size of the onions grown there, as also are the Bermuda Islands. Those of the latter place possess a far milder flavor, a condition due to soil and climate. The flavor of onion, when strong, is unpleasant to some people to a nauseating degree and it is hard to see in it any resemblance to its dainty cousins, the lily and the hyacinth. But when skillfully used it is a valuable and wholesome culinary condiment and is more largely employed by the average cook than the uninitiated ever suspect. Says one author: "The onion is the sheet anchor of the skillful cook. It is impossible to prepare the delicate Bordelaise sauce without resorting to the use of onions and a shade of garlic, ... and it is the judicious use of these two seasonings that stamps the expert cook."

The leek is a member of the onion family, similar in flavor, although milder, and the leaves of which are flat instead of tubular. It has been stated that in England the leek was once considered to be the typical plant, both onion and garlic being but species. The diet of the soldiers of ancient Greece was at one time leeks and cheese, a custom which Bulwer has satirized in a Neo-Greek outburst of rhyme:

> " Away, away, with the helm and greaves,
> Away with the leeks and cheese!
> I have conquered my passion for wounds and blows,
> And the worst that I wish to the worst of my foes
>   Is the glory and gain
>   Of a year's campaign
> On a diet of leeks and cheese!"

Garlic possesses an onion-like bulb around which smaller bulbs cluster, the whole covered by a membranous outer layer. Each bulb is described as a "clove" of garlic and in flavor is far more demonstrative than onion. Shallot, on the contrary, is the daintiest of the onion tribe, growing from a cluster of roots and never forming a compact bulb.

Saffron, a plant of the crocus family, was largely used in mediæval Europe as a condiment, although today its value as a coloring substance is considered of most account. The coloring matter is obtained from the stigmas of the flower, which are of a deep orange hue. The plant grows wild in Asia Minor, is possibly native to Arabia, and has long been extensively cultivated throughout the Mediterranean countries. That

Garlic.

exported from Spain is considered the finest. At one time in Germany the adulteration of saffron was held criminal and punishable by death. History records the burning, in 1444, of a man with his adulterated saffron and, a dozen years later, the burning of two men and a woman for a similar offense. The salutary effect of this penalty was not permanent, however, as it is to-day extensively adulterated with a cheaper article known as safflower. In the Orient, a few nations still add saffron to their rice both for flavor and color while in Europe it is now most largely used for coloring macaroni, vermicelli and other pastes. Saffron is mentioned in the Old Testament in connection with spikenard, cinnamon and other spices, and appears to have been used by the early Greeks medicinally, and as both dye and perfume.

Capers are the unopened flowers of a low, trailing shrub which grows wild in Africa and southern Europe. It is native to Italy and is said to have grown wild upon the walls of ancient Rome. It is cultivated in France, only the small, grayish green, flower buds being of commercial value. They possess an aromatic and slightly pungent flavor and, when preserved as is usual in either salt or vinegar, are used for flavoring gravies, being wellnigh indispensable in the serving of roast mutton. Four or five grades of capers are exported, the finest grade consisting of the tiniest and most perfect buds which gradually diminish in value as they increase in size.

Capers.

Turmeric, while classed with condiments owing to its pungent and aromatic properties, is most extensively used as a coloring agent. It is obtained from the root of the *curcuma longa*, a plant allied to the ginger family and native to India and Annam. It is used as a condiment only by the Orientals who flavor their rice with it, its greatest value to the cooking world being due to the fact that it is one of the chief ingredients of curry powder.

Curry powder is a manufactured condiment, one of the most aromatic and highly seasoned used. It originated in the East Indies, through the skill of whom it is not known. The story goes that the famed and delicious cookery of the Orient came about in this fashion. The early English, French and Dutch, when setting out for the East Indies, each determined to seize and appropriate the islands, spices and all; for fear of being compelled to eat poor and unappetizing food took with them their most accomplished cooks. From the friendly concourse of these chefs arose certain of the celebrated eastern dishes, and from its ingredients it is easy to believe that curry was one of them; for in it are united, with the herbs of the temperate zones, the spices and fruits of the tropics. The ingredients used vary in character and in proportion according to the different houses or localities manufacturing it. One recipe calls for the following: turmeric, black pepper, cayenne pepper, nutmeg, ginger, cloves, cinnamon, allspice, cardamon seeds, coriander seeds, cumin seeds, caraway seeds and fenugreek. In India the following ingredients are sometimes used, besides those above named: anise, almonds, asafœtida, butter (ghee), cocoanut and cocoa oil, cream and curds, various nuts, garlic, lime juice, mangoes, saffron, salt, and tamarinds. In India alone there exist nearly forty different methods of preparing curry, to which list might be added the recipes of the numerous spice houses of Europe and America. The ingredients of curry are always finely ground and well mixed. When lime-juice and butter or oil are added to the curry, a paste is prepared. This is preserved by being packed in earthen jars. The curries and curry pastes of Ceylon and Java (these being often combined with garlic) are quite as celebrated as those of India, while the English and American preparations rank enviably high.

The mustard of commerce consists of the pulverized seed of the mustard plant, which grows wild in England and which may be cultivated in nearly every part of the globe, even in India. The use of mustard as a condiment dates from the Elizabethan age, although it was used medicinally by the most celebrated physicians of antiquity. It was first compounded in its present form for table use by an old lady of Durham, from which circumstance it came to be widely celebrated as "Durham mustard." One of the merchants, to whom this industrious old lady sold her mustard, is credited with saying that he owed his wealth, not to the mustard which people ate but to that which they left on their plates. Two varieties of mustard are cultivated, one producing white seeds, the other, seeds which are tiny and black. Both varieties of seeds are used, whole, in the spicing of pickles. It is requisite that mustard possess good keeping qualities, that it be of a bright yellow color, and have an aromatic as well as pungent flavor.

Mustard.

Horse-radish is a plant allied to the nasturtium and, like the seeds and stems of the latter, possesses a sharply pungent flavor. It is native to England and western Europe although cultivated in nearly all portions of the temperate zone. The root, which is large and fleshy, is grated, mixed with salt and vinegar, and used as a condiment. It may be prepared in season and bottled, either with vinegar or dessicated, keeping for use during the remainder of the year.

Ginger is a flag-like plant, probably native to the East and West Indies, the rhizomatous root of which is the only portion commercially valuable. According to some authorities ginger was known to the earliest of the Greeks and Romans and has been a common spice among the nations of Europe, including England, since the eleventh century. Under the Plantagenets and Tudors ginger was used as a flavoring for meats, unlike the modern custom of using it only in curries, cakes and beverages. To-day ginger is exported from both the Indies, that

Ginger.

from Jamaica being particularly fine, from Africa, from China, from India and from Borneo. The African ginger is of excellent flavor but of dark color. It is chiefly sold to bakers. That from Borneo is good for household use, having a sweet and aromatic flavor and containing very little fibre. From Calcutta the "race" or "hand" ginger is exported, so called because of the palmate shape of the root. It is exported before being decorticated and is not a high grade ginger. The root is often preserved in sugar, being taken when young and succulent. It may be preserved whole or cut into cubes or slices. Both preserved and dried it is largely exported from China and Japan.

Chili Pepper.

Chili is the Spanish name for the pod of the cayenne, the Guinea pepper, and other species of capsicum. Capsicum is a member of the night shade family, in no way related to the true pepper. It is native to tropical America, although now found in nearly all of the warmer countries. Cayenne is the pod of the capsicum pulverized to extreme fineness. It should be of a dull, red color and, if very red, is quite likely to be adulterated, often with red lead or vermilion. Cayenne pepper is, perhaps, the most acrid and pungent aromatic used and is also valuable medicinally. There are many varieties of capsicum, the most noted being the *capsicum annum*, cultivated in the East Indies, in Mexico and southern parts of the United States, and from which cayenne pepper is made; and the *capsicum frutescens*, the Guinea or bird pepper, a much smaller pod and which, dried whole, is most often used in cookery. Chilis are used in enormous quantities by natives of hot countries, a paradoxical custom it appears to be, and the hottest, most "peppery" dishes known have originated where the sunbeam is nearest vertical. Those best known to Americans are the *chili con carne* and the chicken *tomale* of Mexico. In the southern states cayenne is customarily added to all meats, soups and stews. Capsicum is an agreeable and valuable stimulant, having the medicinal effect of alcohol without disastrous results from its use.

Mixed seasonings are now to be found in nearly all markets and in point of convenience deserve to be popular. They consist of the aromatic herbs and spices, mixed and prepared by experts and intended for the seasoning of poultry and meats of all kinds.

Penang or mixed spices, are also a modern preparation and are useful in cooking, pickling and preserving. They consist of aromatic and pungent spices mixed in varying proportions.

Among condiments prepared from animal foods, those of the anchovy, lobster, shrimp, and Yarmouth bloater are the most common. The anchovy is a tiny, silvery fish, caught in the Mediterranean sea in vast quantities. The most famous come from Gorgona, a small island near Leghorn, where they are caught in nets as they come in from the deeper waters for the purpose of depositing spawn. Anchovies were used as a condiment by the most luxurious of the Romans, one preparation, called "garum," consisting of the partly decomposed intestines of this fish mixed with spices. They are now exported for use as a condiment to all parts of the world, being preserved whole as well as in the form of pastes and essences. The pastes are prepared by pressing the fish through a sieve, simple flavorings and some oil being added. The essences consist of the fish steeped in a highly spiced brine or pickle, then strained and bottled. Essences of lobster, shrimp, and various fish are similarly prepared.

Various appetizing mixtures intended to give relish to meats, fish and soups, and composed of vegetables, fruits and divers spices, are known as sauces. "Roots, herbs, vine fruits and salad-flowers, they dish up various ways and find them a very delicious sauce to their meats, both roasted and boiled, fresh and salt." No other sauce made compares with genuine East Indian chutney. It is a thick sauce, made from the mango apple, chilies, spices, lemon juice, raisins, figs, salt and sugar. Those most celebrated are the Bengal Club, Terhoot, Sweet Lucknow and a number of club chutneys. Trinidad chutney is particularly fine. Ceylon chutney is often slightly flavored with garlic. Another kind is "mango chutney, a characteristic Singalese condiment, among the ingredients of which are fresh, grated cocoanut and chilies carefully brayed together in a mortar. This chutney is of a rich roseate hue; and after eating it with his prawn curry the epicure feels like the Grand Turk."

Carachi is a sauce little known in America, although, as it is much liked abroad, I give a recipe for its making, which sufficiently defines its character: one head of garlic, one dessert spoonful of cayenne pepper, three table spoonsful each, of soy, mushroom ketchup, walnut pickle, and mango pickle, five anchovies and a pint of vinegar.

Cassareep consists of the inspissated juice of the root of the bitter cassava, flavored with various spices. From the cassava, or manioc, is prepared tapioca and also cassava flour of which bread is made. The root is poisonous because of the prussic acid contained, this, however, being dissipated by heat. After the juice is extracted, it is boiled down to the color and consistency of molasses, after which spices are added. It is the basis of Worcestershire and many other sauces and is valuable in the flavoring of soups and ragouts. It is largely exported from British Guiana and is used throughout the tropics.

Worcestershire sauce is one of the commonest of table condiments. It is prepared from cassareep and varying proportions of spices, garlic, peppers, and lime-juice, according to the tastes of the various houses manufacturing it.

Both lime-juice and Devonshire sauces are similar in preparation and flavor to Worcestershire, the former being quite acid, owing to the greater proportion of lime-juice used.

Ketchup is a sauce made variously from tomatoes, mushrooms, walnuts, oysters, etc. It should be semi-fluid, about the consistency of a good purée and, although spices may be added, the original flavor of the basic ingredients must always be preserved. Color is one desideratum. In tomato ketchup the sauce is always made of the ripe tomato fruit, although, as the color is sometimes produced artificially, the only safeguard lies in purchasing of reliable manufacturers. The tomato ketchup is a typical American sauce, corresponding in our dietary with the mushroom ketchup of the English.

Soy or *shoyu* is in general use throughout the East, particularly in China and Japan, that from the latter country being acknowledged the finest made. One authority states that our word ketchup is derived from the Chinese name for soy, *kitjap*. The basis of soy, the soy bean, has been cultivated in Japan since the earliest dynasties, and is to-day one of their important crops. The different varieties of the soy bean produce three kinds of soy known as the black, the green and the white. The process of making soy consists in first boiling the beans and mixing them with parched barley and wheat, coarsely ground. This *barm* is fermented and when the whole mixture is covered with fungi it is mixed with brine of a certain strength, which has already been boiled and allowed to cool. This mixture is then kept for fermentation about twenty-five months. It is stirred with a wooden paddle twice a day during winter, three times a day in summer and, when sufficiently fermented, is put through a soy press. It is then heated to 130 degrees Fahrenheit and, after becoming cold again, is put up in bottles and casks. It may be preserved for any length of time. In appearance it resembles Worcestershire sauce aud from a nutritive point of view is superior to any other sauce in our markets.

Soy is manufactured in every part of Japan, no fewer than 10,682 firms being engaged in making it in 1891. It is eaten by the entire Japanese population with every meal and, besides being a sauce, is sufficient as a salt. Used upon fish, beef-steaks and meats, generally, it gives a relish that is impossible to the choicest of cookery otherwise. In Japan it is used by all classes excepting the extremely destitute, who cannot afford to buy it.

Tabasco is a popular sauce, the chief ingredient of which is the pulp of the red pepper. This, a species of chili, came originally from Central America and through cultivation, largely carried on in the South, its strength and flavor have been greatly improved. The sauce is extremely hot with chilis and, as it keeps well in any climate, it is liked by connoisseurs.

There are on the market numerous preparations known as salad dressings. They are useful in cases of inexperience or emergency, but are by no means equal to the freshly made mayonnaise of the home kitchen. There is real art in preparing a good mayonnaise and a Spanish proverb reads: "Four persons are necessary to the making of a salad dressing: a spendthrift for oil, a miser for vinegar, a counsellor for salt and a madman to stir it all up."

Pickles are those articles of food, fruit or vegetables, which are preserved by immersion in vinegar, with or without the addition of salt or spices. Cucumber and green tomato pickles are the commonest varieties. When vegetables are mixed, as with chow-chow, piccalilli and "mixed pickles," cucumbers, small onions, green beans, cabbage, pepper-pods, cauliflower and various spices are used. Fruits, such as apple, melon, peach, crab-apple and pear are also pickled.

One of the choicest of condiments is the olive. It is the fruit of an evergreen tree, native to Syria and lower Asia but now cultivated extensively in southern Europe and California. Unlike most pickles it may be classed as a food, owing to the oil contained. The fruit is picked by hand and carefully sorted about six weeks before it would ripen. It is first placed in strong lye for about twenty-four hours, then removed to fresh water where it may remain several days. After several washings in fresh water the olives are removed and packed in brine. They are ready for use in from one to three months. The residents of the olive districts both in Greece, Spain, and in California often prefer the olive preserved after it has ripened, the oil having then matured and the flavor being finer. Among the export trade there is much prejudice against it owing to its dull, black color. Olives should be of good color, crisp and firm, but never tough. The Spanish and Italian olives are widely popular but are really no finer than the best California products.

The candle-nut, used as a relish and somewhat resembling a green walnut, is the fruit of a tropical tree. It is chopped fine, packed in jars, or bottled, with salt added. As a relish it is highly prized, specially by the natives of the Sandwich Islands.

Candle-nut.

Pickled samphire, although at one time popularly used as a condiment, is now little known outside of England. It is a variety of sea-weed and grows upon dangerous and rocky cliffs. Shakespeare refers to "the samphire gatherer's dangerous trade," and another poet has apostrophized the

"Green girdles and crowns of the sea gods,
Cool blossoms of water and foam,"

quite omitting to mention the fact that the "girdles and crowns" make, when chopped and packed in vinegar, a most delicious pickle. Unlike most condiments, this is, as are all seaweeds, nutritious. The people of the Sandwich Islands, as well as the English, consider samphire, both the true and false varieties, a choice condiment. It is specially liked when served with mutton.

Flavors are used almost entirely in the making of sweetmeats, candies and pastry. Vanilla is perhaps the most choice, being invariably used in the preparation of chocolate and cocoa for the market. The vanilla vine is an orchid, native to Central America, and cultivated in South America, the West Indies, Mexico, and upon the islands of the Indian and southern Pacific oceans. The vanilla of commerce is made from the delicate, volatile oil extracted from the seed-pods. These are several inches in length and great care is exerted in curing that the flavor be not destroyed.

The curing process occupies about six months. The vanilla plant bears fruit when about three years old, remaining productive for thirty or forty years. The best vanilla is exported from Mexico, while that from Brazil is of an inferior quality.

The Tonka bean, called also Tongua and Tonquin bean, is frequently sold as a substitute for or adulterant of vanilla. It belongs to the *leguminosœ*, producing thick, short pods from which an oil, resembling vanilla, is extracted. The tree is common in British Guiana and the tropics and grows to an immense size. It is much cheaper commercially than vanilla.

The extract of bitter almond consists of a tincture made from the kernel of the nut. The tree of the bitter almond originated, it is believed, in Persia, although now growing wild in southern Europe. The flavor obtained from the kernel is due to the prussic acid developed in the process of making the tincture. A similar flavor exists in the kernel and leaves of the peach, a tree allied botanically to the almond. Flavoring extracts are also made from the orange, lemon, strawberry and other fruits. They are also produced chemically, as many alleged fruit-flavors found upon the market prove, from the coal-tar products.

Vanilla Vine and Bean.

The pistachio or pistache nut is particularly liked by confectioners because of its delicate flavor, resembling that of the almond. It is the kernel of a sumac is small and of a light green color. It is native to Europe and the far East.

Cordials or *liqueurs* are used both for flavoring pastries and ices and, in the way of beverages, as aids to the digestion. In the latter case they are taken in very small quantities just at the close of a meal.

Curaçoa is one of the most celebrated of cordials. It was originally made in the island of Curaçoa, whence its name, and is prepared from limes, orange peel and spices. It is still an important source of revenue to its native island.

Noyau is a *liqueur* made from brandy, flavored with bitter almond.

Ratafia is a *liqueur* similar to Curaçoa and noyau, which is flavored with peach and almond extracts and spiced.

Anisette and kümmel have been already mentioned, the former a cordial made by the French and Italians and flavored with aniseed; the latter, a German and Russian *liqueur*, flavored with kümmel or caraway seed.

Absinthe is a bitter and aromatic cordial, the bitterness being due to the use of wormwood in its preparation. It is particularly pernicious and treacherous to use if taken before meals, as is often the custom, instead of afterward. It is largely used by the French.

Maraschino is an aromatic cordial, the flavor of which is produced by the use of the bitter almond and the Italian cherry.

Chartreuse was originally prepared by the monks of a monastery of that name in France. For obvious reasons the Pope prohibited its manufacture by them in 1864 and the original receipt was lost. There are four kinds now made, of which the green is perhaps the most popular. Chartreuse possesses the fragrance of garden herbs, the aroma of various spices, flowers and nuts, and even the balsamy fragrance of the young, green tassel from the pine tree. These cordials are more largely used in France and Italy than anywhere else. Owing to a growing sentiment against their use, they are tolerated to only a limited extent in America although, because of their common use as flavorings, they are here mentioned.

Vegetable acids are also largely used for the flavoring of foods. One of the oldest known is verjuice, used by the ancients as a beverage. Its use in cookery is believed to have originated in mediæval France. It is made from the juice of crab-apples and of unripe grapes.

Vinegar is a developed acid. The word comes from the French *vin-aigre*, meaning sour wine. If simple cane sugar be mixed with water and some ferment, it will turn to grape sugar, then to alcohol, then to vinegar. However, the best vinegar now used is a fruit acid, either from apple or grape. It is also made from the red and white wines and from sour beer, the latter being known as malt vinegar. In England the law allows a per centage of sulphuric acid to be added to malt vinegar while in America both sulphuric and muriatic acids are considered adulterants. Vinegar is the one indispensable ingredient of pickles and various sauces as well as a valuable condiment.

Limes and lemons, similar fruits, contain large quantities of acid which is thoroughly wholesome and agreeable. To some extent these acids are displacing vinegar as condiments, being considered both more health giving and more palatable.

The most complete and instructive exhibition of condiments and spices ever given was held in the Agricultural Building during the World's Columbian Exposition. The nations of all the earth contributed. There were capers and olives from Italy, spices from Java, chutney from Trinidad, Calcutta, and the far away island of Ceylon; ketchup from both England and America, cassareep and pickled limes from British Guiana, soy from China and Japan, and pickles from lands galore. The long, daintily curved, vanilla bean was exhibited side by side with its short, fat, plebeian looking adulterant, the tonka bean. Cordials were sent from every country exhibiting. There was in one portion of the building a small conservatory filled with growing spice plants, among them pimento, ginger, clove, nutmeg, pepper, cassia and cinnamon.

CHAPTER XIII.

MILK AND MILK FOODS.

Milk is perhaps the most perfect of all foods since it is the only one containing all the elements of nutrition in an easily assimilated form. It was primarily intended to promote health and growth in the young animal during the first months of its life but has come into use as an universal and appropriate food for the entire human race. Wherever man and animals together have inhabited any part of the earth, there milk is a common article of diet. Besides the cow, the camel, horse, bison, reindeer, sheep, and goat yield milk for man's use, and many peoples, including the inhabitants of Scandinavia, of Norway, of the Netherlands, of Ireland, of America, even the Bedouins of the desert, depend largely upon it for food. Dr. Edward Smith, while investigating the dietaries of the laboring classes of the European nations, discovered that the English workman consumed about thirty-two ounces of milk weekly, the Welshman, eighty-five ounces, the Scot, one hundred and twenty-five ounces, while the Irishman consumed, during the same length of time, one hundred and thirty-five ounces.

In all stages and conditions of life milk is a valuable and wholesome, often a necessary, food. It is specially valuable to the young, and Dr. Willard Parker was fond of saying, "If you would have your children lambs, give them milk, if lions, feed them upon meat."

The constituents of milk are classed, as in other foods, as protein, carbohydrates, fats, salts and water. Of these, water is by far the greatest in proportion, comprising eighty-seven per cent in an average sample. It serves to hold the other constituents in solution and favors metabolism, the process by which the nutritive elements are assimilated by the plastic tissues of the human system. To this rapid and easy process of assimilation is due the great value of milk as a food for the invalid or the young. It is generally the exclusive diet of the fever patient when nothing else will be tolerated by an enfeebled digestion. The protein or nitrogenous matter comprises both the casein and albuminoids. The carbohydrates consist of the milk sugar which, while classified with the fats as a heat-producer, has still its peculiar value as a food. Dr. Aitkin, chemist of the Highland Society of Edinburgh, has shown that it assists rather in the storing up of fat in organized tissue as well as in effecting a saving in the assimilation of the albuminoids.

The fats, instead of being held in solution as are the other elements, are diffused throughout the liquid in the form of minute oil globules, visible only with the aid of the microscope. These tiny globules, being lighter than the fluid, rise to the surface and, there accumulated, are known as cream. The heat equivalent of fat is two and one-half times that of milk sugar. The amount of cream contained is usually the test quality of milk although, from a nutritive standpoint, this is of minor importance. The amount of casein and albuminoids, which are the flesh forming elements, should become the desideratum rather than the cream, which is chiefly important in the manufacture of butter. The oil globules of milk by chemical analysis consist of many fats which undergo change immediately upon exposure to the atmosphere.

The proportion of fats in milk may be increased by regulating the quality and quantity of the animal's food and, as is well known, differs in amount in different breeds of cattle. The Jerseys have long been famous for producing milk which contains a large percentage of fats and the contest held at the Columbian Exposition between the Jersey, Guernsey and Shorthorn breeds established the reputation of the former as cream producers. The famous Ida Marigold, in her record of producing fifty-two pounds of butter in fourteen days, not only outranked all cows of other breeds but also all other Jerseys.

That both the casein and fats of milk are held in suspension in the fluid and not in solution has been proven by filtering the milk through porcelain. Only a clear fluid, known as milk serum, passes through, holding the salts in solution, leaving as a residue on the filter most of the casein and fats. The ash left after burning the evaporated milk contains the minerals, or salts, which are held in solution, potash, soda, lime, iron and magnesia. The specific gravity of milk is determined by the hydrometer, which also indicates the proportion of solid alimentary substances. Other tests determine the proportion of fatty matter contained but none of these can be relied upon to detect adulterations with accuracy. The food value of milk varies according to the quantity of solid matter contained, this being variable in different grades of milk. Milk which is to be used for butter is tested by the lactometer, an instrument used for ascertaining the quantity of cream contained; if for cheese it is tested by evaporation for the amount of solids, or casein.

The character of milk is perceptibly changed, both in flavor and nutritive value, by the food and surroundings of the cow. Turnips, onions, leeks, or any rank weed of the pastures, when eaten by the cow, ruins the flavor of the milk. One of the largest dairies in Chicago habitually refuses to receive milk from all farmers who feed their cows upon ensilage, or malted food, knowing that any fermented food changes both the quality and the flavor of the milk. This house employs a physician, who is regularly a health officer, to test all samples of milk brought in for the percentages contained of cream, of albuminoids and casein and of salts. Besides this a rigid system of inspection is enforced upon the farmers supplying this milk in regard to the pasturing, feeding and watering of their stock as well as in regard to cleanliness in milking and taking care of the milk. Different pastures determine the constituents to a certain extent, one furnishing a butter-producing milk, another, milk which is valuable to the cheese maker. Cows which are kept away from pasturage in stalls or in unwholesome surroundings, which are fed upon unsuitable food or have access to water contaminated by sewage or surface drainage, produce milk which is wholly unfit for food. It is not only poor in nutrition but likely to be contaminated by disease. The compulsory inspection of milk which is carried on in many of our great cities sufficiently proves that such diseases as typhoid fever, diphtheria and particularly tuberculosis may be the direct result of using infected or unclean milk.

Milk, while variable in the proportion of its constituents, should yet yield about the following analysis (Dr. Letheby):

Nitrogenous matter	4.1
Fats	3.9
Sugar (Lactine)	5.2
Salts	0.8
Water	86.0
	100.0

There is no food more susceptible of change than milk, none better adapted to conveying dirt and disease into the human system, if care and cleanliness be not exercised in the care of the utensils which contain the milk. Unwholesome change in milk is caused by two substances, the unorganized or chemical ferments and the organized or bacterial. The latter class contains divers micro-organisms known as bacteria, which are present in all substances to a certain extent as well as in the atmosphere. No medium is more favorable to their growth and development than warm milk. In a recent bulletin issued by the Agricultural department at Washington a simple experiment in bacterial culture was made with the following result: a specimen of milk was placed for four days in a cool atmosphere, at the end of which time it was found to contain about ten millions of bacteria to the quart. The milk was then placed for seven hours in a warm room, at the end of which time the bacteria had increased in number a hundred fold. This is quite enough to frighten the average person were it not for the fact that non-poisonous bacteria can be digested without harm by one in good health. Only in young children and invalids are they likely to produce gastric disturbances. One variety, the *bacillus lactis*, produces lactic acid, that is, causes the milk to become sour; another bacillus causes it to become bitter; others, blue; others, slimy, etc. Their names and numbers are legion, each variety capable of producing or furthering some change. Climatic conditions influence the development of bacteria in milk, e. g., the rapid souring of milk during thunderstorms and during the sultry weather of "dog-days."

Bacteria may be further classified as those which are innocuous and those which are poison-producing. Although it is a half century since Fuchs discovered bacteria, the science is yet in its infancy, and chemists are still occupied with the discovery of new varieties and with determining their influence in producing changes in milk as well as other foods. Two facts are known, one, that if milk be lowered in temperature immediately after being taken from the cow, the chances of rapid development of bacteria are reduced to a minimum; and the other, that if milk is Pasteurized, that is, sterilized, by being heated to the boiling point, there maintained for a few minutes and then quickly cooled, the germs are killed. Milk so treated can be preserved for an indefinite period of time if kept from contact with the atmosphere and is quite as palatable and far more healthful than before being rendered sterile. When we remember that cows often suffer from tuberculosis and other diseases, and also that milk from a healthy cow is liable to infection from careless or unclean handling, the necessity of sterilization is obvious. Sternberg, in his work on bacteriology, has given the thermal death-point of various poisonous bacteria, of which the bacilli of tuberculosis, of typhoid fever, of diphtheria, the micrococci of pneumonia and of cholera, may be conveyed in milk. Heat destroys the bacilli of typhoid fever at 140° F.; tuberculosis at 160° F.; diphtheria at 140° F.; the micrococci of pneumonia at 160° F.; cholera at 140° F. (Sternberg.)

The necessity of absolute cleanliness in the care of milk should be impressed upon every housewife, particularly upon those who have the care of children. Various chemicals, such as borax, and salicylic acid are used as preservatives, but the results from their use are unsatisfactory, not to mention the injurious effects of these chemicals when taken into the human system. Nothing is so valuable as that ounce of prevention, cleanliness, and nothing, excepting actual infection, is more conducive to the development of disease than dirt. It should be remembered that, while heating to the boiling point is sufficient to sterilize the milk, it by no means destroys all danger from milk which is infected or unclean. The only safeguard aside from this lies in securing milk from a healthy, well-fed cow, chilling it immediately in well cleansed vessels.

Another organic ferment, which produces what is chemically known as alcoholic fermentation when placed in milk, is yeast. Milk so treated is known as koumiss or kumyss. From time immemorial the nomadic tribes of Tartary have used mare's milk so prepared as a beverage, and within the last generation or two koumiss, prepared from cow's milk with the addition of sugar and a small quantity of yeast, has become a valuable liquid food for invalids. Another and similar drink is the "Kefir" of the Caucasus mountains. Matzoon is another milk preparation, which is the result of bacterial culture, caused by the addition of a ferment. The name is simply an Armenian word, meaning "fermented milk," and in the country of its origin all milk is so treated before used as food or for the making of butter. There is an Armenian legend that the ferment was first obtained from heaven, that an angel presented some of it to Father Abraham who divided it generously among his kinsfolk, and it has been used in the Orient ever since. The Matzoon is evidently the result of a pure culture of bacteria which is introduced as a ferment after the milk has been thoroughly sterilized by heating to the boiling point. This is necessary lest the effect of the introduced ferment should be counteracted by other bacteria which inevitably develop in uusterilized milk. The milk is cooled and then agitated, making a light, creamy, most delicious drink, valuable to invalids and somewhat resembling a superior quality of butter-milk, but more nutritious as it contains all the constituents of milk. This was exhibited at the World's Columbian Exposition by two firms. No fresh milk was exhibited excepting as tested for its butter producing quality.

Condensed milk has for many years been manufactured both at home and in European countries. At the Columbian Exposition there were five large exhibits, notable alike for the size and beauty of their pavilions and for the excellence of the milk displayed. The method of preserving milk by evaporation, that is, condensing it, is thoroughly excellent. The milk, in process of evaporation, is sterilized and, if sealed from the air, will keep for almost any length of time and in any climate. In condensing, the milk is first cooled to about 60° F. for the purpose of dissipating all animal heat. It is then quickly heated to a temperature of 185° at which point evaporation of the water takes place. The temperature is not lowered beyond 160° F. until the process is completed, which occurs when four gallons are reduced in bulk to one gallon. The best white sugar is then added, in the proportion of one and one-fourth pounds to one gallon of milk, after which it is sealed in cans. Condensed milk is palatable in coffee and in cookery in which its "scalded" and sweet taste is not objectionable. Its reduced bulk adapts it to transportation and for use on ship-board. It is far too sweet for general use and is objectionable as a food for young children owing to the excess of sugar. It is fattening and the continued use of it may give a child a plump, healthy appearance. But this appearance of health is deceptive for, instead of building up muscular tissue, the flesh becomes less firm, there is an excess of adipose tissue and a child so fed is more liable to succumb to disease than one which is fed rationally. There is a certain Swiss brand which is specially advertised as suitable for children but which, owing to the surplus of sugar, is no more so than the American brands. There is now in the market an unsweetened, condensed milk, which has not only the absence of sugar to recommend it but also the fact that in the process of evaporation it becomes thoroughly sterilized.

The French have a process of condensing milk, a process also used by the Swiss and the product of which is known as solidified milk. To 112 pounds of fresh milk they add twenty-eight pounds of sugar and one teaspoonful of common soda. This is evaporated to a consistency which admits of its being put up in the shape of small bricks. It is preserved simply by a wrapping of tin-foil.

The name of "evaporated cream," an article recently put upon the markets, is a misnomer and one quite likely to mislead purchasers, as such a thing as an evaporated cream is a chemical impossibility. It is simply milk evaporated to the consistency of a thick cream.

CHAPTER XIV.

BUTTER.

UTTER has been used in the countries of the far East for many centuries and is still considered by the descendants of the early Syrian and Israelitish peoples a most necessary food. Both cheese and butter are mentioned in the Hebraic scriptures, the ancient Jewish method of making them being still used by the Arabians and by many of the modern inhabitants of Palestine. For the making of butter the milk is placed in a copper pan over a fire, to it being added either a small quantity of sour milk or the dried intestines of a lamb, the latter used evidently for the pepsin contained, which causes the milk to coagulate. When this is accomplished the milk is gently agitated in a goat skin bag until the butter separates. It is then placed by itself in another pan and, after the addition of a ferment made from wheat, is boiled. The butter collects upon the surface of this mixture from which it is skimmed, a white, ill-flavored article, bearing no resemblance to the fragrant product of an American dairy-farm.

Among the ancient Greeks butter was rarely, if ever, used upon the table as their olive oil must have satisfied the demands of the system for fats. Herodotus relates that the Greeks first learned the use of butter from the nomadic and pastoral Scythians, and, half a century later, we find the physician Galen recommending its use as an ointment. He informs us that cow's milk produces the best butter for such use, goat's milk an inferior quality, while that made from asses' milk is poorest of all. Other writers refer to butter made from sheep's milk as well as to elephant's butter, used by the natives of India for the anointing of wounds. In the second century the Romans learned from the Teutonic races the use of butter as a food.

The butter of the modern dairy farm is almost universally made from cow's milk or, to be more definite, from the floating oil globules contained in the milk. These oil globules, being lighter than the serum of the milk, rise to the surface and may be skimmed off as cream. They are so extremely minute that fifteen hundred of them placed in a row would scarcely reach the distance of an inch. They have no covering, membranous or otherwise, each remaining intact and separate in the form of a drop or tiny globule. Churning or agitation of the cream causes them to adhere to each other, a process that may be facilitated or retarded according to the temperature at which the cream is churned. When the cream takes on a granular form, the agitation should be stopped, the granules gathered and separated from the butter-milk.

Butter is made from milk in two conditions, each method having its adherents. The older and more popular method consists in allowing the milk to stand from twenty to thirty-six hours, the cream being removed when sufficiently "ripened" or soured. The other consists in separating the butter from the whole milk while sweet, butter so produced having a flavor very different and generally not so well liked as that churned from sour cream. There is great diversity of opinion as to whether butter should or should not be washed, recent investigations going to prove that its peculiar and agreeable flavor resides chiefly in the butter-milk, for it is well known that butter may be washed until almost flavorless. The best butter-maker I ever knew was a woman who was reared in the dairy business in Herkimer county, New York. Her butter was uniformly good, had a wide reputation for good keeping qualities and always brought the highest market price. Yet she never washed it nor even allowed water to touch it after it left the churn. In this respect her methods were similar to those used in the Scandinavian countries and the Netherlands, nations world famous for their dairy products. According to the report of the United States consul at

Copenhagen upon the creameries of that country, in one of which, that of Ouroé, the average weekly yield is 1,512 pounds, no water is ever used in the churning, the butter being rinsed with skimmed milk. The churning is stopped when the butter coheres in tiny granules, and the butter is taken up on a sieve from which the milk is drained. In pieces of about one pound each it is pressed with the hands against the sides of a tub, then placed in layers, three drams of salt being used to each pound of butter. It is then cut into pieces perpendicularly through the layers and subjected to the same pressing as before. This operation is repeated ten times before the butter is placed in the cooling box. In these creameries, extensive as many of them are, the butter-milk is all removed by the hands, differing from the method used in American creameries, of pressing it out by machinery. The latter method often destroys the "grain" of the butter, owing to too much working, giving it a greasy appearance.

Butter, like milk, is liable to infection from uncleanliness or disease, as well as vitiation from a foul atmosphere. It is hardly necessary to state that care and cleanliness are absolutely essential, the first essential being milk obtained from a perfectly healthy, well-pastured cow. Just as milk may be infected when taken from a tuberculous or otherwise diseased cow, so is butter, made from such milk. Several years ago German scientists proved that butter made from tuberculous milk was infected and capable of producing disease. Since then Professor Roth of Zurich has investigated the butter made in twenty different cantons in Switzerland. He found that ten per cent of it contained tubercle bacilli. About the same time Dr. Brusaferro of Italy investigated the butter of Italian markets, and found eleven per cent of infected butter. It is not at all probable that so large a proportion of tuberculous butter could be found in American markets, because of the recent systematic efforts made by the bureau of animal industry to root out the disease among cattle. But these examples serve to show with what intelligent and scrupulous care the process of butter making should be carried on, beginning with the food, water and pasturage of the cow and ending only when the butter is deposited in the cooling rooms of the markets. At Copenhagen all butter must pass inspection before judges, whose influence has been inestimable in furthering cleanliness and attention among the dairy population.

But if the American people do not run so great a risk of infected

butter as the poorer classes of Italians, they do run an enormous
risk in eating the unclean products which many of our packing
houses send out. Many a so-called "packing-house" consists of a
single, dirty, damp, and foul-smelling room. To this place butter of
every shade and quality is brought and dumped into a large wooden
vat. Near by stands a pail half-filled with coloring material (an-
nato), in which is a short-handled broom. After the various kinds
of butter are worked into a somewhat homogeneous mass, the coloring liquid is sprinkled in by means of the broom, until the desired
color is obtained. The contents of this vat are then worked and
packed in jars or tubs and go forth as "June grass" or "Orange Co."
butter. I once knew of a creamery which perpetrated this identical
fraud upon its customers by mixing various grades of farmers'
butter; and the "hash" or "ladle" butter which was sent out was
labeled "best creamery butter." Besides the uncleanliness of much
of such butter it will not keep a month without deteriorating in
quality and flavor. Such frauds are the worst enemies with which
the legitimate dairy business has to contend. The wealthier and
more intelligent people can more or less easily avoid these gross
frauds, but not so the poor, the ignorant, and the inmates of various
state institutions, such as our work-houses, poor-houses and certain
of our insane asylums, who are frequently fed on inferior meat and
worse than inferior butter. As yet no systematic investigation has
been made among the eleemosynary institutions of America and, as
an inspiration to some would-be investigator, I quote the following
report, made by F. W. Roswell of England after investigating the
quality of butter furnished to the various workhouses in the
vicinity of London. It is scarcely necessary to say that good butter
should not contain more than from one-half to one ounce of water
to the pound, while one ounce of salt per pound produces salt butter:

Workhouse.	Percentage of Water.	Character of Butter.
St. Saviors	12.6	Fair.
Stepny	16.5	Nasty.
St. Pancreas	12.8	Bad.
Poplar	12.9	Very bad.
Shoreditch	13.2	Bad.
St. Giles	13.2	Tolerably good.
Lambeth	13.2	Exceedingly bad.
Fulham	13.1	Good.
Wardsworth	15.3	Bad.

Workhouse.	Percentage of Water.	Character of Butter.
City of London	13.7	Good.
Hackney	16.6	Tolerable.
St. Olave's	14.3	Fair.
St. Luke's, Chelsea	14.5	Fair.
Camberwell	14.7	Exceedingly bad.
St. George's in the East	15.4	Bad.
Marylebone	18.2	Tolerable.
Greenwich	19.4	Fair.
Holborn	19.7	Middling.
Paddington	23.6	Rather rank.
Kensington	23.7	Wretched.
Salt butter.		
White Chapel	24.9	Very bad.

We might do as the Bedouins, to improve the flavor of butter. They boil aromatic herbs with it, when it is known as Hedjaz. I doubt, however, if any condiment could destroy the flavor of some butter which finds its way into cheap boarding-houses or into certain institutions where the inmates have no choice of foods.

There is evidently far greater need of educating dairy people and farmers to see the necessity of making a uniformly good and pure quality of butter and then of placing it directly into the hands of consumers instead of consigning it to the dubious mercies of a packing-house, than there is in legislating against a wholesome imitation of butter by prohibiting its sale or by placing a tax upon it. For, contrary to the belief of many, butter or a wholesome fat of some kind is an absolute necessity to the human system and has a distinct, nutritive value.

The question of uniformity in butter is a serious one. It is rarely produced twice in succession of uniform quality and flavor by indifferent butter makers, and even the most skillful sometimes fail. Such failure is variously attributed to "dog-days," thunder storms and other atmospheric conditions, occasionally to general "contrariness," never to lack of cleanliness in atmosphere or utensils. But of late years science has come to the rescue. It is now known that to the development of certain bacteria is due the flavor, good or otherwise, of butter. If the butter be made from sour milk, this development begins before churning; if from sweet milk, afterward, in which case the flavor is not generally so well liked. But these bacteria are of divers and manifold varieties and, when the wrong varieties develop, the result is butter of poor, sometimes wretched flavor, and consequently of poor keeping qualities. Chevreul claimed that the *stearine*, *margerine* and *oleine* of butter, with minute quantities of *butyrine* and *caprine*, gave the desired flavor and fragrance. Other scientists believed it to be due to the volatile acids contained, a theory which has been discarded recently by some, owing to the fact that the characteristic aroma of butter has been produced in solutions which contain no fat of butter. But the first reliable investigations made along this line were due to the efforts of the Swedish scientist, Storch, who, after patient research, was able to isolate the bacillus of slightly sour cream which was believed to produce the required butter flavor. Wiegmann later isolated the same class of organisms and introduced them as a ferment into the creameries of Germany with satisfactory results. In Jutland the souring of cream is produced artificially and the dairy-maid is held responsible for the result. A ferment is prepared by allowing sweet milk to become sour, adding this to other cream in small quantities that the souring process may be developed by the action of the required variety of bacteria. By this means the characteristic flavor of "sweet butter" is developed and is always uniform. Still, this very fermentation, if allowed to continue too long, will ultimately destroy all fine flavor and will render it impossible to make the best butter. Certainly, if culture of certain bacteria can be introduced into cheese with success (witness the numerous and widely different varieties of cheese upon our markets), it is not improbable that the fermentation of cream for butter-making can be as successfully accomplished. When that day comes, when to the cleanliness, tact, and housewifely skill of the dairy maid are added the scientific methods of the chemical laboratory, simple though they may be, the day of "all sorts and conditions" of butter will have passed away. It is not too much to predict that, within a few years, the butter of our markets will be more wholesome, clean, and uniform in quality.

CHAPTER XV.

CHEESE.

O THE cheese-maker the organic or bacterial ferments are an absolute necessity for upon them depend the ripening of the cheese, its flavor, in a word, its commercial value. When milk coagulates, either by the action of the bacteria of lactic acid or by the development of some added ferment, a substance called "curd" is formed. This is composed of most of the casein, albumin, fats, sugar and salts of the milk. In this form it is often eaten ice cold with sugar and nutmeg and, called "junket," is regarded as a great delicacy. Dryden refers to "curds and cream, the flower of country fare."

When the liquid portion or whey is well separated the curds may be pressed by the hands into a home-made cheese, known variously as "Dutch" and "cottage" cheese, a variety made and used in nearly every household where milk may be had in abundance. It is customary to make it of skimmed milk, that butter also may be made in the household, and after the curds are well pressed to add butter and cream, with salt and a dash of black pepper. Such cheese is very nutritious, is the result of a natural process of fermentation and was probably the earliest cheese known. That of modern Palestine is similarly made, but, as it is first exceedingly well salted and then allowed to dry to utter hardness in small, round cakes, it compares most unfavorably with the American home-made product.

Cheese is customarily made by the addition to the warmed milk of an organic or digestive ferment known as rennet. This is prepared from the stomach of the calf, and, containing large quantities of pepsin, has the property of coagulating the casein of the milk in a short time, providing the milk be kept at a temperature of about 80° F. In the best or "full cream" cheeses the whole milk is used, the handling and curing of them determining largely their market value. The curd forms in from thirty to fifty minutes, providing the milk be maintained at the proper temperature, and is then ready to be separated from the liquid or whey. Extreme care must be observed in the cutting or breaking of the curd that it may not, owing to the undue pressure or over manipulation, lose a portion of the cream contained. Some cheese makers use a sort of rake for breaking the curd, others a wooden knife, while many prefer the fingers. The curd is allowed to shrink somewhat by the separation of the whey when it is drained and pressed into various shapes in cheese hoops. It is then set away to "cure" or ripen, for a freshly made cheese is far from palatable and has almost no market value.

The ripening process is now known to be due to the action of bacteria. It was Cohn who first discovered these micro-organisms in cheese in 1875. Five years later he found, after experimental observations, that there were numerous varieties and also that if the curd be sterilized or treated in any way with a disinfectant the cheese would fail to ripen. To make cheese without the aid of bacteria is therefore impossible. They exist in fresh, warm milk and multiply rapidly at the temperature necessary for coagulating the curd, now one variety and now another, depending upon atmosphere and surroundings, becoming most numerous. Certain varieties produce a poison, first described by Dr. Vaughan and named *tyrotoxicon*. Says Dr. Vaughan: "Tyrotoxicon may originate in milk on long standing in closed vessels owing to putrefactive change, which is due to minute organisms. The introduction of these organisms into milk hastens putrefaction and consequently the formation of ptomaines. Milk coming from cows kept in filthy stables is likely to undergo speedy putrefaction, and poisonous germs may also adhere to the sides of any vessels which are not kept absolutely clean." He says further, "any cheese which is acid in its reaction should be regarded with suspicion. The old, foul-smelling cheeses, such as Limburger and Schweitzer, are alkaline in reaction and poisoning does not seem to result from their use." In Limburger, as is well known, the bacterial growth is allowed to develop to the verge of putrefaction. At the Arabian encampment upon the Midway Plaisance I was one day invited to taste some cheese made from camel's milk and brought by the Arabs from their desert home. It was hardly pleasant either to taste or sight and must have contained even more bacteria to the ounce than the one hundred and sixty-five millions which ordinary cheese is estimated to contain. These, too, were Arabian bacteria, of wholly characteristic odor and flavor.

Cheese is a highly concentrated and very nutritious food. It is composed almost wholly of protein and, according to Mattieu Williams, there is in every pound of cheese twice as much nutriment as in a pound of the best meat, while, if bones and tendons be included in the weight, cheese has the advantage of three to one. There is much difference of opinion as to the digestibility of cheese, but the fact remains that to the average person it is fully as digestible as it is nutritious. The Scotch and Swiss, who eat it in the place of meat, experience no trouble in digesting it, nor would any one who ate it as rationally as they do. But the American usually considers it a condiment to be eaten at the close of a full dinner, where it often adds to the burden already placed upon an overloaded digestion, not to mention the added nitrogenous matter which the system has no use for and must discard as waste. It is not surprising that the Americans are coming to be known as a nation of dys-

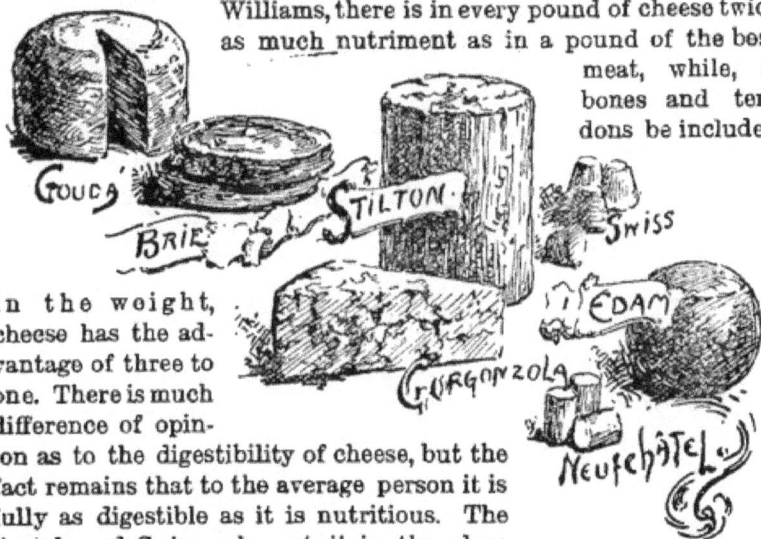

peptics when one considers their universal ignorance of the uses of foods and the needs of the human system. A poor cheese requires longer time for digestion than a good one owing to the smaller amount of fat and the larger amount of casein contained in the former. When used in cookery, as in cheese fondu, custard or soufflé, cheese is rendered more digestible by the addition of a little carbonate of potash to the milk before the cheese is added. This is the result of experiments made by Williams.

The cheese making countries are Great Britain, France, Italy, Germany, the Netherlands, Switzerland, the United States and Canada. The Laplanders make cheese from reindeer's milk, the Bedouins from the milk of sheep. Certain of the French and Swiss cheeses are made from the milk of the sheep and goat, but the ordinary article of export is made from cow's milk.

Perhaps the most famous of all English cheeses is the Cheddar, pale in color, nutty and delicious in flavor. In the process of making a quantity of sour whey is added to the curd just before it is put into the press, the whole being maintained at a temperature of from 00° to 65° F. After being pressed it is placed in a temperature of 70° F. in the curing room, is coated with fat and turned daily. It is cured in from three to six months although said to improve indefinitely with age. At the Columbian Exposition there was a specimen of Cheddar sent by an English firm, which was labeled "Cheddar Cheese, made in 1845." To all appearance it was by no means past its prime. Cheeses similar to the Cheddar are made in America and Canada.

Cheshire cheese, made in the county of Cheshire, resembles Cheddar in appearance although it is stronger in flavor.

The double Gloucester is a cheese which, containing much fat, is excellent in cookery, especially in making Welsh rarebits, and is mild in flavor.

Banbury is a rich cheese about half an inch thick, not so popular now as a few generations ago. It has been described as being "nothing but paring" and, in "Merry Wives of Windsor," Slender is compared to it.

Stilton is one of the choicest of English cheeses and was first made by a Mrs. Paulet who regularly supplied with it an innkeeper of Stilton, a little town in Huntingdon. From that the cheese takes its name. It is a rich cheese, its pale-colored substance marked with greenish veins, and is never eaten until exceedingly well cured.

It was some of this "fine, ripe Stilton" which Charles Lamb purchased and then asked the shopkeeper for a bit of string that he might lead it home! Stilton is small and drum-shaped, and as a dessert cheese is rivaled only by Roquefort or the Italian Gorgonzola.

It is said that no cheese better pleases the true gourmet than Gorgonzola and, although an authority declares it to be "sadly indigestible," it has inspired at least one cheese lover to drop into verse:

> " I have enjoyed it from of old,
> That product of the sunny south—
> The cheese that wears the dainty mould,
> And melts like butter in the mouth;
> And whose consumption oft is graced
> By such a pleasant after taste."

Gorgonzola is a rich, creamy cheese made in the mountainous regions of Italy. It is cured always in exceedingly damp caves, the floors of which are usually covered with water, and the process of curing occupies not less than a year. When cut it is veined with greenish streaks of mold, said to be accomplished by introducing layers of moldy bread crumbs into the curd just before pressing. If this be true the Italian mountaineers well understand the method of introducing a certain culture of bacteria into their cheeses and also how, by dampness and a certain temperature, to best further this bacterial growth.

The Cachio Cavallo di Napolio is a soft, rich cheese which is cured after being put into the stomachs of small animals. It is considered a great delicacy by the Italians and was exhibited in the Italian section at the Columbian Exposition.

Cavallo.

Perhaps the best known of Italian cheeses is the Parmesan as it is used the world over in cooking. It is a skimmed milk cheese, containing very little fat, and so hard that it is used only after being grated. It is made at Parma, Italy, from the milk of cows which are carefully fed upon grass all the year round, and is said to owe its delicious, sweet flavor to the superior quality of the pasturage along the banks of the Po. Parmesan cheeses are of large size and require three years for ripening. However, they may be kept for years without deteriorating, as was proven by the fine flavor and perfect condition of one exhibited at the exposition which was eleven years old and, it is needless to add, as hard as a stone.

Macaroni is never at its best without Parmesan cheese, and certain soups are improved in flavor by its use.

France produces more than forty varieties of cheeses, the most famous among them being Roquefort, Gruyère, Port du Salut, Brie, Camembert and Neufchâtel.

Gruyère is a thick, firm cheese useful in cooking. It is also made in Switzerland, in which country it is usually flavored with herbs.

Neufchâtel is a rich, creamy, white cheese, made in tiny rolls, each wrapped in tin-foil. It is an appropriate dessert cheese.

Port du Salut is a soft, delicately-flavored cheese, made at Bordeaux. It is not considered at its best, the epicures tell us, until it has ripened almost to the verge of decay. It is of a light coffee color and is rarely seen excepting upon club house tables.

Camembert is a small, hand-made cheese covered with blue mold, under which is a white mold. It is made chiefly in Normandy, the dampness and temperature developing the fungous growth upon the outside. After the cheeses are made into shape they are placed upon shelves and turned daily until covered with a white mold, then removed to different atmospheric surroundings until the blue mold is fully developed, when they are ready for use.

Brie, a large, soft cheese, made in the vicinity of Paris, resembles Camembert. It also is covered first with a white, then with a red or blue mold. The development of red mold is the thing desired, Brie of a blue color being less esteemed. This peculiar species of bacteria is due in part to the osier strainers used, which are never washed! Brie ripens in six or eight weeks after pressing.

Roquefort has for many generations been noted for the production of the well known Roquefort cheese. The whole country about this little French town consists of fertile pasture lands which support thousands of sheep, and from the milk of the ewes is produced this famous cheese. It is a rich, creamy cheese, made by the peasantry in their homes. It is made in layers, between which are sprinkled the pulverized crumbs of brown bread, which have been allowed to develop a species of fungous growth. This cheese is therefore the result of direct culture of bacteria. After the loaves of cheese are made the peasant farmers dispose of them to the *maturers*, who own the caves. After reaching the caves the cheeses are brushed over with fat and, with a machine, are pierced with several minute holes to admit the air, a process which would prove destructive to most cheeses. It is stated that in no other place than these caves are the conditions, atmospheric and otherwise, favorable to the growth of the species of bacteria which gives to the Roquefort its characteristic flavor. When cut, the cheese presents a veined appearance, owing to the mold.

The cheeses of Holland are the spice, Gouda and Edam, of which Gouda somewhat resembles the English Cheddar. Edam is a round cheese, the outside of which is artificially colored red, after which it is wrapped in tin-foil. It is a rich though rather hard cheese and of a yellow color, differing from other cheeses in that an acid is used, instead of rennet, for forming the curd.

Limburger cheese has made the little town of Limburg, Belgium, known over most of the globe. It is a rich cheese, ripened until actual putrefaction has set in, and the odor of which is offensively strong. It is disliked by the majority of people and in consistency and general appearance is not unlike new soap. By the uninitiated one article would be as much relished as the other. It is wrapped in tin-foil, probably to facilitate handling it as well as to conceal its fragrance.

Lipton is a famous Bohemian cheese, made from goat's milk. It comes to this country wrapped in tin-foil.

Schweitzer, Ulmetzer and Tyrolean are all well known cheeses made in Germany.

That cheese is a staple food in nearly every land was plainly evidenced by the exhibits made at the Columbian Exposition. Great Britain, France, Italy, Germany, Holland, Belgium, Argentine Republic, Ecuador, Uruguay, Mexico, Canada, our own states and many other countries carried the number of cheeses far into the hundreds. Canada has a reputation for making an excellent cheese, similar to the Cheddar of England. But, not content with this fame, she must needs add to it by making one of enormous size; and there it was, in the center of the Agricultural building, eleven tons in weight and with a spiral stairway leading to its expansive top. The state of Wisconsin ranked first in the number of her cheese exhibits, New York, New Hampshire, Minnesota, Maine and Iowa each adding their quota to the total display. New Jersey has long been known to make large quantities of cheese in imitation of the special, imported brands, but this state made no display at the exposition. In Pennsylvania there is made a cheese which is an excellent imitation of Neufchâtel. It is called *schmierkase*, is made from sour milk, well drained, mixed with cream and butter before pressing, and afterwards ripened. There is also a soft cheese on the market which sells for something like seventy-five cents a pound and which is made from three parts of butter and one part of cheese. It is put up in earthen jars and is a palatable lunch or dessert cheese.

America at the present time has an unenviable reputation for making what are known commercially as "filled" cheeses. They are made of skimmed milk, sufficient fat, either of lard or cotton seed oil, being added to the warm milk to take the place of cream. This mixture is thoroughly emulsified before the curd and whey are separated. and the cheeses are then colored and pressed. When new they can scarcely be distinguished from the honestly made article but they do not cure well and when ripened can easily be detected by their lack of flavor. The consumer gets in such cheese a flavorless and indigestible article of food, and the makers who produce a good cream cheese suffer equally through the reputation which the American product has in foreign markets. That may be one reason why Americans themselves depend so largely upon imported cheese, and this condition will continue until the people realize the value of cheese as a substantial food and until they so thoroughly understand the science of cheese making that results will always be uniform. The curing of cheese is not yet wholly understood but it is probable that before long bacteriological science will make it possible to produce numerous varieties with always uniform results, and that some day the product known as poisonous cheese will be wholly unknown. What the Roquefort peasantry, the makers of Edam, Gruyère, and Camembert, have accomplished after generations of tedious and blundering experiments, the cheese makers of America will at no late date be enabled to accomplish through a scientific understanding of the nature and development of the invisible micro-organisms known as bacteria.

CHAPTER XVI

BUTTERINE.

ONSULTING history, we find that for many decades prior to 1870 the poorer classes of the French, the members of both army and navy, and the inmates of many public institutions, had been the unwilling victims of poor butter; butter so rank and wretched that its only stable quality was its unfailing inferiority. In that year a certain French chemist, one Hyppolyte Mége, awakened to this fact. He determined to give the people a substitute for this intolerable butter, which should be clean, of good flavor, palatable, nutritious, in short, which should possess all the characteristics of the best butter. For he realized that butter or some wholesome fat was by no means a luxury that people might do without, but an absolute necessity as food. Hyppolyte Mége should be accounted one of the benefactors of the human race.

He had observed that poorly fed cows still furnished excellent butter, which, he reasoned, must therefore have been supplied from their own fat instead of from their insufficient supply of food. This led him to establish, just before the Franco-Prussian war, an experimental factory at Poissy. From freshly killed beef he took the kidney and caul fat and from it produced an article which was agreeable to taste, which melted at the same temperature as butter, which did not become rancid nearly as soon as the original article and which was just as useful in cookery. This was the prototype of our modern butterine. The fat thus ob_____ known to be identical with that of milk and the whole_____ of making was far more cleanly than that of the average butter. The method, which was in 1873 finally adopted by M. Mége, was as follows: The best quality of fat from freshly killed beef was obtained, finely cut to separate the membranous or connective tissue, and thrown into a steam-heated tank. To 1000 parts of fat were added 300 parts of water, one part carbonate of potash, and two sheep's or pig's stomachs (the latter containing pepsin and always used for forming the curd in the making of cheese). After two hours, aided by a temperature of 103° F., the pepsin of these stomachs had digested or made soluble the membranous tissue and the melted fat had risen to the surface. That was the basis of his butter.

The fat thus melted away from the membranes is known in some countries as "bosch," in Paris as "siege butter," because it was used during the famous siege. It is pure and wholesome and, from a nutritive standpoint, an adequate substitute for butter, although not to be compared to the later product known as butterine. Butter itself is a raw fat, of a peculiarly sweet taste, but the fat of good beef, when liberated by heat or in water at a low temperature, develops a similar sweet and agreeable flavor, which it does not possess in the raw state.

The modern methods of making butterine have been simplified and consist in using the fat from freshly-killed animals, it being taken only when thoroughly chilled, shredding it finely and heating it by steam to a temperature averaging 150° F. At this point the fat separates and is drawn off into other vats where it is quickly chilled. When cool, it is put into the press which separates the stearin from the olein contained. The stearin is that constituent of the fat which has great solidity and a high melting point. Butter from Jersey cows is characteristically hard because of the large amount of stearin contained. The olein, called "oleo oil" in the factories, is yellow, granular and sweet to the taste, much resembling butter just as it begins to "gather" after churning.

The separated fats are then churned with milk and usually mixed with a greater or lesser quantity of butter. Salt is added, also a sufficient amount of coloring material, and the product is known as butterine or oleomargerine. The coloring material is annatto, which is universally used in the coloring of cheese and butter. There is also added a substance called "neutral" to the olein of the beef suet. It is made from the best leaf lard, which is subjected to the same process as the beef fat and, like it, consists of both oil and a solid fat. The earliest oleomargerine did not contain neutral and it is to-day used because of its value, chemically, when added to the other ingredients. In price it averages higher than beef suet. It improves the grain of artificial butter as well as its quality and reduces the difference between butterine and the best Elgin butter, according to actual chemical analysis, to less than one per cent. I am told on good authority that several creameries are now adding neutral to their butter, finding that it improves the quality.

The best creamery butterine contains about 25 per cent of creamery butter, 30 per cent of neutral, 25 per cent of olein and the remaining 20 per cent of salt and cream, the latter obtained from the milk with which the butterine is churned. Dairy butterine contains a smaller percentage of pure butter. To the cheaper grades of butterine a small quantity of cotton-seed oil is added. This is specially valuable during the winter months, as it renders the butterine less solid.

Each prime beef yields, upon an average, forty pounds of olein, while the leaf lard from each animal produces about six pounds of neutral.

Here is the whole process of making an article of food which many people look upon with horror, which the government taxes outrageously, and yet which, it is well known, is produced in the most cleanly manner and according to the most scientific principles, and which the leading scientists of both Europe and America have pronounced to be clean, wholesome and possessing the same nutritive value as the very best butter. Let us examine its constituents. The basis is beef suet which every housewife prizes, the one indispensable ingredient of her suet puddings. The olein is the delicious granular fat which we call "drippings." In the frugal homes of England it is commonly salted and eaten upon bread, particularly by the children. Lard is indispensable, so we think, to pastry, pies and doughnuts and is often used upon bread by the Germans instead of butter. The cotton-seed oil we daily use, under its attractive pseudonym, olive oil, in the preparation of our salads.

Yet no article of food has ever been so persistently fought; its most ponderous and (if the truth must be told) most ignorant opponent, the government of the United States; its most shrewd and unscrupulous antagonist, the middleman or butter dealer. The government endeavors to protect the butter makers of the country; the butter dealer, who makes fifty per cent in the handling of low grades of butter, to protect himself. According to the law, all manufacturers of butterine must furnish bonds, pay special and internal revenue taxes, give monthly reports of all material used, and must furnish samples for governmental inspection whenever requested. It is nothing less than a travesty upon the scientific and enlightened American people that the makers of a food which is pronounced by scientists to be excellent and nutritious and in no respect whatever objectionable, and which was first made to give the poor a wholesome food, should be compelled to pay a tax of two cents upon each pound put forth; that each wholesale dealer must pay a tax of $40 per month and each retailer, $4.00.

In Michigan it is illegal to use butterine in any public institution although it is by no means probable that the criminals, paupers and insane of that state are fed upon the finest and most gilt-edged of dairy products or upon that which is even palatable. In Ohio any hotel keeper who places butterine before his guests is liable to indictment, if it can be proven that it is not butter, by no means an easy thing to do. In Massachusetts it is illegal to color butterine yellow. In New York its sale is all but prohibited. But it is useless to multiply examples. It were far more to the credit of this nation had it commissioned our chemists, as did the French government, to produce an adequate substitute for butter, and had then given it the stamp of public recognition and approval.

But butterine has survived these attacks. Why? Because chemistry has proven it to be all that the manufacturers claimed for it and chemistry is a careful and never bigoted investigator. Let us see what the scientists report: Says the noted Professor Chandler of Columbia College, "It is palatable and wholesome and I regard it as a most valuable article of food." Says Henry Morton of the Stevens Institute of Technology, New Jersey, "It is essentially identical with the best fresh butter, and is superior to much of the butter made from cream alone found in the market." Says S. W. Johnson, Professor of Agricultural Chemistry in Yale College, "It is a product that is entirely attractive and wholesome as food, and one that for all ordinary and culinary purposes is the full equivalent of good butter made from cream. I regard the manufacture of oleo-margerine as a legitimate and beneficent industry." Prof. W. O. Atwater, Director of the Government Experiment Station in Connecticut, and one of the foremost authorities on foods, states that butterine "contains essentially the same ingredients as butter made from cow's milk. It is perfectly wholesome and healthy and has a high nutritive value."

From one of the state asylums for the insane where butterine has been recently prohibited the resident physician lately wrote me: "I have myself inspected the entire process of manufacture in the factory and I know of no product of food in which more apparent care and cleanliness were exercised in the selection of material and preparation of the finished product. It is a cheaper article than butter and uniformly more satisfactory in an institution of this character. There was no difficulty in keeping it clean and sweet in the amount we ordered, usually twelve hundred pounds. (It was used until prohibited.) I believe it to be a wholesome and healthy food product and more desirable than much of the butter that is presented in the markets for sale."

It is easy to ascertain why scientists and authorities on foods universally approve this article, in spite of popular prejudice against it. First of all, chemistry has shown it to contain all the elements of the best butter, the nutritive value of both being identical. Next, the process of making is absolutely cleanly. I have known the butter making industry of various rural districts for twenty-five years, I have also visited numerous creameries and butterine factories and, as far as cleanliness is concerned, I unhesitatingly prefer butterine to butter of which I do not know the history of making. No place could be more sweet and clean and odorless, more free from every indication of dirt, than the butterine factories which I have visited. Steam, the best known deodorizer and germicide, is the principle agent of cleanliness. The immense vats, floors, pipes, all are daily cleansed by steam. No dairy-maid as she daintily pats her rolls of butter could be more cleanly than the girls who, in white caps and aprons, stand about the tables of the finishing room, wrapping each pound of butterine in oiled paper, preparatory to the final packing.

While in the South some two years ago, I investigated both the butter and butterine of the markets. Although at that time strongly prejudiced, my verdict was unfailingly in favor of the latter article. It is true, however, that the butter of our southern markets is not generally of so good a quality as that of the North.

Again, the heat which is used to separate the oil from the membranous fatty tissues kills many of the germs and renders the product less liable to changes in flavor than is butter. To this fact is due its excellent keeping qualities and its uniform flavor. The greatest danger of infection is encountered in the milk and butter which are mixed with the best grades of butterine after the heating process.

During the Columbian Exposition, where butterine was extensively exhibited, an experienced hotel proprietor from one of our metropolitan cities said to me: "I am at last converted to the use of butterine, and it happened in this way. We had been having butter not up to the usual standard for some time. I told the steward he must make a change. A month passed and he asked me how I liked the butter. 'Excellent,' said I, 'procure that quality and there will be no complaint.' He then told me that during the past month he had been serving butterine. We have had butterine ever since." The hotel referred to is a wealthy and high class family hotel.

During the year ending in June, 1893, there were produced in the United States, according to governmental report of internal revenues, 67,685,549 pounds. The commissioner reported that "the production of oleomargerine or butterine has nearly doubled during the past five years," and he further stated that "this has become a recognized article of food and its manufacture is one of the recognized industries of the country. There is in nearly all the states an increased demand for it under its proper name and that by persons fully informed of the nature of the substance. While it is used as a substitute for butter its production and sale have not, as shown by commercial reports and statistics, reduced the price of the higher grades of butter. The most reliable writers in this country on food products and those who have given the subject careful study state that oleomargerine, if carefully and properly prepared, is a healthful article of diet, a wholesome substitute for butter, and can be furnished at less cost. The special taxes imposed upon wholesale dealers ($480 yearly) and retail ($48) are exorbitant compared with the special taxes imposed upon other occupations, and I respectfully submit for your consideration the propriety of a reduction of the special taxes imposed upon wholesale dealers in oleomargerine to $120 and the tax imposed upon retail dealers to $12 per year. I am satisfied that the reduction of the taxes to the sums above named would not result in loss of revenue."

It was Brillat Savarin who said: "The discovery of a new dish does more for the happiness of the human race than the discovery of a star." Butterine is certainly a new food, recognized by chemists and hygienists everywhere as palatable, wholesome, pure and nutritious. Yet our government persistently places it under the ban. I do not object to the rigid governmental inspection. It were far better if our butter were subjected to the same examination, as well as most of our foods. But the tax is unreasonable and undemocratic. It keeps the price of this article beyond the purses of the very people who need it most, the illy-nourished laboring classes. The price of the best butter will never be affected by any reduction whatever in the price of butterine and inferior qualities ought to be swept out of existence, for that the quality of butter will be affected by competition with butterine is certain. It will have to become purer and more uniform in flavor. Certain classes will always eat butter and will pay high prices for it, for the best butter can never be produced as cheaply as butterine. But the unprejudiced and the poor should not be compelled to pay a special tax (amounting to about three cents upon each pound consumed) upon a food which is not a luxury but a necessity. The state laws against butterine have been enacted, it is very evident, by men ignorant alike of the methods of making and of its food value to that class of people who are usually the victims of inferior butter. The relentless war which has been waged against butterine has been actuated by commercial and mercenary, not by scientific nor humanitarian motives.

CHAPTER XVII

ONTRARY to general belief, these constitute a large and very important group of
food products. It has been already shown
that fat of some kind is an absolute necessity to the maintenance of health although,
if used exclusively, not sufficient to sustain
life for any length of time. The scientists
who have most recently investigated the
dietaries of the laboring classes have
found that about two and one-half ounces
of fat should be taken daily in addition to
other food, while one ounce or less is sadly
insufficient. Various diseases of a scrofulous nature are believed
to be induced or furthered by a lack of fat in the foods taken into
the system and, as is well known, the time-honored cure for all
such ills is cod-liver oil. The French agricultural chemists have
proven by experiments that, however varied and abundant their
food, animals more quickly fattened and were put into prime condition more easily by the addition of a small quantity of fat to their
food supply.

All people use fats in a greater or lesser degree, and there is a
physiological reason for the natural craving of the system for them.
Fats are heat producers and are most largely consumed in the cold
climates, e. g., the whale and seal blubber in the Arctic regions. But
all people depend upon fats and oils of some kind, and even the natives of the tropics are abundantly satisfied by the oils contained
in the nuts which they consume.

The following table by Youmans indicates the percentage of fat or oil contained in average samples of every-day foods:

Yolk of egg	28.75	Wheat flour, 1 to	2
Ordinary meat (Liebig)	14.03	Barley meal	2
Indian corn	9.00	Potatoes (dried)	1
Oatmeal	6.00	Rice	0.8
Cow's milk (variable)	3.13	Buckwheat	0.4
Rye flour	3.5		

Vegetable oils are both fixed and volatile, the former comprising that class which resembles animal oils in many particulars and which may be subdivided into *true* and *drying* oils. Only that class of fixed oils available for food will here be mentioned.

Nearly every substance belonging to the vegetable kingdom contains more or less fat among its tissues. In some plants it exists in minute quantities, in others it is so abundant as to be easily obtained and transformed into an article of commerce. One of the most important of our oils is extracted from a substance that until recently was accounted a waste product. I refer to that pressed from the seed of the cotton-plant. For years the cotton seed of our southern plantations sorely taxed the ingenuity of the owners in its disposal. It persistently accumulated and persistently refused to perish. If thrown into the streams it simply choked them, if used upon land as a fertilizer its slow transformation into soil rendered it practically useless. Quantities were used for feeding cattle, although that was but a partial solution of the problem. The disposal of this so-called waste product became a grave question, owing to its utter imperishability. But that very quality kept it before the people and finally resulted in an attempt to extract the oil from the fatty seeds. The attempt was successful, the oil being at first utilized in the manufacture of soap, then as a lubricating oil for machinery, then for illuminating, later as a substitute for linseed oil in the mixing of paints. But in no one of these offices did it quite give satisfaction, for as yet the subtle and refined characteristics of this product of King Cotton were little understood. Later it was more highly refined with all the skill of modern chemistry and behold the result!—a clear, amber-colored, flavorless, odorless, limpid, bland oil, the rival of that other which has held sway for ages in the culinary world, the oil of the olive. How popular and how extensively used it has become, figures can best explain. In 1872 the export from the United States amounted to 547,165 gallons, valued at $293,546. During 1893, but little more than a decade later, the quantity exported seems fabulous—almost nine and one-half millions of gallons, valued at nearly $4,000,000. So valuable has this oil become since refining and so universally is it liked as a food, that it is now annually exported to forty-two different nations. It is interesting to note that France last year bought 1,205,108 gallons, Italy 462,244 gallons, and Spain 5,000, when one remembers that these are the countries of the olive tree and the exporting bureaus of olive oil. Just how much of it returns to our shores in dainty, wicker flasks, labeled "*huile d'olive*" we shall never know; yet it is a fact that at all the Mediterranean ports from which olive oil is exported, hundreds of barrels of cotton-seed oil are annually unloaded. Holland takes nearly two-fifths of our entire supply and uses it in the manufacturing of butter. This butter, so-called, is enclosed in hermetically sealed cans and shipped to India, the West India Islands, and to Central and South America. Germany buys annually over one million gallons, England nearly that amount, while Austria and the other European countries consume smaller quantities. Each year increases the number of gallons taken by the West Indies, particularly Cuba, by Central and South America, in all of which countries it comes into direct competition with the olive oil from Spain. During the last year Mexico purchased 671,000 gallons, Brazil, 304,155, the British and French West Indies more than a quarter million, while Africa and Australia took a like quantity. Throughout the Atlantic and Pacific coasts of the United States immense quantities are annually used in the canning factories for the preserving of fish, as well as millions of gallons, combined with animal fats, in the production of various lard and suet compounds, such as cottolene, cotosuet, vegetol, suetol, etc. The commercial importance of the cotton seed oil industry of the United States is enormous, to say nothing of its food value. It is one of the most wholesome of fats and, when perfectly refined, a process that has been but recently perfected, is valuable in cookery and in the preparation of salads. It has not the delicate flavor of olive oil although, when skilfully combined with the other ingredients of a salad dressing, none but an epicure could detect the difference. The fact that of itself it is almost flavorless accounts for the possibility of largely adulterating olive oil with it without danger of detection.

There is something significant in the fact that this distinctly

American product was so scantily displayed at the Columbian Exposition. The states which produce the largest quantities ignored its existence. Louisiana made a small exhibit, the New York Cotton-oil company, which refines the oil, one somewhat larger. It is in every way nutritious, pure, wholesome, and palatable, and should have been as largely exhibited by the states producing it as was olive oil by Spain, Italy, France and Algiers. It argues a snobbishness quite unworthy of democratic America to sell this product to European countries and then buy it from them six months later, transferred from barrel to bottle, renamed, and with the price many times doubled. We should place this oil upon our tables labeled with its right name, proud that it is a distinctively American product, equal in all essential respects to any oil produced.

But the oil *par excellence* is that of the olive. The tree dates back to patriarchal times, having been one of the special blessings of the Promised Land, and it has always been abundant throughout

Olives.

Palestine, although now extensively cultivated throughout the Mediterranean countries, in Algiers, and in Asia. Its value as a food has increased with the centuries of its usage until to-day it, or an unsuspected adulterant, is to be found in nearly every household. Its high price alone prevents a more extended use, although in the countries where it is produced the poorest among the peasantry use it daily. Even the soap originally used in Palestine was made from olive oil and from a potash extracted from the alkaline plants about the Dead Sea. The tree was brought to the United States by missionaries who planted it in Mexico and California where, owing to care and cultivation, it has become an important source of revenue. It is claimed that the olive can be grown to perfection in the southeastern Atlantic States but, as the fruit ripens at just the time of cotton-picking, it could not be attended to with profit. The tree is an evergreen which attains to great beauty and immense size after cultivation although in its wild state it is small, ungainly, and covered with thorns. It reaches a remarkable age and, as it always produces abundantly, is most valuable. The wood possesses great beauty of grain; and among the historic Greeks no greater honor could be conferred upon an illustrious poet, sculptor or combatant than a simple crown or circlet of the tiny, leathery, dark, grayish-green leaves.

The olive tree produces fruit at six years of age which, of little value in its fresh state, forms, when pickled, a delicate, valuable and nutritious condiment. From the fleshy pericarp an oil is expressed, clear and beautiful, delicate of flavor and altogether the daintiest known for medicinal, table or culinary usage. The oil of the European countries is estimated to keep "sweet" for four years while that from California, when carefully pressed from properly cared-for, unbruised fruit, has been known to resist damaging changes for an entire decade. This is probably due to the greater cleanliness and more scientific care used in the modern industry in California than is the case in tradition-bound Italy and Spain. In many of the olive producing countries of Europe the oil is expressed by the present generation much as it was by their fathers, with total lack of labor-saving appliances or of scientific care. One writer (Mr. Hayne of California) describes an olive oil mill recently visited by him in Nice "in which there were two mules, eight people, three dogs, kitchen, manure heap, wash tubs, oil tanks, presses, heaps of olives, and a smoky fire, all in one cellar, the walls of which were covered with smoky grease. After dinner I sat down in this pen and saw eight well-filled pipes lighted up." This is by no means a typical picture, for cleanliness and skill are and must be inevitable factors in the making of the best grades of European oil. But it is nevertheless true that the people of California have the great advantage of being unhampered by traditional processes which are usually at variance with modern science.

The methods of producing olive oil differ widely in detail but are yet substantially as follows: The fruit is picked by hand before it is quite ripe, the oil being expressed soon after gathering. Bruising the fruit or leaving it in piles to "sweat" or ferment has a most detrimental effect upon the color and particularly the flavor of the oil. The freshly gathered fruit is first crushed in a mill, the pulp being then pressed much as is apple pulp in making cider, the oil which first flows from the press constituting the lightest and best grade, known as virgin oil. This is filtered of impurities by various means, a filter of cotton being used in California, and the beautiful, limpid, delicious oil of our tables is then bottled for sale and export.

It would be to our advantage if olive oil could be as easily and cheaply obtained in America as is the case in certain localities of Europe, for the superiority of vegetable over animal products is, from the standpoint of health and purity, unquestioned. At present there is so much prejudice against the home product that the general public prefers to pay a double price for the foreign article, the customary adulteration of which is well known. During a recent visit in California I was told that the best olive oil could not be produced at any profit in that state for less than two dollars per gallon. At the same time the retail stores in San Francisco were selling "best imported olive oil" for one dollar and twenty-five cents per gallon. The inference made is obvious. But it is our own fault. We have two distinctively American products, both excellent from a chemical as well as from a nutritive standpoint; one, the product of the stately western tree, the other, of the invaluable cotton plant of our southern states. Both should be found in every household and in every market throughout the land, sold unadulterated and under their own names, one oil of course being much higher in price than the other. We should be loyal to both, and not, by unreasonable demands for "genuine" olive oil at a low price, tempt our own makers to adulterate their product as the makers of Europe have done. The olive growers of California are working enthusiastically along scientific lines and it is not too much to predict that if they are encouraged by the good sense and loyalty of the American people the olive oil of our far western state will come to be known as the purest and most superior in the world.

The largest exhibit of olive oil made at the World's Columbian Exposition was in the California state building. No one who saw it can forget the great columns of the bottled oil, clear as crystal, and of most delicate color and flavor.

If California led in the immensity of her exhibit, Spain excelled in number of exhibitors, of which there were nearly one hundred.

Spain has a well earned reputation for producing excellent oil.

Italy made a fine exhibit of Lucca oil, which was put up in dainty flasks. This is reputed to be the best in the world.

Algiers sent twenty-two exhibits of oil which, while good, was not equal to the Spanish or Italian, owing probably to the crude method of extracting it.

France exhibited largely of a very superior oil.

Peanut oil is produced from the fatty, subterranean nut of a leguminous plant, believed to have been native to Africa. It is very generally cultivated in warm climates and there are allied species in the southern states of North America where it is an important agricultural product. It is largely eaten, having a high nutritive value, but is of greater importance in the production of oil. The peanut contains from forty to fifty per cent of oil, clear, odorless, colorless, resembling olive oil in many respects, and having the property of resisting change under all ordinary exposure for a great length of time. The fact that it is largely exported to European countries fully warrants the suspicion that quantities of it are returned to us as "pure olive oil" for table use. While it is one of our most important southern industries it was not exhibited at the Columbian Exposition excepting by certain of the French colonies; and many a fastidious American who could never have countenanced oil made from the plebeian southern "goober," expressed wholly epicurean admiration for the dainty bottles filled with amber oil and labeled "*Huile, pistache de terre*"

Peanut.

Both Argentine Republic and Russia exhibited largely of turnip seed oil. It is produced from the seed of the turnip plant, growing wild in parts of Russia and Scandinavia, and which is, as Grant Allen would say, first cousin to both cabbage and mustard. It is cultivated in nearly all temperate climates and, where greatly improved by cultivation, the root, a succulent vegetable, is used for food. The seed is rich in a bland, almost colorless, oil which possesses many of the properties of the oil of the cotton-seed. In the countries in which it is produced it takes important rank as a food, and much resembles the oil produced from rape seed.

The rape seed, a plant of the turnip family, is to be found in abundance throughout Europe, where it is cultivated. When young and succulent the tender green leaves are used much as is spinach, both in the making of salads and as a pot-herb. It is largely used as a forage plant, although its greatest value lies in the oil expressed from the seeds. Both Japan and Russia exhibited quantities of rape-seed oil, which was tasteless, odorless, and a wholly desirable oil for table or kitchen use.

The sunflower, although a tropical plant, is extensively culti-vated in temperate Europe and America, and is a garden favorite. In Russia it is cultivated for the seed, which produces about forty per cent of oil and which, when refined, is useful for culinary pur-poses. A large exhibit was sent to the Columbian Exposition by Russia.

Almond oil is produced from the kernel of the nut of the almond tree, common to southern Europe and Asia. There are two varieties, known as the bitter and the sweet, from the latter being ex-pressed the almond oil of commerce, although oil from the bitter al-mond is also produced, a cheap-er product commercially. The sweet almond oil is clear, odorless, and valuable medi-cinally as well as in the prep-aration of foods for the table. The tree is now extensively grown in southern California, although no oil is expressed

Palm oil Strainer.

from the nuts, owing to the great demand for them as a table nut.

Oil is also obtained from the fibrous second coating of the fruit of a species of palm, allied to the cocoanut palm and native to Africa. The oil is clear, limpid, agreeable to the taste and having the odor of violets. In Liberia it is clarified of the fibrous particles contained in it after being expressed by straining through a dipper of woven twigs. The fibrous residue is boiled down and from it is obtained a palm butter, used by the poorer classes.

One of the most valuable of oils is that of the cocoa-nut, the fruit of a palm indigenous to Ceylon but common to most tropical countries. It is delicious of flavor and useful both for cooking and as a table oil. It is usually not entirely extracted from the nut, a small quantity being retained that the edible portion may be further utilized by drying and desiccating. The desiccated cocoanut exhibited at the Exposition by Ceylon was far superior, in points of nutrition and flavor, to the American product, owing to the fact that none of the oil was extracted. The cocoa-nut palm tree grows luxuriantly and is an article of absolute necessity to the natives of the tropics. Without it they could scarcely manage to exist. The tender, green fruit or "cabbage" is eaten. From its juice is made a drink called "toddy," which, by boiling, is converted into the native sugar, "jaggery." The trunks, small and large, are used for nearly everything from water pipes to posts; the leaves for thatching; from the fibrous covering of the fruit are woven ropes, mats and garments. Whittier, in his beautiful little poem on the palm tree has sung its praises more justly than I can do:

Is it the palm, the cocoa-palm,
On the Indian Sea, by the isles of balm?
Or is it a ship in the breezeless calm?

A ship whose keel is of palm beneath,
Whose ribs of palm have a palm-bark sheath,
And a rudder of palm it steereth with.

Branches of palm are its spars and rails,
Fibres of palm are its woven sails,
And the rope is of palm that idly trails!

What does the good ship bear so well?
The cocoanut with its stony shell
And the milky sap of its inner cell.

What are its jars so smooth and fine,
But hollowed nuts, filled with oil and wine,
And the cabbage that ripens under the Line?

Who smokes his nargileh, cool and calm?
The master, whose cunning and skill could charm
Cargo and ship from the bounteous palm.

In the cabin he sits on a palm-mat soft,
From a beaker of palm his drink is quaffed,
And a palm-thatch shields from the sun aloft!

His dress is woven of palmy strands,
And he holds a palm leaf scroll in his hands,
Traced with the Prophet's wise commands!

11

The turban folded about his head
Was daintily wrought of the palm-leaf braid,
And the fan that cools him of palm was made.

Of threads of palm was the carpet spun
Whereon he kneels when the day is done,
And the foreheads of Islam are bowed as one!

To him the palm is a gift divine,
Wherein all uses of man combine,—
House, and raiment, and food, and wine!

And in the hour of his great release,
His need of the palm shall only cease
With the shroud wherein he lieth in peace.

"Allah il Allah!" he sings his psalm,
On the Indian Sea by the isles of balm;
"Thanks to Allah who gives the palm!"

Cocoa butter is a fat which at ordinary temperatures is solid but which melts at about 90° F. It is obtained from the seeds of the *Cacoa theobroma*, a tree native to Mexico, from the seeds of which chocolate and cocoa are also produced. This fat has the excellent quality of keeping "sweet," and of retaining its fine flavor much longer than oils in general. It constitutes nearly fifty per cent of the cocoa seeds or beans and is expressed from them by crushing, grinding and the application of heat. The use of cocoa butter is very general throughout the countries in which it is produced, but it is high priced in foreign markets, owing to the fact that its use is almost wholly medicinal. Like all of the vegetable fats and oils it deserves recognition and more extended use because of its nutritive value.

CHAPTER XVIII.

CEREALS.

HEN Sir Richard Bannister of London, judge upon agricultural products at the World's Columbian Exposition, was asked to give his opinion of America, he replied: "The agricultural resources of your land, particularly of the great West, have surprised and interested me more than all else. In these rest the future, the marvelous future, of America." He was right. If Ceres hovers over any land to-day, that land is America, with her astonishing crops of vegetables and fruits and her millions of acres of grain. She possesses the greatest agricultural district in the modern world, if greatness be measured by advanced methods in the planting, tillage and harvesting of cereals as well as by extent. She has profited richly by the experiences of the older nations; Egypt, the land of corn and wheat; Rome with her wealth of agricultural interests, immortalized by Virgil and Cato; Saracenic Spain, Saxon England, and peasant Italy, France and Germany. No country possesses soil and climate more appropriate to the growth of cereal crops than America and none other promises so lavishly for the future.

The greatest food crops of the world are cereals: wheat, rice, corn, oats, barley, rye, and millet, all belonging to the *graminea* or grass family, the herbage and seed of nearly all members of which are valuable foods for both animal and man. By common consent, wheat takes first rank, being richest of all cereals in protein, and old Homer was not wrong when he defined it as "the marrow of men." There are now more than one hundred and fifty varieties, due to variation of soil, climate and cultivation, the origin of them all being so lost in antiquity that it cannot be traced. But chemist and botanist have analyzed the tiny kernel until it has divulged to a curious world all the secrets entrusted to its care by the sunshine, the soil and the showers. The botanist alone has revealed the poetic side of its evolution, for he tells us that wheat is simply a degenerate lily, which, away back when the world was young, swung gaily on its stem beside its sister lilies. But, unlike many of its kindred, it depended upon the wind for fertilization and not upon meandering insects. So it needed no brightly colored petals with which to attract these insects, only long, quivering stamens from which pollen would fly at a breath and sensitive, feathery pistils to which the tiniest atom of pollen would cling. As a result not many blossoms became fertile and, that the seeds which did develop should have the best chances for existence, nature stored each little kernel well with gluten, starch and fat for the development of the young plant. Thus this lily came to have an unimportant blossom and a very important seed. Local differences of soil and climate differentiated the species and, after cultivation, our various cereals came into being. Says Grant Allen, the author of this theory as to the origin of wheat: "We thus trace the whole pedigree of wheat from the time its ancestors first diverged from the common stock of lilies and water plantains, to the time when savage man found it growing wild among the untilled plains of prehistoric Asia and took it under his special protection in the little garden plots around his wattled hut, until it has gradually altered under his constant selection into the golden grain that now covers half the lowland tilth of Europe and America."

Egypt cultivated wheat two thousand years before the Christian era while the Chinese claim precedence of even that marvelous date by seven hundred years. The lake-dwellers of prehistoric Switzerland have left indubitable evidence of its cultivation and since most ancient of times it has been carried from one country to another by explorers and hostile invaders as well as by philanthropists. Said Pliny: "The people of Rome for three hundred years together used no other food than groats made from common wheat." It was introduced into Mexico by Cortez and into Peru by a Spanish lady. Gosnold, the explorer, brought it to Massachusetts in the seventeenth century and later we find that enterprising colony exporting quantities of it to Holland. The price, as late as 1635, was sixty cents a bushel, while fifty years later it brought in Maine $1.25. In 1611 wheat was introduced into Virginia although, so zealous were the agriculturists in their cultivation of tobacco, the growing of it was almost wholly neglected for fifty years.

Wheat is most extensively cultivated to-day in the western and northwestern portions of the United States, in Russia, which ranks next to America in extent of acreage, in France as well as in other European countries, and in India.

A kernel of wheat examined under the microscope is seen to have several integuments or layers upon its surface, the outer one hard, wholly indigestible and therefore of no nutritive value. This is defined as husk or bran. The next layers are rich in nitrogenous matter and salts, are composed of gluten cells and constitute the most nutritious portion of the kernel. Beneath these are the cerealine cells, giving color and flavor, while the body or interior of the grain is composed almost entirely of starch, a substance of minor nutritive value. At the lower end of the grain is the tiny germ or embryo, for the nourishment of which are provided all these curiously wrought integuments.

Section of Wheat Grain, Magnified.

Wheats are variously classified as hard and soft, red and white, spring and winter, and subdivided occasionally into bearded and beardless varieties. The hardness and softness of the grain depends both upon its maturity and upon the amount of gluten contained. In either or any variety an unripened grain is less hard and far less nutritious than if fully matured. The hard wheats are relatively more nutritious than the soft, being more largely composed of starch. In general the hard wheats are produced in climates in which long summers allow the grain to perfectly mature, while the wheats of colder climates are softer and more fragile.

Any variety may be either a spring or a winter wheat, depending upon the time of sowing. The other subdivisions depend upon the color of the grain, whether red or white, and upon whether or not the variety contain awns or beards.

Besides the value of wheaten preparations in the making of bread and macaroni, it has various minor uses. The whole grain may be cooked until soft, a lengthy process, and eaten with milk or sugar. It may also be combined with milk and eggs into a pudding, which is palatable but rather indigestible, owing to the tough outer coating of the grain. Cracked wheat, rolled wheat, germ meal and various other wheaten preparations now upon the markets, attest to its wide usage as a breakfast food. A recent preparation is made from the shredded grain formed into oblong cakes and slightly baked. Almost numberless wheaten preparations are to be found in the market described as infant's or invalid's foods. Unfortunately, many of them contain little if any gluten, the strength-giving and easily digested substance, while consisting almost wholly of starch, a food most taxing to an already enfeebled digestion and which does not contain tissue-building elements.

The display of wheat at the Columbian Exposition was marvelously complete. The varieties sent from Russia, from our own northwestern states, from Venezuela, and from the Mediterranean countries, particularly Italy, were conceded to be the finest. That from the latter country possesses a long, slender grain, and is of the hard, red variety, specially used in the manufacture of macaroni.

Indian corn, Zea Mays, or more commonly maize, is indigenous to America, particularly, it is believed, to Central Mexico. The earliest explorers found it a staple food of the Indians and recent investigations of the Cliff Dwellers' homes in Colorado indicate that it was grown also by these prehistoric people. Specimens of ears of corn, three and four inches in length, were exhibited among the relics of Peruvian mummy pits at the Columbian Exposition, proving it to have been quite as anciently a South American product.

According to the Indian legend, maize was a gift from the Great Spirit who came to earth ages ago as a youth dressed in splendid garments of green and yellow and promising them great good should he be wrestled with and overthrown. Hiawatha, fasting, leaped from his bed of branches and for seven nights contested with the youth in physical combat. At last he slew him. He buried the wrestler and tenderly watched his grave for many moons, keeping away the raven and all insects,

> " Till at length a small, green feather
> From the earth shot slowly upward,
> Then another and another,
> And before the summer ended
> Stood the maize in all its beauty
> With its shining robes about it,

And its long, soft yellow tresses.

.   .   .   .   .   .

" And still later, when the autumn
Changed the long, green leaves to yellow,
And the soft and juicy kernels
Grew like wampum, hard and yellow,
Then the ripened ears he gathered,
Stripped the withered husks from off them
As he once had stripped the wrestler,
Gave the first Feast of Mondamin,
And made known unto the people
This new gift of the Great Spirit."

In appearance the maize plant is tall, stately, of extraordinary beauty and tropical luxuriance of growth. Nothing could be more beautiful than the plant in full bloom, crowned with its waving, feathery tassel of staminate flowers, while below, nestled among a profusion of rustling leaves, hang out the long pink and green, silken styles of the corn ear. The ear varies greatly throughout the three hundred species cultivated, both in color, size, and size of grain. The grain may be white, yellow, red, purple or occasionally mottled, and may also vary in nutritive value. Some varieties require also a much greater length of time for growth than do others.

From a nutritive standpoint corn is inferior to hard wheat, although containing about the same amount of nitrogenous matter as the soft varieties of wheat and fully five times as much fat. Owing to the lack of gluten it cannot be used in making a "light" or yeast bread. But its usefulness, nevertheless, is wide-reaching. When green it makes an excellent and nourishing food for cattle, for which purpose it is often planted in drills like wheat that the ears may not develop, leaving the stalks richer in sugar. The sweet varieties are used green as table corn, and "sugar corn" is extensively put up at many canning factories. In Mexico the stalks are utilized in extracting a syrup by pressure, which, when fermented, is made into a drink called "chica." Probably upon no food product is there put such a premium for misappropriation as upon corn. From a western paper I clip the following: "Corn in Nebraska sells for twenty-five cents per bushel. This, distilled, makes four and one-half gallons of spirits. After being manipulated by the distillers, this makes nine gallons of whiskey. This pays to the United States government ninety cents a gallon, which is a revenue of $8.10 from one bushel of corn. This retails to the customer at ten cents a drink. Thus the nine gallons of whiskey bring $54, all from one bushel of corn at twenty-five cents." For many years the corn of our western prairies had so low a market value that it was raised at a profit only when utilized for feeding hogs, which thereby brought a higher market price. This is much to be regretted, as corn meal or flour, properly prepared, is one of our most valuable cereal foods. Corn starch is an important product of the grain as well as corn flour. But corn meal, rich, yellow corn-meal, sung of poets and honored of sages, is the homespun dish which is common to all lands wherein corn is grown. The "pone" and "hoe-cake" of the south, eaten alike by negro and planter, the northern "johnny-cake" or corn bread, the Boston brown bread of the east, the *tortilla* and *pinole* of Mexico, the mush, hasty pudding and samp of New England, all bear eloquent, even though silent, testimony to its homely value. Says Whittier:

> " There, richer than the fabled gift
>   Apollo showered of old,
> Fair hands the broken grain shall sift,
>   And knead its meal of gold.

> " Let vapid idlers loll in silk
>   Around their costly board;
> Give us the bowl of samp and milk,
>   By homespun beauty poured."

Effort has been made to introduce corn and corn flour into Europe. It is grown but little there, as, owing to its extreme susceptibility to frosts or even cool weather, it could not be grown profitably excepting in the Mediterranean portions. In England "corn" refers to wheat, in Scotland, to oats.' But it is exported only to a limited extent, owing to the fact that if not well cured, either in the ear or the meal, it deteriorates in flavor; while, if not thoroughly dried before being ground into meal its sweetness is lost. It is at its best only when perfectly cured and freshly ground, and few American housewives will order it even in small quantities, unless certain that it is "new" or fresh. It is said that the North American Indian kept the flavor of corn unchanged by carefully drying the ears, then, after shelling, drying the grain. After this process was finished it was carefully stored away in the ground, protected by various mats or coverings. The Mexican method of parching corn is also unique, and is as follows: "An iron pot filled with sand is heated over the fire until very hot. Into this hot sand are placed two or three pounds of the corn which is mixed with the hot sand by stirring until each grain bursts and throws out a white substance

of twice its bigness. It is separated from the sand by sifting."
Eight ounces of this is considered quite sufficient for one day's food
supply. The variety used must be analogous to the variety known
in the United States as "pop-corn." The bursting is due to the ex-
pansion of the starch granules and also, probably, to the generating
of a gas which causes the explosive sound.

The origin of the barley plant is related only in legends and to
what land it is indigenous is therefore unknown. The Egyptians
hold that the art of cultivating this grain was imparted to them
anciently by the divine Isis, who herself brought it to them in a
wild state, teaching them how to improve it in quality by care. In
Exodus they are described as cultivators of flax and barley, of wheat
and rye.

Barley has been found in the lake dwellings of Switzerland, and
is mentioned by Pliny as the first grain to have been used for the
nourishment of man. Hippocrates and Galen both prescribed it
medicinally, for its nourishing and soothing qualities.

According to the Indian legend, related by a chief of the Sus-
quehanna tribe to Dr. Franklin: "In the beginning, our fathers
subsisted only upon the flesh of animals and, if the hunt was unsuccessful, they had but one alternative, starvation. One day, two of
our young hunters having killed a deer, they cooked it over their
fire and were preparing to eat when a beautiful young woman appeared from the clouds. She seated herself upon the hill which
you see yonder, among the blue mountains. They said to each other,
'It is a spirit who has smelled our venison and wishes to eat of it.
Let us give her some.' So they gave her the tongue. She was
greatly pleased and said, 'Your kindness shall be rewarded. Come
to this place in thirteen moons and you will find something that
will be for the nourishing of yourselves and your children unto the
latest generation.' They came, thirteen moons later, and there
found growing barley and maize."

The cultivation of barley may be extended over a wider range
than that of any other cereal, as it bears well both heat and cold
and matures rapidly. It may thus be planted later and harvested
earlier than wheat and in warm climates two crops a year may be
produced, one in the spring from winter-sown grain and one in the
autumn from seed sown in the spring.

Barley contains more starch and less gluten than wheat, being
for the latter reason unadapted for making light bread, and also

contains seven parts in a hundred of saccharine matter not found in
wheat. It has been highly valued as a food since most ancient
periods, in Greece, Rome, and countries of the Orient. According
to Pliny the Roman gladiators were called *hordearii* from their use
of this grain as food. In Japan one of the staple foods, *miso-miso*,
is prepared by combining the soy-bean and a preparation of barley.
In Great Britain, particularly in Scotland, both a coarse barley
meal and a finer or patent barley meal are extensively used. Pearl
barley, the preparation best known in America, consists of the
whole grain, decorticated, rounded, and polished by attrition.
Barley broth and barley water are widely commended as nourishing
and refreshing drinks for invalids and children.

Like all cereal foods, barley is made the basis of alcoholic
drinks, an industry which began with the Egyptians and was continued by the Greeks. It is not to be wondered at that poverty and
famine inevitably follow in the train of so perverted a usage.

Dr. Johnson, in his dictionary, characteristically defined oats as
"a grain which in England is given to horses, but which in Scotland
supports the people." This definition, although the grouty old
doctor did not so intend it, speaks volumes for the wisdom and
economy of the Scotch people in recognizing
the value of so important a food. Like wheat,
it is a member of the grass family, differing,
however, in that the spikelets grow in the
shape of a loose panicle, each tiny, closely-
husked grain having a long beard or awn.

Its origin either as to native place or species is unknown. According to De Candolle it
was unknown to the Egyptians, Hebrews, Greeks
or ancient Romans, although in all probability
cultivated by the aboriginal Swiss and perhaps
by the ancient Germans. It is now grown, a
plant of numerous varieties, over most of the
temperate zone.

Nutritively, it stands high in the list of
cereal foods, although it is unsuitable for making into a light bread because of the lack of
gluten. Its chief use is in the form of a por-
ridge, in preparing it for which the husk is removed and the grain
then crushed by rollers or cut by steel knives. When left whole

Asiatic Millet.

it is called "groats" or "grits." There is an oven-baked preparation
which is specially fine. The best American preparations are partially
cooked by steam after which their adaptation in the household is
a comparatively easy matter. If slowly cooked in boiling water, the
mixture being kept rather thin, a delicious porridge of jelly-like
consistency is the result. If strained and allowed to cool, you have
a nutritious jelly or blanc mange. Oatmeal, chiefly a breakfast
dish, is more extensively used in America by the well-to-do classes
than by the poor, a fact to be regretted, for it is the latter class which
most needs cheap, nourishing foods.

In Ireland oatmeal is combined with corn meal in a porridge.
In Scotland it is truly the national dish. It is there frequently
boiled in beef-stock when it is called "beef-brose," or in water in
which cabbage has been cooked, making "kale-brose." It is the
chief and typical food of the peasantry. Said a Scotch mother
when asked how she persuaded her children to eat oatmeal, the de-
spair of many an American mother, "I tell them that if they first
eat their bowl of porridge they may have whatever else they wish.
By the time that has been eaten they are satisfied."

The consular report of 1889, relative to the condition of the
poor of the great cities of Scotland, is significant. It states that
porridge had so long been the main food of the poorer Scotch that
the eating of it came to be considered a mark of poverty. So the
city poor began substituting for it baker's bread and tea without
adding sufficient of either milk or meat to their diet to bring it to a
health-giving standard. The result: diseases of childhood, traceable
directly to the lack of nutritious food. The report further states
that projects are on foot to furnish the poor a bowl of good porridge and milk for a penny, and it closes with these words: "Whatever else is done for the redemption of the 100,000 poor, and much
is certain to be done, nothing will be wholly efficacious without a
return to the diet that made their ancestors the finest soldiers and
the most stalwart workers in the British Islands."

Millet is indigenous to the East Indies but has been cultivated
in southern Europe since the days of the Greeks. It is almost unused in America excepting as a food for animals, but in Russia and
India forms a staple article of diet. During the recent Russian
famine millet bread was for a long time the only food remaining between the peasantry and starvation. Millet flour, although very
white and nutritious, does not make good bread unless combined

with wheaten flour. The flour is, by the Orientals, made into a paste with fat, called *kaddel*, although the grain is also eaten whole in the form of groats.

Millet ought to be a profitable cereal crop as the plant is very prolific, capable of yielding per acre five times as much as would wheat. The Asiatic millet reaches even a greater height than the American maize and is a plant of great beauty, owing to its delicate, feathery, profuse infloresence. The name comes from the Latin *mille*, a thousand, owing to its numberless tiny seeds, of which one kind, containing black seeds, is most used for the feeding of birds and poultry. Edwin Arnold describes the self-torture of a *Yogi* of ancient India, who

> " Meted a thousand grains of millet out,
> Ate it with famished patience, seed by seed,
> And so starved on."

Rye is a cereal of comparatively recent cultivation, and is grown extensively only in northern Germany, Russia and Scandinavia, north of the wheat limit. It is lower in nutritive value than wheat, although containing sufficient gluten to enable it to be made into bread, the rye bread, kümmel-brod and "pumpernickel" of the German bake-shop. In America rye, excepting as an ingredient of Boston brown bread, is used chiefly by the foreign element. The sour taste developed when made into bread is due to the rapid fermentation of the sugar contained. In appearance the rye plant resembles both wheat and barley. In Great Britain the plant, while green, is used as forage for cattle and horses. Its chief use is in the distilling of liquors.

Buckwheat is not a cereal but a showy, herbaceous plant, related to the rhubarb and sorrel, the name of which was originally beech wheat, owing to the three-sided, angular shape of the seeds. The meal is used much as are the cereal flours,

Rice.   although suitable only for the making of small batter-cakes, owing to deficiency in gluten. In Russia the seeds are used in the form of groats, particularly by the soldiery, and are cooked with butter or oil. The flour of buckwheat compares unfavorably with that of wheat in point of nutrition.

Rice, the origin of which is variously ascribed to India and to China, has been for thousands of years one of the most widely used cereals of the world. It is not alluded to in the Bible and was anciently unknown to the Greeks, Romans and probably to the inhabitants of the Holy Land. But for thousands of years the chief nations of the Orient have partially subsisted upon it, from the divine Buddha who begged it from house to house after the custom of the hermits of ancient India, to the poorest of his brothers. It was thrown to the blue and purple fish of the lotus-pools, and, "boiled with sandal and fine spice," was laid upon sacrificial altars. In China, more than four thousand years ago, was established a custom according to which, once in every year, the Emperor sows the seeds of rice with his own hands. China, Japan, India, Java, Siam and Ceylon to-day regard rice as their staple food.

In appearance the rice grain resembles barley, and the plant itself, the other cereals and grasses to which it is allied. The grains possess each separate pedicles springing from a branching main stalk. Each is enclosed in a rough, yellow husk which, in the bearded varieties, terminates in an awn. There are numerous species, Japan alone claiming more than one hundred, although they may be classified simply as farina rice, composed almost wholly of starch, and a second variety containing a larger proportion of gluten. Chemically, rice contains far less gluten than wheat, oats, barley or maize and therefore ranks much below these cereals, nutritively. Professor Atwater states that a rice-fed people are invariably weak physically, and it has been demonstrated by others that they lack invention and enterprise, a condition certainly true of the poorer classes among the Orientals. To counteract the faultiness of a diet composed of so much starch and so little protein, rice is usually combined in cooking with fat, salt and curry, and those of the Orientals who can procure other food consume large quantities of fish and poultry.

The cultivation of rice in America is of recent origin. In 1761, in a treatise written upon the British plantations of America, it was recorded that the first seed rice which found its way into America was left by the officers of a brigantine from Madagascar, which happened to put into port along the Carolina coast. The rice was given to a gentleman named Woodward, who began the cultivation of it. A little later a Mr. Dubois of the East Indian Company sent to the colonies a small bag of seed rice. It is believed that from these two sources came our two varieties of Carolina rice, the

white and the red. This classification is due to the color of the
inner husk, the grains of both varieties being similar when cleaned.

But, however it came to the "rice-swamp, dank and lone" of the
Carolinas, the lowlands, periodically flooded by tides and rivers,
were well adapted by nature to its growing. From its revenues the
states of North and South Carolina,
Georgia, and Louisiana have become
greatly enriched.

It is fortunate for the people of rice-
growing states that this cereal was not
introduced until an abundant and varied
diet had already been established. Even
in case of total failure of the rice crop,
there could be no danger of famine
owing to the abundance of other foods,
while in those countries in which it
forms the main dependence of the poorer
classes, failure of the crop
means the gravest famine and
destitution. As said Ricardo,
one of the earliest of political
economists, "When the laboring classes have fewest wants
and are contented with the
cheapest food, the people are
exposed to the greatest vicissi-
tudes and miseries. They have
no refuge from calamity. On
any deficiency of the chief
article of subsistence, there
are few substitutes of which
they can avail themselves, and
dearth is attended on all sides
by famine."

Javanese Rice Cooker.

No people cook rice so deliciously as the nations of the Orient.
At the Columbian Exposition the Javanese not only brought their
own rice, which they think superior to any other, but their own
cooking utensils. They customarily prepare it by steaming, the rice
being placed in a conical basket of loosely woven twigs, the basket
being placed over a tall brass vessel half filled with water. Placed

over the fire, the steam from the heated water penetrates every portion of the basket and its contents, and a fragrant, snowy dish, each grain separate and dry, is the result. It is commonly eaten with curry or chilies and a meat gravy of some kind. The largest exhibit of rice was made by the Japanese. Each preparation was accompanied by its analysis, made at the Agricultural College at Tokio. Several of the most unique merit description. *Shir-a-ta-ma* is made from the glutinous varieties, which are first steeped in water, then ground and washed through fine sieves. The residue obtained is dried over a coal fire, then made into small, round balls of dough which, when steamed, are eaten both with soups and with sweets. *Ame,* prepared from malt and the flour of glutinous rice, greatly resembles glucose. It is a delicious sweet-meat. Its making dates from one hundred years, B. C., when sugar was unknown. *Do-mo-ji* is rice steamed, dried and then ground into flour. It may be prepared for use whenever wanted by the addition of water and is eaten with sugar. It is specially valuable to travelers and to an army on long marches. *Kori-mochi* is made from steamed rice, beaten into a paste and then frozen. Water is poured upon it to soften it, and it is served with sugar. It was quite surprising to the American to observe the varied and dainty preparations of so homely an article as simple rice. Like our own cereals, it is fermented by the Japanese and distilled into a liquor called *sake,* which is highly intoxicating.

CHAPTER XIX.

HE bread of the modern world is an evolution; its making, the result of centuries of experiment, beginning with the crudest of materials and most primitive of methods, and ending with the modern bakery of automatic, thousand-loaf capacity. The "raised" or light loaf of to-day was unknown to the ancients, theirs being an unleavened bread or cake. The Egyptians, long before the Christian era, made a loaf of wheat and meal; in what proportions history does not state. The early Britons made cakes of crushed acorns long before cereals were grown upon their island. The bread of the ancient Syrians was made from mulberries, dried and ground to flour.

But the Greeks were the best bread-makers of antiquity, as became a race whose tables were considered to be sumptuously laden when containing plain meat, "roasted on a spit and dusted with flour," wheaten bread, and wine. Both barley and wheat were used, ground in small hand mills by the women slaves of each household, and made into a well-salted, unleavened dough. Plato's ideal of barley-pudding and bread, the sole food of the dwellers of the *Republic*, was well nigh realized in his own Greece, for bread was as indispensable a food among the aristocrats as among the poor and it was publicly vended in all markets.

By the citizens of the Roman republic bread was universally used in all households, partly owing to the fact that machinery for grinding the wheat had superseded the primitive hand-mill. All classes, patrician, plebeian and slave, could be supplied with this article from governmental bakeries. When the Romans first visited the islands of Great Britain they found the Scotch in both the highlands and lowlands making oaten cakes which they baked upon flat stones,

12

heated in front of the fire. To these stones the Romans gave the
name of *grerdiol*, from which our word "griddle" is evidently derived.
It was written, "when the soldier hath eaten meat so long that he
begins to loath it, he casteth the stone (which he always carried
with him in his wallet of meal) into the fire; he moisteneth the meal
with water and when the plate is heated he layeth the paste thereon
and maketh a little cake; the which he eateth to comfort his
stomach." In later days, Bobbie Burns pronounced "the oat
cake, kneaded out with the knuckles and toasted over real embers
of wood, on a gridiron," to be remarkably fine eating. The Scots
did not know the wheaten loaf until the end of the sixteenth
century, cakes or "bannocks" of oat, barley and peas meal constituting their house-
hold bread.

Apache Grain Mortars.

In Wales the peo-
ple of those times
used a baking utensil
similar to the Scotch
griddle and known as
the bake-stone. Their
bread was close and
heavy, resembling in
shape, extent and
thickness, a small cart
wheel.

Oaths were form-
erly sworn by bread,
possibly because it
symbolized the neces-
sities of life. Says Rich, in describing the customs of old Ireland:
"I will trust him better that offereth to swear by bread and salt
than him that offereth to swear by the Bible."

England was indebted to the Romans for the first knowledge of
the art of making wheaten flour into a loaf. For centuries this was
a wholly domestic occupation, and even as late as 1804 the city of
Manchester did not contain a single public bakery. Until the last
two or three centuries there was lack of the best material for bread-
making. Wheaten bread was a luxury to be enjoyed by the rich,
only, and, in a book published in 1576, it is stated that the poor of
that time contented themselves with rye and barley bread, with

bread of peas, beans or oats, and sometimes with that made from all these ingredients, to which were added acorns; food more nutritious, probably, than palatable.

Bread of some sort and savor is a universal food among even the primitive nations of to-day. The North American Indian combines berries, pemican, and the bark of certain trees into a cake or loaf. The Bedouin woman makes from finely crushed grains and water a dough, which is manipulated before baking until the thinness of a wafer. It is then baked upon the concave surface of a shallow iron pan which is turned, face down, over the smoky fire. The result is a very tasty bit of toast, not quite relishable because of a lack of salt. *Tortilla,* a cake made from corn and baked in the ashes, is still the national bread of the Mexican. In Sweden, Norway, Lapland, and Iceland there is made a nutritious loaf from crushed grains and flour of fish, dried and then finely ground. In times of distress the Irish and Icelanders, as well as the Russians, have utilized a species of nutritious moss which makes not an inferior nor unpalatable food. The natives of South America, Jamaica, and British Guiana have long made a bread from the dried and ground root of the cassava or tapioca plant. It is known as cassava bread and is very nutritious. Several countries exhibited this at the Columbian Exposition.

But the bread of modern America and much of Europe is primarily wheaten. This is as it should be for wheat contains a larger proportion of protein, the purely nourishing element, than any of the other cereals. Other constituents are starch and dextrine (carbohydrates), fatty matter, and important mineral substances, such as the phosphates of lime and soda, salts of potash and silica.

The following table by Payen compares the nutritive value of our principal cereals:

COMPOSITION OF VARIOUS DRIED CEREALS.

	Hard Wheat.	Soft Wheat.	Oats.	Maize.	Rice.	Barley.	Rye.
Protein ...	22.75	12.65	14.39	12.50	7.55	12.96	12.50
Starch	58.62	76.51	60.59	67.55	88.65	66.43	64.65
Dextrine..	9.50	6.05	9.25	4.00	1.00	10.00	14.90
Cellulose..	3.50	2.80	7.06	5.90	1.10	4.75	3.10
Fats.......	2.61	1.87	5.50	8.80	0.80	2.76	2.25
Salts	3.02	2.12	3.25	1.25	0.90	3.10	2.60
	100.00	100.00	100.00	100.00	100.00	100.00	100.00

The protein or nitrogenous matter of wheat is known as *gluten* and upon this its commercial value is based. If you visit the Chicago Board of Trade you will see there men testing flour. They do this by mixing with it a sufficient quantity of water to form a stiff dough, their mixing pan being usually the palm of the left hand while the mixing is done with a finger of the right. They first pull the dough, to "test its strength," they will tell you, and then break it forcibly into two parts. If it is tough, tenacious and leathery it contains a high per cent of gluten and is therefore excellent, nutritious and "strong." If it is soft, non-elastic and breaks apart with a short fracture it is starchy and non-glutinous, probably from soft wheat, or because the gluten has been taken from it during the process of milling.

But the selection of a hard or glutinous wheat is not the only requisite for a nutritious quality of flour, for the modern miller produces many sorts of flour from the starchiest of grains and many more sorts from the most glutinous. The miller of ancient days crushed and ground the cereals in little hand mills, or grinding mortars. The product was given to the consumer filched of none of its strength-giving elements. To-day, milling is a complicated industry; and the honest little grain, crushed and divided, hurried through spout-like conveyors and over rollers, elevated, purified, sifted, and bolted to astonishing fineness, is resolved at the end of its astonishing journey into many grades of flour. Four different grades are made in all mills—often more—first and second patent, and first and second baker's. The reasons for this division are, that consumers in general demand a white flour; that one quality is superior for bread, quite another for pastry; and that by this separation and division there is greater profit to the producer. Flour for the best bread making should contain a large quantity of gluten, a condition easily ascertained by its creamy tint and by testing the tenacity of the dough. That for pastry should be starchy, as little tenacious as possible and thus of course less nutritious. A glutin-

ous flour will invariably make tough cake and pie-crust. The first patent contains more gluten than the second, and both contain more than the first and second baker's.

To the bread maker of the present age yeast seems to be as indispensable as flour, and it is hard to believe that such has not always been the case. Pliny tells us that the Gauls leavened their bread with a yeast made from the lye of beer, although the use of this ferment was early abandoned and not revived until the seventeenth century. When the bakers of France re-established its use physicians universally denounced it as deleterious to health and in 1666 it was finally prohibited by law. The bakers waged such incessant war against the decree that it was at length repealed, with the proviso, however, that only beer freshly made in Paris or vicinity should be used. Since then the use of yeast has spread over all lands in which wheaten bread is made.

Yeast, scientists have determined, is a plant, a microscopic fungus, with capacity for marvelous growth if nourished amid favorable surroundings. It deserves the same consideration as the geranium in your window. Warmth, moisture and nourishment are as necessary to its growth as to that of your plant. Hot water will kill it, a low temperature will arrest its development. Just as your plant can be forced so rapidly as to injure or kill it, so can the yeast plant. The nourishment to be supplied is flour, upon which it develops by multiplying its own cellular growth with marvelous rapidity. Carbonic acid gas is developed, the mixture "rises," and a so-called lively sponge is the result. It is essential that yeast be fresh to produce rapid alcoholic fermentation. The best known is compressed yeast, obtained from the distillation of rye. It consists of the scum, drained upon cloths and pressed into cakes, the action of which, when fresh, is rapid and uniformly satisfactory. The action of all yeast is somewhat quickened by the addition of a spoonful of sugar. Too high a temperature induces the development of an acid ferment in yeast, a temperature too low retards its action and causes sour bread. Yeast best develops at 70° to 80° F.

Now when to water and flour, in proper proportions, is added yeast, the latter, if maintained at the proper temperature, feeds upon the flour and begins to rapidly multiply its cells. The gluten of the flour, becoming hydrated, i. e., well mixed with water, causes the dough to become tenacious and elastic; carbonic acid gas is developed by the action of the yeast and endeavors to escape. But,

entangled in the glutinous fibres of the dough, the gas is held.
Heat causes it to still further expand and the sponge "rises." That
is the philosophy of the process, in which, if allowed to continue too
long, the yeast plant ceases its rapid development, owing to the ex-
haustion of its food supply, the elasticity departs, and the sponge
"falls." That means failure. So at the critical point the housewife
or baker adds a quantity of flour to the sponge, making a dough, and
the kneading process is begun. This has a two-fold object: to insure uniform distribution of the gas and to develop the gluten of
the flour. It requires two kneadings, each usually from twenty to
thirty minutes in length. The uncouth old Bedouin woman of the
Midway Plaisance furnished a daily object lesson to hundreds of
visitors on the possibilities of the development of gluten by kneading.

By rapid and deft manipulation she converted a small piece of unleavened dough
into a flat, tenacious and immense wafer,
round as a pie tin and twenty inches in
diameter. The housekeeper uses her
hands in the kneading process and the
baker, machinery. The result is the

A Bedouin Oven.

same in both cases.

The next essential to good bread is prolonged baking at not too
high a temperature. This is to assist the transformation of the
starch, of which the bread is so largely composed, into dextrine,
which must occur to all starchy foods either within or without the
body before they can be assimilated. Heat is one agent for this
conversion without the body. The brown crust on a loaf is almost
pure dextrine, of which a good example is the crust of Vienna
bread, nutty, fragrant and sweet, by all odds the most delicious part
of the loaf and by far the most easily digested. This may explain
why toast and crust coffee are such appropriate invalid dishes. If
the bread has been well baked there is incipient conversion of
the starch throughout the entire loaf.

In the making of leavened bread, water and flour are first mixed
into a thin sponge and allowed to stand until fermentation sets in.
A portion of this leaven is then added to new dough, the slight acidity
being corrected by the use of carbonate of soda, a substitute for
the wood ashes of former days. A delicious loaf is the result.
Parts of the leavened dough are always saved to be used as leaven
for the next baking. A treatise written long before yeast was

known to the bread-making world runs as follows: "It must be well leavened, for without leaven it is good for no man; it ought to be light, for thereby the clamminess is gone; it ought to be well-baked, otherwise it is indigestible; it must be temperately salted for bread over sweet is a stopper and bread over salt is a drier; finally, this ideal bread should be made of wheat, hard, thick, heavy, yellow, light, full ripe, clean, and grown in a fat soil."

Salt rising bread is leavened by means of a ferment developed from salt, flour and water, combined. If these ingredients are left in a warm temperature for a few hours a gas is formed, resulting from the chemical reaction between the flour, water and salt. By the addition of more flour it is made into a dough, kneaded, and allowed to rise a second time, after which it is baked. If fermentation be not checked at just the proper time a highly offensive odor will result, hence the great care necessary in using this kind of ferment. One author denounces it as bread in the highest stage of putrefaction and wholly unfit to eat.

Aerated bread is lightened by carbonic acid gas which is forced through the dough by means of machinery. The process is the invention of a Dr. Danglish of Edinburg. The bread is light and sweet, though without the agreeable flavor of the best yeast bread, and is very popular in England. All fermentation, with its possible evils, is avoided and, as bread can be made by this process in one hour and a half (not including the time consumed in baking), it is much to be commended. For some reason it has not become popular in America excepting, to a limited extent, in the East.

Germ bread is another variety of local fame and which, consisting as it does of the germ or embryo of the wheat grain, is very nutritious. The germ is separated from the kernel in all mills because it not only darkens the flour, if ground, but affects the flavor. It is more commonly known as a breakfast food, under the names of germina, semolina, wheatena and others.

In the eastern states a most famous food is "Boston brown bread," made from rye, corn meal, and graham flour, well sweetened and usually served smoking hot. It is nutritious, not quite as digestible as wheaten bread, but the accompaniment, always and ever, of baked beans.

Fifty years ago Rev. Sylvester Graham of Boston waged moral war against the ordinary wheat bread of the bakeries, doubtless with good reason, for at that time the nutritive value of flour was

pretty generally considered of secondary importance to its whiteness. He advocated the grinding of the whole wheat kernel and
"Graham bread" was the result. His idea was excellent but he was
not enough of a scientist to carry it to perfection, and it is certainly
true that neither himself nor his followers brought glory to his
cause by reason of superior health or great longevity. It is, on the
other hand, also true that many a person has been made dys-
peptic by its constant use, and for the following reason: In his
effort to retain all the nourishing qualities of the little brown kernel
Mr. Graham retained the tough, outer layers of the wheat grain which
are not only innutritious but wholly indigestible. Chemically, they
are soluble only in strong solutions of acid and alkali, while the
acid and alkaline secretions of the human system, the saliva, gastric
juice and biliary fluid are very weak, only sufficient, in fact, to
digest or make soluble the pure starches. These tough coatings or
"bran" therefore act only as irritants upon the tender mucous
surfaces of the digestive tract, and cause a large proportion of the
food to be simply hurried through the system before assimilation
can take place, thus promoting waste of nutritive material. This
has been proven but recently by the experiments of Atwater in
America and Voit in Germany. Says one authority, "The ardent
dietetic morality which extolled the bread that was coarsest, brown-
est, stalest and most truly home made, and caused fine, white bread
to be swallowed as if it were a sin against nature is classed among
the 'isms' of forty years ago." However, I by no means advocate
the abolition of graham flour, although it should be well sifted before being used.

Flour is, generally speaking, one of our purest foods, although
it has at times been adulterated with such articles as peas, beans
or peanuts, dried and pulverized. These are wholly healthful and
more nourishing than the whitest grades of flour, although, if such
adulterations are introduced into wheaten flour the consumer
should not be deceived. In old Pompeii, as exploration has proven,
it was not unusual to make loaves entirely of pea flour. Alum has
been frequently used in minute quantities to produce whiteness,
though just why it has that effect, says Williams, is still a chemical
puzzle.

Much has been written pro and con the price of bread at the
present time. It is certainly unfair to the tenement house population of our great cities, which depends largely upon baker's bread,

to charge as much for a loaf with wheat at less than fifty cents a bushel as was paid when it cost a dollar and a quarter. A barrel of flour produces, it has been estimated, three hundred loaves of bread and the baker expects to make a clear profit of twelve or fourteen dollars from every barrel he makes up, even at the former high price. A pound of flour absorbs half that quantity of water. It is therefore easy to see that a loaf weighing a pound is sold at a good profit even if the best quality of flour is used, which is rarely the case among bakers.

A miller from Glasgow, Scotland, while in Chicago, recently, gave some interesting items in regard to the baker's bread of his own land. The flour used in the Scotch bakeries is principally American, although some is imported from Hungary. Certain of the bakeries use three thousand sacks a week, each sack weighing two hundred and eighty pounds. The weight of the bread is regulated by law. The loaf is large and square, known as the quartern loaf, and must weigh four ponnds twenty-four hours after it is baked. The family baker gets five pence (ten cents) for the quartern loaf and half that price for the smaller loaf of two pounds. It is baked on the bare floor of the oven. The yeast used is that prepared by the bakers themselves from malt. One wonders how the Scotch people can import American flour and then sell their bread at the above rate, while in America, with wheat so low in price at present that it is used for fattening stock, we pay five cents for a loaf made in many cases from inferior flour and often weighing less than a pound. The fact that the Scotch bakers do not take back unsold bread, and that wages are lower abroad, are not satisfactory reasons for this difference in price. The wealthy and well-to-do classes bake their own bread. It is the people with little ready money, no knowledge of foods or their proper selection, who depend upon the frequently innutritious bread of the bakeries. With the possibility of furnishing a good bowl of soup for a penny, at little if any profit but certainly at no loss, a cheaper loaf of bread is not a distant probability.

Mexican Grinding Stone.

What bread is to the American macaroni is to the Italian, an universal and nourishing food. Macaroni, as we know it, might be defined as a hollow tube of paste which in American kitchens is all too frequently spoiled in cooking. But originally it consisted of lumps of flour paste and cheese, compressed into little balls. The Italian name, "maccheroni", is derived from "maccare," to crush; vermicelli is, as the name indicates, worm-like in shape while spaghetti means a cord. These three varieties are the best known of Italian pastes, although there are fancy pastes, large and small, whose number is legion.

It is not known in what land or by what people this paste was originally made, although it was manufactured in China at a remote date. It is believed that the Germans obtained their knowledge from the Chinese, they, in turn, imparting it to the Italians, who have come to consider it, through centuries of usage, their one indispensable food.

On the other hand, the Japanese claim priority in the making of this paste, having used it for many hundreds of years. We first know of its use in Italy in the fourteenth century, and the secret of its manufacture and preparation was confined to that country by its jealous cooks for nearly a hundred years. It was then introduced into France and we hear of Louis XIII. ordering it from an innkeeper of Tours, who had established a great reputation for its preparation. From that time its use became general throughout all the Latin countries.

The favorite dish of Lord Byron, even in the land of the boar's head and sirloin, was macaroni, served with truffles.

At one time the composer Rossini was invited to dine with Prince Napoleon, in company with Dumas *fils* and Doré. Rossini was the guest of the hour and in his honor macaroni was served, a dish of which he was excessively fond. Not long after, Costa, a conductor of the Covent Garden opera, wished Rossini's opinion of an oratorio of his own composing and, to win the great musician's favor, sent with it a box of macaroni. Days and weeks passed without acknowledgement. At the end of a month Costa received this note, "My dear Costa: Thanks for the oratorio and the macaroni. The latter was excellent. G. Rossini."

For many years it has been claimed that no country could produce so excellent a macaroni as Italy, a circumstance long believed to be due to the species of wheat grown there. It is of the hard variety, having a horny grain and containing a large amount of gluten. However, the hard, flinty wheats of Algeria, of Tangarok,

Russia, of Argentine Republic, of the United States, particularly of the Dakotas, are as rich in the element needed for the making of macaroni, *i. e.*, gluten, as the best varieties of the Italian farms.

The raw material used in making these pastes is a coarsely ground flour, called "semoula" or "farinola," which is chiefly glutinous, most of the starch having been eliminated. Macaroni cannot be successfully manufactured from a starchy flour because, in cooking, the starch granules so expand as to cause the pipes of macaroni to break or else to become pasty and cohesive.

Let us follow the process of making as it is conducted in the large manufactories of the United States, the material being flour from the excellent, hard wheat of Dakota. One hundred pounds of this glutinous flour is placed in a wooden box with a small quantity of warm water, seemingly quite insufficient to moisten it. The mixing is done by machinery and when that process is completed the dough has much the appearance as well as the tenacity of India rubber. It is then kneaded for some time under a three-ton pressure that all the tenacious possibilities of the gluten may be developed. The dough, cut in pieces, is placed into cylinders about two feet in depth by nine or ten inches in diameter, and which are warmed by a jacket of steam. A pressure of one thousand pounds to the square inch is then applied by means of slowly revolving screws and the mass of dough is forced through tiny cylindrical holes at the bottom of the cylinder. Owing to the stiffness of the dough this process is lengthy, occupying about an hour. At the core or center of each of the holes with which the copper plates at the bottom of the large cylinders are pierced is a steel pin. This it is that renders macaroni tubular in form; and through these holes the macaroni pipes slowly emerge until the dough in the cylinder is exhausted. The macaroni pipes are cut into the required lengths by boys and girls who sort them, laying aside all imperfect pieces, and place them on long frames to dry. These frames are wooden, latticed with twine, upon which is laid heavy manilla paper. Upon this the macaroni is placed, the heat from the cylinder having so dried it that there is no danger of its adhesion to the paper. The handling of the long, tenacious, undried tubes, the cutting into exact lengths and the careful assorting are important details of the work which, if carefully attended to, greatly diminish waste and facilitate the final packing. The drying requires a few days' time during which the greatest care must be observed. The rooms are large and perfectly ventilated. After the frames of macaroni are placed, tier above tier, the temperature is carefully watched that it may not vary, and all draughts are excluded. Too moist a temperature causes the paste to sour or mildew, too much heat injures it by quick drying; let a draught of air enter and the macaroni cracks. No infant is ever more carefully attended to than is this product by the successful manufacturer.

When thoroughly dried the pieces are weighed, rolled into pound packages and labeled. In one of our largest American factories I watched this process, standing at the long tables by the side of the deft-fingered girls. Only a small proportion of the daily output was marked in English letters. The greater proportion, by far, sported Italian labels, purporting to come from Naples, and a quantity likewise was splendidly labeled in French. This is due, as I was told, to the great prejudice existing in this country in favor of the far-famed Italian pastes.

Vermicelli, spaghetti, and all the fancy pastes are made from the same dough and, excepting the final shaping, pass through the identical process. There is a ribbon macaroni, wide and with fluted edge, a fluted pipe known as "celery macaroni," as well as numberless tiny pastes of fancy shapes, alphabetical, seed, ring, and star shapes, which are a pretty addition to clear soups. The larger fancy shapes are, however, difficult to cook and serve unbroken, as well as quite puzzling, at times, to the uninitiated eater of them. There is also a variety known as the German noodle. It is colored yellow with saffron, giving it a flavor much liked by certain classes, and imitating the color of the original German noodle which is always made with eggs. It is the *tagliarini* or *lasagnette* of the Italians.

There are several grades of macaroni upon the markets, the cheaper containing a large proportion of starch, a condition at once determined by cooking. The best are made from the same sort of flour used in making the best bread, with, however, part of the starch eliminated; hence the higher price. The foreign macaronis are sometimes cheapened by adulteration with wheaten flour and that of corn, beans and peas, articles which, as they do not change the appearance nor detract from the weight of the paste, are rarely detected until the only infallible test is made, that of cooking. The cooking of macaroni is not often successfully accomplished by the unskilful, for the delicate tubes should come to the table whole, separate, and without any pastiness. The best may be injured by soaking, by being washed carelessly, or by being put into cold water to cook. Macaroni should be plunged into boiling water,—plenty of water,—to which there has been added salt. Continue the boiling until the macaroni is tender, from twenty to thirty minutes, when the tubes should have become double their original size. Drain the macaroni and plunge it into cold water for a moment, to prevent breaking and cohesion, and it is then ready to be dressed for the table. It is an ideal dish when properly prepared, simple, delicious, nourishing, and cheap.

It may be dressed with butter and cream, with Parmesan cheese, although American cheese is suitable; with tomatoes or with meat gravies; it may take the place of rice or barley in a soup, and is delicious if scalloped with oysters or bits of cooked meat. It is to be regretted that macaroni does not enter more largely into the dietary of the working classes in America, not less because of its cheapness and the ease with which it may be prepared than because of its nourishing qualities.

No food product at the Columbian Exposition created more discussion among the judges, none elicited more careful comparison, none received more accurate tests than did the macaroni and pastes. This was partially owing to the general apprehension that no good pastes were produced outside of Italy and France, and partially to the fact that the American macaroni seemed to be equally as good as the Italian. This, after tests and analyses, was found to be the case, and I am convinced that our best macaroni compares favorably with the best Italian. Chemical analysis has long since proven that our hard wheats are as valuable in its manufacture as the best of those grown by the Mediterranean. Our manufacturers are, with scarcely an exception, Frenchmen or Italians, who followed the same business when abroad. One, who has been a maker of pastes for nearly a quarter of a century, assured me that the only points of difference between the manufacturing of macaroni here and abroad lay in the method of drying. In

Fancy Pastes.

Italy, owing to the mildness of the climate, all pastes are dried out of doors in the sunshine, a process which somewhat bleaches them so that the French, Spanish and Italian products are whiter than the American. But the American pastes have the advantage of a process much more cleanly, for dust from streets and highways has easy access to the foreign pastes, a fact of much account to the consumers in this age, with all humanity at war against microbes. In Italy the mixing of the dough is accomplished by hand excepting in a few of the largest manufactories, and nearly the entire amount of macaroni produced in that country is consumed at home. The bulk of the imported article, which we know, comes from France. The best quality of American macaroni is in every way equal to the best of the foreign products, and it is much to be regretted that cheaper qualities are manufactured. It is undoubtedly done to satisfy the demands of the poorer classes of foreigners living here, who prefer it to almost any other food. As yet it is not largely used among the American born population, although to be invariably found in the best restaurants and hotels.

The largest exhibit of pastes at the Columbian Exposition was made by Italy. Macaroni in most wonderful shapes, vermicelli, spaghetti, fancy pastes of all descriptions, placed the exhibit ahead of all others in point of completeness. A large quantity was also sent from Spain.

Costa Rica presented a great variety of pastes, not, however, of specially excellent quality. Their bright yellow color was produced by saffron, owing probably to the impression that the dye is a protection from weevils, the pests of tropical countries.

The quality of the pastes from Jamaica and those from Mexico was not of the best. They were in the form of vermicelli and, from having been dried on hot plates, consisted of a network of worm-like threads, closely massed.

The pastes from Russia, as well as from the Argentine Republic, in both of which countries excellent, hard wheat is produced, were of superior quality although unattractive appearance.

The principality of Monaco exhibited very excellent pastes, equal to the best from any country, most of which were put up in fancy shapes.

Japan made a large exhibit of vermicelli, unlike any other pastes in taste as well as appearance. The dough had been salted in the process of mixing, disproving the European theory that salting the dough ruins it. The Japanese spin the dough into threads of astonishing fineness, the entire process being accomplished by hand. The threads which, owing to the extreme tenacity of the dough, are of great length, are hung over bamboo sticks to dry, after which they are cut into lengths of six, eight or ten inches. These are tied into bundles about an inch in diameter and are then packed, ready for sale or export, in boxes holding one dozen bundles each. Unlike the other pastes, this vermicelli is peculiarly flexible and the tiny bundles are almost as pliable as a bundle of coarse bristles. If eaten, uncooked, it does not remain hard, but is readily soluble. When cooked each thread expands, retaining its shape perfectly.

At a dinner given to the judges one summer day at the Japanese Tea House, one course consisted of vermicelli. It had been cooked, by boiling, in unbroken lengths of about eight inches. These, on being served, were dropped into glasses half filled with cracked ice. Accompanying each glass was a tiny bowl of soy, that distinctively Japanese sauce. We were allowed to choose either forks or chop-sticks with which to eat, a process which involved winding a few threads of the glutinous paste upon the fork, dipping them into the soy and conveying them to the mouth. It was quite as difficult as carrying an armful of eels, and scarcely more successfully done. In swallowing the paste, the long threads, cold as ice, appeared to slowly unwind as they traveled adown the throat, and were quite suggestive of frozen angle worms. However, the paste is notably superior both in nutrition and flavor.

Only three American firms exhibited at the exposition, although it is claimed that New York alone has thirty. All these houses presented extensive and creditable exhibits, the capacity of each averaging, it is estimated, five or six thousand pounds each day. About thirty million pounds is each year manufactured in America, consuming five million bushels of our best wheat.

CHAPTER XX.

I N MANY respects the edible fungi comprise the most singular and interesting class of substances to be found in the entire range of food products. Their growth is always nocturnal, they are the most delicate and perishable of all vegetables, they assimilate materials and thrive amid surroundings that would be absolutely fatal to almost any other species of vegetation. In flavor as well as nutritively they closely approximate animal foods while, if kept until decomposition sets in, their odor is similar to that of decayed meat. They belong, nevertheless, to the vegetable kingdom, and one wonders that naturalists were for so many years undecided upon that point. The writer of a quaint little English book, published by Charles Knight of London in 1832 and entitled "Substances of Food," says: "Some refer them to the animal, some to the vegetable, others to the mineral world, while one naturalist has asserted that these fungi ought to be excluded from all these divisions and considered as intermediate beings." This scientific indecision appears the more singular when one recalls the fact that mushrooms have been used as food since the early days of Greece and Rome. They are frequently mentioned by Pliny as well as by Galen, the accomplished old physician of Pergamus.

The greatest difference between edible fungi and vegetables is to be found in the amount of nitrogenous matter or protein contained. Nutritively they rank higher than the cereals, legumes, or even lean beef. The following table (adapted from analyses made

13

by both Dr. Letheby and Payen) indicates the comparative value of
our principal foods, including fungi, from a strictly strength-giving
standpoint:

Per Cent of Nitrogenous Matter.		Per Cent of Nitrogenous Matter.	
Lean beef	27.60	Beans	25.50
Lean mutton	18.30	Potatoes	2.50
Veal	16.50	Parsnips	1.10
Calf's liver	20.10	Mushrooms (dried)	52.00
Dried bacon	8.80	Morels "	44.00
Hard wheat	22.75	White truffles "	36.00
Rice	7.55	Black truffles "	31.00

Discussion has long been rife as to the digestibility of the edible
varieties of fungi, reminding one of the complaints often lodged
against cheese as well as occasional other articles rich in proteids.

The fact is, complaints of indigestibility are
heard only among certain classes of people who
understand nothing of the chemical properties
of mushrooms and who usually combine them
with other foods in wholly unscientific proportions. Now the system does not demand,
neither can it assimilate, more than a certain
amount of nitrogenous food; and for that reason mushrooms should be eaten, not as a luxurious accompaniment to the more nutritious
foods, such as meats, but in the place of them. In America mushrooms are an expensive luxury, whether home-grown or imported,
and are used only by the well-to-do classes. There is no necessity
for economy and consequently, at hotels and restaurants even more
than in private houses, we see such dishes as beef steak smothered
in mushrooms, boned turkey with truffles, ragout of beef with
mushrooms, truffled omelet, or the more common "omelette aux
champignons." In not a few cases the overloaded stomach rebels
and indigestion is the legitimate result. From our own country-
people who occasionally gather them, from the European peasantry,
or from the people of China and Japan, who use them only in combination with such starchy foods as potatoes, bread or rice, we hear
no complaints of indigestibility. In individual cases, however, it
makes a great difference whether the person be of an active or
sedentary habit of life.

Edible fungi may be generally classified as mushrooms, morels,

Common Mushroom.

and truffles. Of the former, more than one thousand edible varieties are known to exist, although a comparatively small number are commonly used as food. They have also been classified according to the color of the spores, as white, pink, iron-color, purple, brown, and black. In describing the best known varieties I have chiefly relied upon reports made by Dr. Thomas Taylor, one of our most careful investigators and leading mycologists, and who has been for some years connected with the Agricultural Department at Washington. His services, in investigating both the edible as well as the poisonous varieties of fungi, have been invaluable.

The common meadow mushroom, *agaricus campestris*, is, always excepting the imported "button" mushroom, the variety best known in America and England. It is usually gathered in the autumn, being most plentifully found just after the early frosts in September. It is delicate in appearance and flavor, is most delicious when cooked, and may be known by its shape, its white color, pink gills, and by the pleasant odor exhaled when it is bruised. From it an excellent ketchup may be made.

The fairy ring champignon, *marasmius oreades*, is to be found in dry meadows, occasionally upon lawns, and is so named because of its peculiar manner of growth. The mushrooms, which are small in size, invariably arrange themselves in rings or circles with astonishing regularity. If two rings chance to meet while forming, each elongates in the form of an ellipse. If the ring be interrupted by a stone or stick the obliging little fungi simply unite and continue the ring on the other side of the obstruction. No scientific explanation of this manner of growth has ever been advanced.

The giant puff-ball, *lycoperdon giganteum*, is well known in country places, owing to its commonness, and is noticeable because of its immense size. It consists of a simple ball, white or cream-colored, and from ten to twenty inches in diameter. It is edible only

Fairy Ring Champignon. when unripe, the flesh being white, elastic, and fragrant. If allowed to ripen the mass becomes at first streaked with yellow, later, transformed into a mass of powdery spores. The puff-ball grows upon prairie lands, particularly throughout the prairies of Nebraska, and should, because of its nourishing properties, become, in that state, an important source of food supply. As the western people are, however, ignorant of its value it is rarely if ever eaten. An Italian mycologist, Vittadini, states that if a giant puff-ball be found in good condition a slice may be taken off each day for a week, providing care be taken not to disturb its growth.

A species of mushroom grown in the hot-houses of both Europe and America is known botanically as *lepiota cepoestipes*. It possesses a delicate flavor when cooked, and is white in color, its surface being covered with tiny projections or tufts. It requires cultivation and has never been known to grow in the open air.

The morel, or *morchella esculenta*, grows abundantly throughout the wooded portions of the United States, from Missouri to Maryland and from Virginia to Michigan and Wisconsin. Its use is restricted, however, to a comparatively small number of people who know its value while in the European countries in which it grows profusely it is greatly esteemed as a food. In my own state, Michigan, the morel may

Lepiota Cepoestipes.

be always gathered in the months of April and May in beech and maple forests and, where it is most abundant of all, in elm swamps, near streams. In appearance it is far from attractive, having a somewhat conical head, which is deeply honeycombed and of a light brown color. But, whether stewed or sautéed, it is tender, meaty in consistency, and delicious in flavor.

It is not generally known in America that nearly all of the edible mushrooms may be cultivated with a minimum of care and a maximum of result, but such is nevertheless the case. Given a quantity of properly prepared compost, a darkened area, such as a cellar, in which the compost may be placed, a temperature not rising above 80° F., occasional watering after the spawn has been planted, and in six or eight weeks a crop of mushrooms will appear, rewarding ten-fold the slight expenditure of trouble and expense incurred in starting the beds. It is quite unnecessary to give specific directions in this place as they will be furnished by any reliable seed house at which the spawn may be obtained. However, information much more complete is to be found in the reports published by Dr. Thomas Taylor, Chief of the Division of Microscopy at Washington, D. C. I should advise everyone interested in the subject to send for these reports, as they embody the most important contributions made during recent years to the science of mycology. They may be obtained by addressing the United States Department of Agriculture.

There is probably not a grocery house of any account in our entire land which does not display upon its shelves "Imported Button Mushrooms from France," indicating that in that country, at least, the cultivation of the mushroom has reached astonishing proportions. They are usually cultivated in caves, the quarries and even the catacombs about Paris being thus utilized. One cave alone contains more than twenty-three miles of beds, which produce thousands of pounds of these delicious fungi daily. One can never be certain, when eating a juicy fillet of beef or a tenderloin, garnished with mushrooms, that the innocent little "buttons" did not draw their sustenance from the ashes of some illustrious Gaul! These fungi are analogous to the common meadow mushroom of England and America, and are gathered for export long before they are fully matured. The consumer thus gets an article which is leathery in texture, undeveloped in flavor, and ridiculously high in price. It seems little less than farcical that we should persist in importing a product which is indigenous to our own soil, which may be cheaply and easily cultivated, and which might thus be obtained with its growth matured, its flavor fully developed, and its delicacy of texture unimpaired. In China the government has recently published an "Anti-famine Herbal" of six volumes, containing descriptions and illustrations of over four hundred edible plants. It is to be deplored that our government does not emulate so good an example, giving the edible mushrooms special recognition. I do not mean to say that mushrooms have never been cultivated in this country, for a small number of market-gardeners, particularly in

Morels.

the vicinity of the large eastern cities, have long cultivated them, more or less extensively, at enormous profits. But the secrets of their trade have been jealously guarded and, until the last decade, the growers have been regarded by the mass of people as exponents of a science that, from a horticultural point of view, was thoroughly occult. The government reports issued from time to time have been the principal agents in disposing of this fallacy.

The uninitiated gatherer of mushrooms is likely to become sorely perplexed in the endeavor to distinguish the true from the false varieties, particularly if guided only by the popular theories or so-called "tests." But neither the onion nor the silver spoon tests are in all cases infallible. It is well to remember that poisonous varieties have usually an offensive odor; that the gills of the edible varieties are never perfectly white but have usually a yellow or pink tinge. The only safe-guard is perfect familiarity with the appearance of certain species, which may be gained from the fungi themselves, or from colored drawings, such as those contained in Dr. Taylor's reports.

Truffles, from the standpoint of natural science, are even less understood than mushrooms. They possess neither root nor branch, neither flower nor seed, growing in subterranean clusters without attaching themselves to any support. They develop a few

Black and White Truffles.

inches below the surface of the soil and can be detected only by their aroma, which, when powerful, is slightly nauseating. Dogs and pigs have long been trained to burrow for them, guided by the odor, and, although the reason for it is not known, they flourish best in oak forests. The most famous of the few truffle-producing localities of the world is Perigord, France, although they are also found in other portions of France, in Italy, in England, and in Japan. Unlike mushrooms, they have never been produced under cultivation, and they are as yet unknown in America excepting in bottles, with their flavor much impaired and their price correspondingly high. Those of finest flavor come from Perigord; the English or Hampshire truffle is somewhat inferior, while still less delicate varieties are eaten by the natives of Algeria and the Bedouins of western Asia.

The truffle was earliest mentioned by Theophrastus, who described it as a rootless plant, engendered by the thunderstorms of autumn. It was known to the epicures of Greece and Rome, but was apparently lost sight of during the Middle Ages to be revived in France only after the dawn of the Renaissance. Said a famous French gourmet of recent days, "There must be two at the eating of a truffled turkey, the eater and the turkey."

In appearance the truffle is far from attractive. It is spherical in shape, light in color when quite young but dark, nearly black, at maturity, and having a rough, warty exterior. Of the two varieties, the white and black, the latter is most valuable, owing to its more delicious flavor, and is the variety known to fame as "Truffe au Perigord." The best are the size of an English walnut, while those weighing three or four ounces are considered large. Truffles are still occasionally found which weigh a pound and it has been stated that specimens from ten to fourteen pounds in weight have been gathered in Italian forests. As may be readily believed, the scarcity of this product as well as the uncertainty of its harvests are quite as important factors in the esteem with which it is held by the epicurean and the wealthy as are its marvelously delicate aroma and flavor. As Brillat-Savarin, high-priest of epicureanism, once remarked, "Perhaps if they were not expensive, but were within reach of everybody, *we* should not prize them so highly." It is almost unnecessary to state that; owing to their chemical composition which approximates that of meat, all the edible fungi require cooking. They are unfit to be eaten in the raw state.

Whoever investigated the foods exhibited by the Japanese at the World's Columbian Exposition must have been astonished at the immense quantities of mushrooms there exhibited. They were in a dried state, so light in color, so clean and attractive, that the visitor was quite prepared to learn of mushrooms as not only one of the most valued articles of food in the far-off island of the Orient, but one of the chief articles of export. They are cultivated by the Japanese upon decaying logs, a method peculiar to that people, and are dried for export. Tons upon tons are exported to China and quantities find their way to the Chinese shops of other lands. In San Francisco I found dried mushrooms in all the Chinese groceries selling at fifty cents a pound, an astonishingly low price when one remembers how considerably drying reduces them in weight and bulk, while the hotels and restaurants of America are paying a dollar a pound for them in a fresh state.

The Chinese import quantities of mushrooms from Japan, besides growing them extensively, thus furnishing to their densely populated communities, which subsist chiefly upon rice, a nitrogenous food, taking the place of meat in their dietaries.

New Zealand also exports large quantities, although none were exhibited at Chicago, and the Terra del Fuegans have long lived upon little besides mushrooms and fish.

Models of all the edible mushrooms of America were exhibited, in all the glory of their numerous varieties, at the Government building at the exposition, and about them was always to be seen a wondering, admiring crowd. No exhibits were made by private growers.

CHAPTER XXI.

R O M a nutritive standpoint the edible legumes are of more importance than any other vegetable, always excepting the esculent fungi. Commercially they rank next to cereals, although much richer than these in protein. They are peculiarly adapted to garden culture and are noticeable for their delicate vines and beautiful papilionaceous or butterfly shaped flowers. The sweet-pea is a variety cultivated exclusively for its delicate, fragrant flower, as is frequently the kidney-bean or "scarlet runner." Indeed, the latter legume, for fully a hundred dred years after its introduction into England from South America, was cultivated only for use in bouquets, and as an ornamental vine.

The legumes, under the name of "pulse," which in general includes all the edible varieties, are spoken of in the Old Testament and are known to be of great antiquity. It was simple pulse that Daniel preferred to all the luxuries of the king's table, an example which leads one to exclaim with Milton:

"If all the world
Should i⸱ a fit of temperance feed on pulse!"

The legumes in common use are few in number, comprising only the bean, pea, chick-pea, and lentil. The esculent portion consists simply of the fruits or berries, which are eaten both green and dried as well as with or without the seed pod in which they develop. Of them the bean can boast of greatest antiquity as to origin, although even to-day ranking as a plebeian, rather than an aristocratic, food product.

The bean is believed to have originated in Egypt, probably because of its early mention by the Egyptian priests, who regarded it as an article unfit for food. This prejudice continued among the Greeks for some time after beans were introduced into their land. Wild beans have long been used in Persia and the inhabitants of Barbary have long eaten them, stewed with oil and garlic. But numerous varieties have been developed from the original wild stock, and to-day we have the navy bean, kidney bean, Lima bean, French or haricot bean, in fact, a hundred species, more or less, all of which, however, possess the same general characteristics.

Beans are specially valuable to densely populated communities because they furnish so large a proportion of protein to a given area of land. We find them, as well as other legumes, a standard food in the older nations such as China, Japan, India, France, Germany and most of Europe. Says one author: "A given area of land cropped with legumes and cereals will support a population more than three times as numerous as that which can be sustained on the same land devoted to the growth of cattle." According to Payen the analysis of beans gives: protein, 25.50; starch, 55.70; cellulose, 2.90; fats, 2.80; salts, 3.20; water, 9.90. As will be seen, they contain more protein than the best hard wheat and twice as much as the soft. Since the sixteenth century it has been customary to substitute beans, or other of the legumes, for meat during Lent, particularly on the fourth or Pas on Sunday. According to an old writer, "After the sallad we eat fried beanes, by which we understand confession. When we would have beanes well sooden, we lay them in steepe, for otherwise they will never seeth kindly."

Chick-pea.

The Egyptians had a saying that children fed upon beans were

well educated, a foreshadowing of the truth later established by
science, that no child, unless well nourished, can fully develop
mentally.

At the Columbian Exposition more varieties (about one hundred) were exhibited by Brazil than by any other nation, showing
how largely beans entered into the dietaries of that country and
also how important a factor cultivation is in the differentiation of
any species. Japan sent a large exhibit of the soy bean (*vide* chapter on condiments), as well as a bean product called *tofu*. This was
lso exhibited by China. It consists of the coagulated albumen of
the bean, pressed into square cakes. It is white as snow, is sold in
all villages and country places in the Orient, and in the Chinese
markets in San Francisco. When frozen and dried the *tofu* becomes of a spongy texture. All these preparations were accompanied
by analyses, showing them to be high in point of nutrition.

Mexico also exhibited beans. These, called "frijoles," when
boiled with fat and flavored with capsicum and garlic, make a
savory dish, but one not at all to the taste of the average American.

The Boston method of baking beans has done a great deal to
popularize the use of this food among Americans. The beans are
cooked or baked very slowly, with the addition of just the right
quantities of water and sugar, and a piece of either fat pork or bacon.
The result is a thoroughly hygienic dish, one which in its proportions of protein, fats and carbohydrates, is an almost perfect and
complete food itself.

But the use of beans is by no means confined to the dried
article, although that is most valuable, especially in the army or on
shipboard, because it supplies so much nutriment in so little bulk.
Green beans contain valuable organic salts and are cooked either
in the pods, as "string beans," or when mature, shelled. One of our
finest dishes, a combination of sweet corn and green beans, originated with the Indians, and is known as succotash from the Indian
word, "su-sich-qua-tash." The deservedly anonymous author of a
little English work, published in 1832, naïvely assures us that "the
bean in its green state is well known as a culinary vegetable; when
mature and dried it is never used as human food in this country,
but is then considered good, though coarse, nourishment for labour-
ing horses."

Peas have been cultivated for food since the days of the Greeks,
and it is believed that they were grown during still earlier periods

in both China and India. The varieties known to-day were introduced into England from the continent in the seventeenth century and were long regarded only as "fit dainties for ladies; they come so far and cost so dear."

Like beans, peas are used both in the green and the dried states and of one variety, grown chiefly in Europe, both pod and seed are used, being gathered when quite immature.

The green pea, although far less nutritious than the dried, is considered much more of a delicacy because of its finer flavor. The Romans knew nothing about the use of peas green, and it was a Frenchman, one Michaux, who not only discovered that they were edible but food fit for the gods, as well. That rare combination, lamb with mint and green peas, is alone enough to make one heartily thankful for the privilege of living in the modern world.

Dried peas are most commonly met with in "split-pea" soup, the indigestible outer skin having been removed.

Pea flour is also valuable, although, as it may be easily adulterated, it is advisable to buy the split peas whenever practicable. The flour, when formed into small cakes by the addition of a small quantity of fat, is a welcome addition to soups. In Germany, the "erbswurst," so much used by the army, is prepared from pea-flour, fat and condiments. It is so nutritious that but a small amount is sufficient for a long march. Like beans, dried peas require slow and prolonged cooking. They contain only slightly less protein than dried beans.

The *garbanza* or chick-pea is little known in America, although it is a common article of diet in all the Mediterranean countries of Europe. It is much larger than the common pea and grows singly in dainty, round pods, its wrinkled surface giving it so odd an appearance that one would not at first believe it to be a member of the *leguminosæ*. It is believed that this pea was the "parched pulse" of the ancient Hebrews, and it is still purchased by travelers who are obliged to carry their own provisions across the wastes of the Oriental countries. Parched or dried chick-peas have long been sold in the shops of Cairo and Damascus.

But the chick-pea of modern days is chiefly famous as an ingredient of that distinctively Spanish dish, "olla podrida." As are chowder and Boston baked beans to the New Englander, macaroni to the Italian or cheese to the Swiss, all that and more is the "olla podrida" to the Spaniard. The chick-pea does not become soft and pasty during the process of cooking, but each retains its own assertive little individuality so that, besides being an ingredient among others of soups, it may also be placed about meat or vegetables as a garnish.

Spain exhibited the *garbanza* quite lavishly at the Columbian Exposition and one of the officials in that department displayed some surprise at my negative reply to the question, "And you never have *olla podrida* in America?" Said he, "Let me write you the receipt for making, for he who has never eaten *olla podrida* knows not what is fine eating!" The receipt was at length finished and presented to me with much ceremony. It occupied two entire pages of fool's cap paper. This was the first sentence: "It requires an entire day to make *olla podrida* for the six o'clock dinner"; and this, the second, "cook very slowly over a charcoal fire." Imagine, if you can, an American woman spending an entire day over a mess of soup, with only the murky and doubtful assistance of a charcoal fire! My Spanish friend must have been a bachelor who, while the peas were simmering, comfortably read, smoked and dozed amid the savory odors, quietly anticipating, perhaps, a trio of friends to share with him the evening meal.

Lentils, although as valuable nutritively as peas and beans, are but little used in America, excepting by foreigners. This is probably due to the fact that our abundant food supply renders the use of them quite unnecessary. Like split peas, they are to be found in nearly all markets, and when used, in soups or stews, are universally liked in spite of their dark and unattractive color. The mess of pottage for which Esau sold his birthright was undoubtedly made from lentils, and, from the earliest times until to-day, they have always been obtained in the shops and from the gardens of the Orient. Three varieties are now cultivated in both Germany and France, one of which closely resembles the common pea; the second is a larger, yellowish variety, and the third, the small brown lentil whose delicate flavor is much prized in soups. Lentil soup should always be made in the form of a purée, the indigestible outer skin being removed by straining, and a bit of pork, bacon or, if preferred, butter added to supply the necessary amount of fat. Lentil meal is also combined with sugar and sold as a sweetmeat, or, under the name of *ervalenta Arabica*, as an infant's food. The use of the starchy foods, such as rice or lentil meal, as the basis of sweetmeats and candies is peculiar to the Orientals. The plant greatly resembles the pea-vine, the pods, which grow in clusters, containing never more than three or four seeds.

CHAPTER XXII

F THE large family of plants which produce tubers, the potato (*solanum tuberosum*) is our best-known type. No plant grown, always excepting wheat, to-day occupies a more important place in the dietary of the nations of the western world, although it is far more valuable commercially than nutritively, and was all but unknown until a comparatively recent date. Authorities differ as to where the potato was first discovered or by whom first cultivated, although probably in South America, as the Spaniards there found it under cultivation by the natives in the sixteenth century. One author states that in Ireland the potato was used as early as 1565, while Dr. Campbell, in his *Political Survey*, declares that it was not there introduced until 1610. Not until 1728 was it considered important enough to be cultivated in Scotland.

It was introduced into that land by one Thomas Prentice, a day laborer, in spite of great opposition from the higher classes, who objected to it on religious grounds. "Potatoes," they said, "are not mentioned in the Bible." But 1742 and 1743 were years of famine and consequently of high prices for the scanty food that was obtained. "The destitute wandered in the fields, seeking to prolong the misery of existence by devouring the leaves of pease, beans,

sorrel, and other wild plants, while not a few perished from absolute want. Still more were carried off by the diseases which always
follow famine, and this state of things naturally called attention to
the cultivation of the potato."

In England it was not grown outside of kitchen-gardens until
after 1770, but it so rapidly grew in public esteem that a quarter of a
century later, "seventeen hundred acres were planted with this
tuber, in Essex county alone, for the London markets." An English
writer of the last century referred to it as "a root found in the New
World consisting of knobs held together by strings, and which, perhaps, if you boil with dates, may serve to keep body and soul together among those who can find nothing better." From which it
may be inferred that a few Philistines were still to be encountered
long after the potato won not only popular favor but even the recognition of royalty, for, in 1584, Raleigh is said to have obtained a
patent from Queen Elizabeth "for
discovering and planting new countries, not possessed by Christians,"
with potatoes.

Bishop Heber, in speaking of its
introduction into India, says "it has
been attended with most satisfactory
results and, by degrees, its cultivation is becoming more and more extended. It is held in much esteem
by the Musselmen as a very useful
absorbent in their greasy messes. . . .
A dry season is prejudicial to the rice
crop while it is favorable to the potato; therefore, nature makes one
crop a substitute for the other."

In 1827 the potato was the most
important field crop of entire Poland.

Potato.

For more than a hundred years before that date it had been extensively grown in Sweden, where it was commonly used, after being
dried and ground, as a substitute for flour in the making of bread.
But it did not reach Saxony until 1740, and, half a century later,
prejudice continued to be so strong in that country against the use
of potatoes that Count Rumford, when desirous of using them
for the celebrated soups with which he so long fed the poor of

Munich, was obliged to smuggle them into his rooms. They were secreted in the basement and there cooked and reduced to a pulp before being added to the soups. The improvement in his cookery was so marked that when Count Rumford at last told of the reason the despised tuber rose immediately in public esteem.

The Indians of North America have long used the wild potato, although they seem to know nothing of its cultivation. At the Columbian Exposition wild potatoes were exhibited by the Nez Perces tribe, under the direction of Miss Alice Fletcher. They were combined, after having been mashed and dried, with jerked meat and also with berries, very sensible and nutritious combinations of food. It is difficult to believe that the potato of our commerce, so universally used as food, and the varieties of which number far into the hundreds, has been developed from the insignificant wild root of the prairie.

No vegetable has proven more tractable in the hands of the cultivator. The edible portion develops perfectly only underground and comprises the roots or tubers, which are simply the underground stem, greatly enlarged at its free end. From the buds or "eyes" of these tubers the plant is propagated. New varieties, however, are usually the result of propagation by the seed. Its cultivation is limited by about the same climatic conditions as that of wheat, the lighter soils producing, in general, larger crops than the heavier. This is due to the fact that the tubers have less resistance to overcome in the process of their growth in a light soil and are not forced to develop partially above ground as is the case with the wild variety. From an English horticultural report I quote the following: "Some careful cultivators pinch off the blossoms as they appear on the plant. This increases the yield about a ton an acre. . . . The reason is that the sap which gives sustenance alike to the tuber and blossom will be exerted for the enlargement of the root." Whether this expedient is a common one I do not know. In America the finest potatoes I have ever seen were grown in Montana and Washington, their uniformity in quality and size being due to irrigation. Excellent potatoes are also grown in the lighter soil of Michigan, as well as in most of the other states, although the crops are not always uniform, owing to occasional drouth.

In regard to the nutritive value of potatoes we have made no comparisons which are, broadly speaking, much more reliable than those made by Sir Humphrey Davy half a century ago in England.

14

According to him, "the nutritive power of wheat to that of potatoes is about as seven to two, or two pounds of wheat afford as much sustenance as seven pounds of potatoes. . . . The weight of the two kinds of food from the same extent of land is nearly as one to eight. Now if we assume that the consumption of an individual is 480 pounds of wheat, its equivalent in potatoes would be 1680 pounds. Then one acre of wheat will produce enough food for three persons while one acre of potatoes will feed six and five-sixths." This latter deduction is quite likely to be misleading. For modern dietetic science has clearly proven that a person whose principal food is potatoes, no matter in how abundant quantities they might be consumed, would be far less sufficiently nourished than one whose staple food is wheat. The analysis given by Dr. Letheby is as follows:

Protein	2.10	Salts	0.70
Starch	18.80	Water	75.00
Sugar	3.20		
Fat	0 20		100.00

Potatoes should be considered as an auxiliary to other foods, rather than a food in themselves. Owing to their deficiency in protein they are wholly unable, unless reinforced by nitrogenous articles of diet, to satisfy the needs of the human system, while they contain a wholly disproportionate amount of starch. Used alone they cannot sustain the health or strength of the system for more than a short time. It is related, however, that in Saxony during the latter part of the seventeenth century a detachment of French troops was cut off, for a period of ten days, from all supplies. During that time the soldiers subsisted entirely, without inconvenience, upon potatoes from neighboring fields.

But all people who consume them as a daily food, year after year, reinforce their diet with articles rich in proteids. The Irish use quantities of milk, more per capita than any other nation, according to Dr. Smith; the Scotch, an abundance of oatmeal and cheese; the Swiss and Germans, cheese and flesh foods, and the English and Americans, quantities of meat. But in no place are potatoes more prized than on shipboard, owing to their anti-scorbutic qualities. They are an invaluable adjunct to the salt meat of a sailor's diet, which, unless accompanied by vegetables or acid fruits of some kind, soon develops scurvy. In the excited days of '49 the value of potatoes became apparent when scurvy developed among certain communities of miners on the Pacific coast, who were subsisting almost entirely upon salt meat and flour. The disease yielded readily to a diet of raw potatoes, which at one time are reputed to have sold at a dollar apiece.

The starch of potatoes is an important commercial product while potato flour is even more valuable as it contains all the chemical constituents of the tuber. In Russia the latter preparation is largely used, for soups, stews or, in combination with wheaten flour, for the making of bread. Meal is also made from potatoes, pared, sliced, then thoroughly dried and ground. Potato flour was exhibited by Russia at the exposition.

In the early history of the tuber opinions were rife as to whether it should be converted, in cooking, into a savory or a sweet dish. Certainly the following receipt, given to an inquiring world by one Hannah Wooley in 1770, should have settled that question forever: "Have your pie-dish lined with a crust. Lay in butter and potatoes, boiled until very tender, with whole spice, marrow, dates, the yolks of hard-boiled eggs, blanched almonds, pistachio nuts, candied peels of orange, citron and lemon. Close the pie with a crust, bake, and serve with wine, butter and sugar."

The Irish prefer potatoes boiled with their "jackets on," that is, unpeeled. This has the advantage of retaining all the salts which would otherwise escape into the water in which they were boiled. There are infinite ways of preparing this vegetable for the table which have the cardinal virtues of simplicity and healthfulness, but in doing which the average housewife is far from skilled. To quote the expressive sentences of Sidney Smith, who depended greatly upon potatoes during a certain period of life when he was too poor to buy meat: "At this moment (1830) there are few French cooks who can boil, mash, fry, pulverize, or roast a loafer in such appetizing forms as necessity, the mother of invention, forced me to learn. It is a thousand pities that English women know no more how to dress vegetables than I do how to dance on the tight rope."

Although the use of the sweet potato antedates that of the common potato, its origin is quite as mysterious, as it is not to be found growing in any country in a wild state. It is probably native to both hemispheres and was brought to Spain from the Malayan peninsula long before the white potato was introduced into Europe. That to which Shakespeare has referred is believed to have been of this variety. Botanically, the two are wholly unrelated, the sweet potato (*batatas edulis*) belonging to the convolvulus family, possessing a delicate, climbing vine and flowers which are only a little less attractive than the garden morning-glory.

Its cultivation is limited to the warmer parts of our temperate climates and in America it is peculiarly a product of the cotton and tobacco-producing states. Several, although not many, varieties exist.

Sweet potatoes yield about the same per cent of protein and starch as the white, although containing ten per cent or more of sugar. They are, on account of this excess of sugar, less mealy and somewhat more mucilaginous than the white, when cooked.

The people of America and Europe regard the sweet potato simply as a vegetable, while those of Siam, Johore and East India preserve it as a sweetmeat. A large exhibit of these preserves, put up in a clear syrup, palatable to the taste and attractive in appearance, was sent to the Columbian Exposition from these countries. Japan exhibited sweet potato flour and also the same vegetable dried. For the latter process the potatoes are first peeled, then immersed in hot water for a time, then taken out, sliced, and placed upon mats in the sun. Drying has been attempted in the South of our own country but has not been done successfully as yet.

It is related that Marion, an American general of the Revolution, once dined an English officer upon sweet potatoes, baked in the ashes of his camp-fire and served upon strips of bark. The officer later resigned his commission and returned to England, saying that it would be impossible to conquer a people who were willing to live upon sweet potatoes!

Jerusalem Artichoke.

The yam is the fleshy, tuberous root of an ornamental vine of the *dioscorea* family, and is probably native to the East Indies. The name is commonly but incorrectly applied to those varieties of the sweet potato which contain most sugar and which are better liked in the South than the starchier kinds. Botanically it is wholly unrelated to either the white or sweet potatoes, although its root resembles that of the latter and is cooked and used in the same way. The tuber is less delicate of flavor, developing to an astonishing size, some of those gathered in the East Indies weighing twenty-five, occasionally thirty, pounds. The plant was brought to this country from the West Indies in 1733 but not until more than a century later was it generally used as food, and only then (in 1845) on account of the disaster wrought by potato disease. It will probably never be extensively grown on account of the extreme difficulty of gathering the crop. The tubers, which are larger at the base than at any other portion, grow perpendicularly downward and have to be carefully dug out, as, owing to their brittleness, they break if pulled. There are two principal, and more than a hundred minor, varieties.

Salep is the tuberous root of the *orchis mascula*, a small plant native to the East Indies, and highly valued throughout Turkey, Syria, Persia and, in fact, nearly all countries of the Orient. It is there regarded as a specific for nervousness, but is really no more than a simple and nutritious vegetable. The root contains about fifty per cent of a mucilage or jelly known as bassorin, and about thirty per cent of starch. It is prepared for use by being heated until transparent, then dried, usually in the sun. When needed for food the little, bulbous roots are either immersed in boiling water or crushed into a powder. A century ago it was commonly used by the working classes in the Orient, but "the salep-stall has long been replaced by the coffee-stall." It is but little known in either Europe or America.

Taro is the Hawaiian name for the root of the *colocasia esculenta*, which is cultivated by the natives of the Sandwich Islands for the sake of its large, fleshy tubers. Like our potatoes, they are eaten both roasted and boiled, and are an important ingredient of the national dish, *poi*, a mucilaginous, slightly fermented dish, tasting quite like sour paste, eaten with the fingers from the calabash and prized beyond all other food. The leaves of the *taro*, which rise directly from the root, are used much as we use spinach. The *taro* has recently been introduced into southern California where it grows well, but, as yet, the demand for it is not extensive.

The Jerusalem artichoke is not the artichoke proper but a plant of the sun-flower family, which is cultivated for its edible tubers. It is native to Brazil and, possibly, Mexico, but is cultivated to only a small extent either in America or England, probably because other foods are so abundant as to make the use of it quite unnecessary. The plant produces large numbers of tubers which, although extremely ugly in shape, resemble potatoes. They are not injured by freezing and are usually allowed to remain in the ground all winter. Chemical analysis shows them to contain but a very small percentage of starch but nevertheless to be slightly more nutritious than potatoes. The tubers may be cooked or eaten raw as a salad.

The arrow-root, a plant native to both the East and West Indies, is chiefly valuable for the starch extracted from the fleshy roots. It is particularly useful in the preparation of invalid dishes, although often adulterated with the starch of the cassava or the potato. It is credited by the native East Indians with various medicinal virtues which it does not actually possess.

One of the most remarkable of our products is the cassava or manioc plant, the fleshy, starch-producing tubers of which furnish food for so large a proportion of our tropical and sub-tropical nations. It is known botanically as *jatropha manihot*. The two principal varieties are the sweet cassava, which may be known by its five-cleft palmate leaves, and the bitter or poisonous, the leaves of which are seven parted. The bitter variety is most common in the tropics. It is fit for food only after the poisonous properties of the root, which are due to the prussic acid contained, are dissipated by heat. From the pulp, well washed and heated, the tapioca of commerce is prepared. The manioc

Sweet Cassava.

which poisoned Stanley's rear-guard in Africa was simply the root of the bitter cassava which was eaten raw. From the juice of this variety a substance known as *cassareep* is made (*vide* condiments) and from the flour, a delicate, palatable bread, not, however, as high in nutritive value as the best wheaten bread. From it an alcoholic drink is prepared which is, unfortunately, too highly esteemed by the natives of the cassava-producing countries.

The native method of extracting the juice is unique. The

Indians weave from reeds a curiously shaped, tubular press or strainer, closed at the bottom. Into this the ground pulp of the root of the bitter cassava is placed, and the press is suspended with a stone tied to the handle shaped bottom. The weight of the stone lengthens out the press and the poisonous juice is squeezed through the interstices.

The root of the sweet cassava (*manihot utilissima*) is used much as are potatoes, the juice being innocuous. This variety has recently been introduced into Florida. It was exhibited at the Columbian Exposition. Cassava grows well in the sandy lands of the South, a valuable food for animals as well as man. According to the analysis made by H. W. Wiley, chemist of the United States Department of Agriculture, the roots contain 3.47 per cent of albuminoids (protein) and 71.85 per cent of starch. They attain a weight of several pounds and, as many tubers are produced by each plant, the crop is a profitable one, yielding as high as five tons to the acre. Besides starch, which is always valuable commercially, glucose is prepared from the roots, also a small proportion of cane sugar and a superior tapioca. The cassava will inevitably take a high place among our starch producing plants as it becomes more generally known.

The succulent roots, like the tubers, are used merely as adjuncts to other foods, although they contain a much smaller percentage of starch. They are liked because of their flavors, which are quite distinctive, and are valuable because of the organic salts contained.

The turnip (*brassica rapex*) has been cultivated since the days of the Greeks, although the wild variety is still to be found growing in the fields of Europe. The object of cultivation has been to increase the size of the root without sacrificing

Cassava Strainer. tenderness and flavor. While at first only a product of the kitchen garden the turnip is now grown, like potatoes, in fields. The two chief varieties are the white and the yellow. The uses of it in cookery are well known, but it is doubtful if the gastronomic skill of modern days can ever

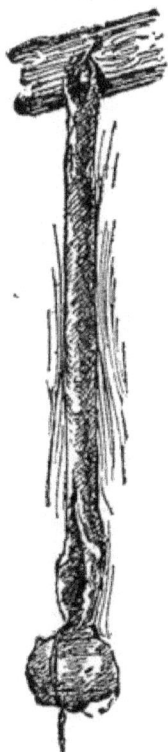

equal that of an ancient, royal cook. It is related that the king of Bythnia, while on an expedition against the Scythians was, one winter day, seized with a desperate longing for a certain small fish, a pilchard or herring, one writer says a loach. The sea lay at some distance and a fish was quite out of the question. So the ingenious cook procured a turnip, cut it into the shape of a fish, cooked it in oil, salted, seasoned, and well powdered it with grains of black poppies, and served it to the king as the particular fish he so much desired. His majesty could not have been hypercritical as to food, for he was exquisitely deceived and praised the root to his guests as a "most excellent fish."

In Rome, in the days of Pliny, turnips were worth a sestertius, about two-pence, each, the best being brought from the district of the Sabines. Pliny relates that the roots occasionally weighed forty pounds, a weight that no region of modern days, unless it be our own state of Washington, can equal.

In England, during the years of 1629 and 1630, there was such dearth of food that a bread was made from equal parts of turnip, which was deprived of most of its moisture, and flour. It was known as turnip bread and, although not very nutritious, was an acceptable substitute for the cereals, then so much in demand. One is reminded of the sarcastic Jeames Yellowplush who said that the most "unexceptionable swarry" he ever sat down to consisted of due proportions of mutton and turnips.

In Russia turnips are considered quite a luxury by all classes and are frequently eaten as fruits. Even among the nobility, according to one author, thinly sliced, raw turnip is served with tiny glasses of brandy, as a relish.

The fondness of the Laplanders for this vegetable is even more remarkable. They will often exchange a whole cheese for one turnip, thereby displaying an ignorance of the relative nutritive values of the two articles that is certainly ludicrous, for the turnip is not only rather indigestible unless cooked, on account of its large proportion of cellulose or woody fibre, but is most innutritious. I think the adage, "you cannot get blood from a turnip," must have been inspired by the doctrines of certain thin-blooded philosophers who insist upon a diet of "bran-bread" and vegetables.

The carrot (daucus carota) is indigenous to many portions of Europe, although only the cultivated varieties are sufficiently sweet and tender to find ready favor as food. It was introduced into

England from Flanders during the reign of Elizabeth and was a favorite vegetable in the time of James I. The ladies of the court adorned their hair with its leaves, which were light, graceful, and a good substitute for the traditional feathers. From being exclusively a garden vegetable the carrot was easily adapted to field culture, two principal varieties being developed, the large, and the short or horn carrot. The root is valuable for feeding cows as, unlike the turnip, it does not impart any flavor to the milk.

A transverse section of the carrot reveals two distinct portions, the outer, which is deep red in color, pulpy in consistency and containing a large proportion of saccharine matter; and the heart or core which is light yellow, less sweet and, when mature, fibrous or woody. The gardeners of all times have exerted their best efforts to produce a carrot which should contain the greatest possible proportion of outer pulp. The carrot is more used by the French than by ourselves, both as a vegetable and as a savory addition to soups and stews. When raw it is believed to possess antiseptic properties. It is, like turnips and all succulent roots, very low in nutritive value, containing but little starch or sugar, and consisting principally of water which, according to Letheby, constitutes eighty-three per cent.

The beet (*beta vulgaris*) has been cultivated since the time of the early Romans and is described by Pliny. By these people it was undoubtedly introduced into England, at what date is not known. It is now extensively used in Europe and America, the red variety being more attractive for table use than the white or yellow. When young the plant, leaf, stalk and root, is boiled as "greens," making a truly appetizing dish which may be served either with butter or some acid as dressing. Beets produce abundantly and it is said that in Guernsey one hundred tons to the acre have been raised. A specially sweet variety is now cultivated in France, Germany, Russia, and the United States for the sugar contained, which is of a high quality.

Salsify.

The parsnip (*pastinaca sativa*), like the carrot, is a biennial. It also possesses similar characteristics and habits of growth. There are four varieties. The root is not injured by frosts but may be left in the ground all winter. It contains somewhat more starch than the carrot and, when slowly roasted in the ashes, appears to be nearly as farinaceous and mealy as the potato. In the north of Scotland the peasantry prepare a dish composed of equal parts of parsnip and potato, to which are added butter and simple seasonings. In Catholic communities the use of it, combined with salt fish, is general during Lent.

The salsify (*tragopogon porrifolius*) is commonly known in America as the oyster plant or vegetable oyster owing to its flavor, which approximates quite closely that of the delicious bivalve. It is related to the lettuce and dandelion although the only edible portion is the long, tapering root. It is native to England, and the original variety has been so much improved by cultivation, in size as well as flavor, that few gardens on either side of the Atlantic are to be found without it.

The black oyster plant (*scorzonera hispanica*) was earliest cultivated in Spain to which it is indigenous. The Moors valued it for its supposed medicinal properties, believing, as did also the people of Africa, that it was a specific for snake bite; hence its name, from *scurzo*, a species of snake.

Like salsify the plant has a milky juice and a flavor resembling that of the oyster. But, as it is a darker, coarser, and somewhat inferior vegetable, there is little to recommend its use if salsify is to be obtained instead. The flesh is white, having a slightly bitter flavor, which is dissipated by thorough soaking in cold water before cooking. The root has long been used in Spain as a vegetable although not introduced from that country into France until the seventeenth century.

CHAPTER XXIII.

ACETARIOUS OR SALAD PLANTS.

HE salad plants contain no appreciable amount of nutriment, yet are, owing to their crispness and cooling properties, an indispensable portion of the ideal dinner and are aids to the digestion by virtue of the acids and other condiments with which they are dressed. It is to the French that credit must be given for using salad plants at their tables the year around. A salad of simple vegetables, occasionally combined with lobster, shrimp, or meats, over which is poured the equally simple dressing of oil and vinegar or lemon juice, is daily served by almost every housewife in the land. The Germans and Americans use salad plants extensively, although with somewhat less of favor than did the ancients. More than two centuries ago the Irish used salads of sorrel, dressed with vinegar, sugar, and mustard.

The early Jews ate at the Passover lettuce, tansy, camomile, dandelion and mint, the "bitter herbs" of the Paschal feast, all of which were combined with oil and vinegar. Tansy was frequently eaten at the Easter day dinners of Europe as late as the sixteenth century.

The Romans early regulated the use of vegetables by penal statute which compelled the people to combine them freely with meats in their dietaries. That they loved salads Virgil bears cordial witness. From the Cowper translation I quote the following description of the way in which they were made by the ancient Roman:

"With hasty steps his garden round he sought;
There, delving with his hands, he first displaced
Four plants of garlic, large and rooted fast;
The tender tops of parsley next he culls,
Then the old rue bush shudders as he pulls,
And coriander last to these succeeds,
That hangs on slightest thread her trembling seeds.
Placed near his fire, he now demands
The mortar at his sable servant's hands,
When, stripping all his garlic first, he tore
The exterior coats, and cast them on the floor,
Then cast away with like contempt the skin,
Flimsier concealment of the cloves within;
These, searched and perfect found, he, one by one,
Rinsed and disposed within the hollow stone.
Salt added, and a lump of cheese,
With his injected herbs he covered these,
And tucking with left hand his tunic tight,
And seizing fast the pestle with his right,
The garlic bruising first, he soon expressed
And mixed the various juices of the rest.
He grinds, and by degrees his herbs below,
Lost in each other, their own powers forego,
And, with the cheese in compound, to the sight
Nor wholly green appear, nor wholly white.
The work proceeds; not roughly turns he now
The pestle, but in circles smooth and slow,
With cautious hand that grudges what it spills,
Some drops of olive oil he next instills,
Then vinegar, with caution scarcely less,
And gathering to a ball the mealy mess,
Last, with two fingers frugally applied,
Sweeps the small remnant from the mortar's side,
And thus, complete in color and in kind,
Obtains at length the salad he designed."

In Oriental countries flowers are frequently used in salads, probably quite as much for ornament as for flavor, and it is said that the Japanese even serve their national flower, the chrysanthemum, at their tables. Flowers were also added to the salads of fourteenth century England, according to Evelyn, violets and hawthorn-blossoms, primroses and marigolds, daisies, elder flowers, roses, cowslips, orange blossoms, and even the tender buds of the hop vine.

Shakespeare testifies to the English appreciation of the salad as a cooling dish when he makes Jack Cade say (punning upon the word "sallet," which meant at that time a helmet as well as a mixture of herbs and green vegetables): "Wherefore, on a brick wall have I climbed into this garden, to see if I can eat grass or pick a sallet another while, which is not amiss to cool a man's stomach this hot weather. And I think this word sallet was born to do me good; for many a time, but for a sallet, my brain-pan had been cleft with a brown bill; and, many a time, when I have been dry, and bravely marching, it hath served me instead of a quart-pot to drink in; and now the word sallet must serve me to feed on."

For many sorts of salads does this world feed on, from the carefully mortared preparation of the Roman to the dish of modern America, all pink and green and white, with its ingredients, whatever they may be, cool, crisp, and individual, no triturated preparation, but one just enough bruised and broken to yield to mixture, "frescoed with waves of golden mayonnaise," fragrant as country flowers, and as dainty, spruce and cool as a floating sea-weed.

Artichoke.

Chief among salad plants is lettuce, known to the botanist as *lactuca sativa*, owing to its milky juice. The ancients held it in peculiar esteem, possibly because it was the fragrance from a bed of wild lettuce that revived the wounded Adonis when he was placed upon its soothing leaves by the weeping goddess, Venus. The plant was used by the ancients at the close of a meal, its cooling properties being believed to counteract the heating effects of wine. Says Pope:

——"If your wish be rest,
Lettuce and cowslip wine *probatum est.*"

There are two main varieties of lettuce, with numbers of variations, the cabbage shaped, which forms in heads, and the Cos lettuce, curly and broad leaved. It is not known when or at what place lettuce was first cultivated, probably on some of the Greek islands of the Mediterranean, such as Cos. In 1520 it was first introduced into England from Flanders, and, ten years later, under Henry VII, we read that the gardener at York Place received a reward for bringing "lettuze" and cherries to Hampton Court. To-day it is universally cultivated in both hot houses and gardens, a rapid, unchecked growth being induced for the sake of tenderness, crispness, blanching at the center, and to prevent the development of the bitter principle. It is wholesome at breakfast, excellent at lunch, and almost necessary at dinner; good for yourself to eat and most dainty to serve to your friends; of all salad plants the most delicate and most prized.

The inspissated juice of the lettuce, which possesses in a mild form the medicinal virtues of opium, has held a place for many years among pharmaceutical preparations. It is obtained from the flower stalk just as the flowers are about to open. The stem is cut with a sharp knife just below the buds, the milk oozes from the incision, quickly dries, and hardens into a brown scale. This is taken off, another section of the stalk is made, another scale is formed, and this process is repeated over and over again until the juice is exhausted or, perchance, the weather interferes. Although this procedure is both laborious and slow, owners of lettuce farms have reported satisfactory profits even during unfavorable years.

Endive (*cichorium endivia*), usually called winter lettuce, belongs, like lettuce proper, to the dandelion family. It was earliest under cultivation in China and Japan, whence it was introduced into the European countries during the sixteenth century. The plant produces an immense mass of leaves from the crown of the root, which are smooth of surface but deeply serrated at the edges. Although more acrid and tough, when exposed to the air, than lettuce, the leaves when blanched become crisp, tender, and appetizing. Blanching is done in various ways: by keeping the mass of leaves tightly tied together, by covering the whole plant with a pot or, again, by partially covering with earth. Endive is blanched to perfection by the German gardeners in the vicinity of our large cities, and is particularly valuable because it may be obtained in the winter when there is dearth of other salad plants. It is closely allied to the chicory of England and France.

The radish (*raphanus sativus*), although its succulent root is the part used, is properly one of the acetarious plants, because it is eaten as a relish. In many countries the tender, young leaves, as well as the seed pods, are used for salad but, owing to its pungency, the root is looked upon as a condiment rather than a food. The garden varieties are two, one possessing a long fusiform root, the other, small and turnip-shaped. Either kind may be yellowish, black, or white, in color, although the brilliant red roots are far preferable, specially for garnishing. The field varieties are larger, coarser in texture, and stronger in flavor. The radish has been known and cultivated in India since a remote period but was not introduced into England until the sixteenth century.

Celery (*apium graveolens*) has become so changed and improved under cultivation that it bears little resemblance to the original wild plant. There are the red, white and green varieties, the latter being almost universally whitened by blanching. The desideratum is not size but tenderness and delicacy of flavor, although under favorable conditions and in rich soil it develops enormously. In the state of Washington plants occasionally attain a weight of six pounds, and it is recorded that a head of celery, cultivated in the vicinity of Manchester, England, in 1815, weighed nine pounds and measured four and one-half feet in height. Celeriac, or the turnip-rooted celery, is also used for salads, the root being boiled and, when cold, sliced with acids and other condiments.

The nasturtium or Indian cress (*tropaeolum majus*) is an excellent salad plant, although cultivated in America chiefly for its brilliant flowers. Leaves, stems and

Kohl-rabi.

flower buds give a pungent and appetizing flavor to a salad, while the seeds, if pickled in brine similar to capers, may be used as a condiment. The plant is called nasturtium erroneously, but the misnaming of it is undoubtedly due to its acrid, pungent flavor, the name being derived from two Latin words, *nasus* and *tortus*, meaning nose-torturing. The true nasturtium is known as the common water cress.

Water cress (*nasturtium officinale*) belongs to the mustard family. It grows wild in abundance throughout portions of Europe and America, at the edges of ponds, near springs, and upon the banks of small streams, always under water. It is now cultivated for the market by sowing the seed in tanks of water in which a deep layer of sand has been placed or, better still, at the margins of natural creeks or streams. The cultivated cress is larger and more tender than the wild while containing all of the aromatic pungency so much prized. The garden variety, which is even more acrid and pungent than water cress, is known as "pepper grass." It is useful both as flavor and garnish.

The sorrel (*rumex acetosella*) is a hardy plant that is much better known in Europe than in America, although well adapted to garden culture. It is a member of the buckwheat family. The leaves of the variety known as French sorrel are slightly more acid than the common garden sorrel.

Corn salad or lamb's lettuce (*valerianella olitoria*) grows wild in southern and central Europe, but is cultivated throughout the continent. Like chicory, it is an admirable substitute for lettuce during the spring and winter months.

Spinach (*spinacia oleracea*) belongs to the beet family. It was originally called *hispanach* or Spanish plant, having been first used by the monks of Spain during fast days. The plant is native to Japan and New Zealand, probably also to southern Europe, although it was not introduced into England until the sixteenth century. Several varieties are cultivated in our gardens during both spring and winter. The leaves are boiled and dressed with butter or with acids and the simpler condiments. The leaves as well as the root of the common beet (*beta vulgaris*) are boiled and dressed like spinach while young and tender, and an excellent dish may be prepared from the whole, young plant, boiled and dressed in the same way. Swiss chard is still another variety of beet, cultivated for its leaves but particularly for its large, fleshy leaf-stalks which, when cooked, are almost as delicate as asparagus.

The artichoke (*cynara scolymus*) is cultivated solely for the sake of its immature flowerheads, which are not only cooked but are served raw with condiments in the form of a salad. It somewhat resembles the thistle, to which it is botanically related, and is believed to thrive best in those countries which border upon salt water. Since 1473 the plant has been cultivated in Venice and, in fact, throughout Italy as well as other of the Mediterranean countries. It was first introduced into England during the reign of Henry VIII., and in the Harleian library there is still preserved a paper written in the time of Queen Mary and relating to the "best settynge and keepynge of artichokes." The vegetable is still more largely used upon the continent than elsewhere, and is but little known in America. Quantities of canned artichokes were sent by Italy to the Columbian Exposition.

One of the earliest and most delicate of our garden products is asparagus (*asparagus officinalis*), in appearance and manner of growth resembling the salad plants but usually boiled and dressed as a vegetable. The stalk is the portion used and, although containing very little nutriment, is prized for its flavor. It is best grown on well manured soil which is treated annually to a top-dressing of salt. In some countries it grows luxuriantly on light, sandy soil which is heavily dressed with seaweed. The plant has been cultivated since the days of the Greeks and Romans, and was mentioned by the poet Cratinus in the fifth century B. C. Cato speaks of it in his treatise, "De Re Rustica," and about a hundred years later Pliny discusses its care and cultivation in his work on natural history. He asserts that three heads of asparagus, grown in the neighborhood of Ravenna, have been known to weigh a pound.

The green seed-pods of okra (*hibiscus esculentus*), a plant native to the West Indies but cultivated in the southern states, are stewed and served like asparagus. When dried, the pods are chiefly used for thickening soups, or making "gumbo." The plant belongs to the mallow family, all members of which possess the mucilaginous properties which distinguish the okra.

Rhubarb (*rheum rhaponticum*) is a member of the buckwheat family and, like sorrel, possesses an acid flavor. Only the fleshy petioles or leaf-stalks are used for food but the plant is particularly valued because it is ready for use in the spring long before any fruits or even the principal salad plants are to be had. The petioles, stewed and sweetened, are a good substitute for fruit. Several varieties are cultivated, the root of one (*rheum palmatum*) being used as a medicine. It is native to Tartary. The common garden variety, known as pie-plant, wine-plant, and in England as monk rhubarb, is also indigenous to portions of Asia and was not introduced into Europe until the sixteenth century.

The cabbage (*brassica oleracca capitata*) is that particular member of the brassica family in which the broad leaves, arising directly from the root stalk, are gathered or folded together in a compact head. Owing to their compression and exclusion

Brussels Sprouts.

15

from the light the leaves become crisp, tender, and blanched. It is impossible to determine when or just where the cabbage was originally cultivated, possibly by the Germans or early Saxons. One authority states that the old Saxon word for sprout-kale was given to the month of February, as that was the month in which sprouts were earliest gathered from the old stalks. The cabbage was in common use in Rome as food for both freemen and slaves. It was introduced into England at an early date but not generally cultivated until after many years. It was Ben Jonson who said, referring to the customary importation of this vegetable, "He hath news from the low countries in cabbages." The plant may have been introduced into Scotland by German fishermen, although more probably by the English soldiers of Cromwell. But, however it came, the cabbage has long occupied a unique place in Scottish national cookery and particularly that of the common people. The Irish have a dish which somewhat corresponds to the kale-brose of the Scotch, which they have named "kolcannon," and which consists of a bit of salt pork, boiled with potatoes, cabbage, and seasonings.

The cabbage when crisp and tender is commonly dressed for the table raw, delicately sliced and combined with vinegar and oil or mayonnaise. It is also prepared for winter use by being cut or sliced and packed into casks with a little salt. After fermentation this is known as "sauer kraut," and the making of it is quite an industry both in the United States and in Germany. Sauer kraut is of special value to sailors as an anti-scorbutic, and is quite as efficacious as lemon juice or green vegetables.

All the plants of the *brassica* family have a tendency "to sport or run into varieties and monstrosities," although still retaining to a marked degree the flavor peculiar to cabbage. Chief among these varieties are the kale, kohl-rabi, Brussels sprouts, colewort, broccoli, and cauliflower. Kale, also called borecole and German greens, differs from its kinfolk in that the leaves do not form a head but branch out, each separate, from the main stalk. In kohl-rabi, or turnip-cabbage, the stem is greatly developed above the ground into a turnip-like bulb, which is the part used. Brussels sprouts have been cultivated near Brussels and in other parts of Belgium since the early part of the thirteenth century. The sprouts are miniature cabbage heads, one or two inches in diameter, branching upon the main stalk. Colewort or "collards" consists of a large, open-headed cabbage or mass of leaves, growing loosely upon the rather tall,

central stem. Broccoli is a variety of cauliflower, differing mainly
in that the head is loosely divided into smaller heads. The cauliflower itself, dainty, delicious, the one white rose of our kitchen
gardens, might be defined as the cabbage in the highest state of
evolution. It is of Italian origin, was early cultivated in Cyprus,
and at the time of the French Revolution was exported into England, Holland, Germany and France. It was introduced into
England at the beginning of the seventeenth century, and soon at-
tained great perfection under cultivation. We have no vegetable
more delicious, none more satisfactory, in the hands of a skillful
cook. But, alas! the water-soaked, overcooked, maimed, and dis-
colored article that is to be seen upon many an elaborate table
testifies that skillful cooks are all too rare. When properly served,
like a miniature mountain of snow, with a simple white sauce or
au gratin with a sprinkling of Parmesan
cheese, one is fain to exclaim with Dr. Johnson, "Of all flowers I like cauliflowers
best."

The onion (*allium cepa*) and its confrères,
the leek, garlic, shallot and chives, are
more remarkable for flavor than for any
other quality. But all are largely used as
ingredients of salads, particularly in France
and Germany. Owing to their medicinal
and antiseptic virtues they occupy a unique
place among our vegetable foods, and there

Okra.

is not a little truth in the old couplet,
"Eat onions in May
And all the year after physicians may play."

The plant is of great antiquity and was worshipped in Egypt 2000
years B. C., and to this day Egyptians devoutly hope that the onion
may be numbered among the viands of Paradise. It is usually
eaten by them roasted, with meat. Alexander the Great found the
onion in Egypt and, believing that it would excite martial ardor,
brought it back to Greece with him and furnished it to his army.
It also figured in Druidic worship, a custom that may have descended from the equally mysterious rites of the divine Isis. Literature is full of allusions to the onion, perhaps because of its distinguished lineage. Macauley wrote to a friend one Michaelmas time of

"The churchman gay, who will wallow to-day
In apple-sauce, onions and sage";

and years before this Cervantes bestowed upon it an enviable immortality when he made Sancho Pansa say, "To tell the truth, what I eat in my corner without compliments or ceremonies, though it be nothing but bread and an onion, relishes better than turkey at other folk's tables." Both the leek and garlic have been mentioned as condiments but they are also used in salads. Garlic grows wild along the shores of the Mediterranean and a wild variety found in Kamtchatka and Russia is much prized as a vegetable by the poor of those countries.

Chives is a hardy plant which grows wild throughout the hilly districts of both Europe and Asiatic Russia. It is cultivated for the sake of its delicate, green, tubular leaves, which are a good substitute for onions, particularly in soups and stews.

Two of our garden fruits, because of the way in which they are customarily prepared for the table, are properly classed as salad plants. These are the tomato (*lycopersicum esculentum*) and the cucumber (*cucumis sativus*). The tomato (from the Mexican word, *tomatl*) was formerly known as the love apple. It is native to India, possibly to the warmer portions of Europe and America, but is now very generally cultivated. There are many varieties and the tendency among cultivators seems to be to increase the size without sacrificing the deep red color or the firmness of the flesh. When green the fruit is used for pickles and preserves; when ripe, it may be stewed as a vegetable, made into a ketchup, or, better still, sliced raw for a salad. When so used and simply dressed with oil, vinegar, pepper, and salt nothing can be more appetizing and delicious. The value of the tomato crop of the United States is annually increasing, the largest output being from Maryland and New Jersey.

The cucumber, of which there are several varieties, belongs to the melon family. That it has been cultivated since the earliest of historic times, particularly in Syria and Egypt, is proven by the occasional reference made to it in the Old Testament. The cucumber of Syria is to-day grown in open fields, so extensive as to require the constant presence of a watcher, a custom dating from an ancient period and alluded to in the Bible. It has been known in England since the reign of Edward III. but did not come into general use until the seventeenth century. The cucumber is always plucked green, and is usually dressed for the table like the tomato. It is very largely made into pickles, specially a prickly variety known as gherkin, which is cultivated wholly for that purpose.

Among other plants which are occasionally cultivated for salads is the cardoon (*cynara cardunculus*). This is little known outside of England and the south of France, where, like its cousin the artichoke, it is greatly prized. Only the tender, crisp, blanched leaf-stalks are used. But numbers of our uncultivated herbaceous plants are also used, not a few of them being considered wholly epicurean. Among these are the marsh marigold or cowslip, tender, young nettles, hop sprigs. young milkweed shoots, even borage and comfrey. Still humbler confrères are the narrow-leaved dock and the dandelion, the latter now being extensively cultivated by the eastern market gardeners. Tender, uncurled leaves of fern make a pleasant salad and tarragon leaves are also useful as a flavor. In England a salad is often made from seaweed, boiled and chopped with condiments. A specially favored variety is samphire, which is, however, usually pickled for use.

CHAPTER XXIV.

H E history of our cultivated fruits, it may be
stated without much exaggeration, is the history of civilization. Wherever communities
are to be found existing in a condition of
rudeness or barbarity, there the cultivation of
fruits is a science quite unknown. On the
other hand, in lands governed by the arts and higher industries we
see attributed to the science of horticulture great importance.
Only when the industries and luxuries of civilization are introduced,
whether by conquest or commerce it matters little, do the native
fruits come to be improved by cultivation; only then are those of
other lands imported and acclimatized. The fruits of the early
Britons, in fact, of all the early uncivilized nations of northern
Europe, were few in number, among them being the acorn, the hazel
nut, and a most insignificant variety of apple. The very ones that
we have come to believe indigenous to Europe to-day, the peach,
pear, apple, cherry, and plum, were introduced into these lands by
the Roman conquerors, who in turn had first obtained them from
the Orient. The Europeans later carried them to the newly found
land of America and a century later, says Humboldt, "the Spaniards
spread the cultivation of the European vegetables along the ridges
of the Cordilleras, from one extremity of the continent to the

other." Whenever pioneer work is undertaken we find the transportation of fruits from the old lands to the new an almost inevitable result.

The systematic cultivation of fruits did not begin until the eighth century. The monks were the earliest and most successful gardeners and fruiterers, in fact, they seem to have virtually monopolized that industry, and up to the fifteenth century the monastic gardens and orchards were celebrated throughout all Europe. The industrial classes in general did not realize the value of horticulture and not until the decline of monasticism did they generally engage in it. Queen Elizabeth was one of its most enthusiastic patrons and during her reign, besides practical gardeners, numbers of scientific men, among them Fitzherbert and Gerard, contributed their share of labor in the form of voluminous treatises. Not later than the reign of Charles II. was the management of hot houses so well understood that the king's garden was occasionally supplied with strawberries and other small fruits entirely out of season. Writers of the period of Charles I. record that there were cultivated at that time fifty-eight varieties of apples, sixty-four of pears, sixty-one of plums, twenty-one of peaches, thirty-six of cherries, and twenty-three of grapes. Prior to that Lord Bacon had enumerated, among the fruits of an Elizabethan dessert, apricots, pears, grapes, apples, peaches, nectarines, wardens (a variety of pear, and of which Perdita's pies were made), quinces, medlars, barberries, filberts, and muskmelons. When we consider with what intelligent care many of our originally sub-tropical fruits have been acclimatized and improved by the gardeners of our temperate regions it appears scarcely possible to overestimate the marvelous future of this science of horticulture.

Fruits may be roughly classified as fleshy or pulpy, as drupaceous or stony, and as nuts or hard, dry fruits. The fleshy fruits comprise all of the *citrus* family, the citron, orange, lemon, lime, and grape-fruit or shaddock; the guava, banana, pomegranate, pawpaw, and fig, of the tropics; all of the berried fruits, including the currant, grape, raspberry, gooseberry, cranberry, elderberry, huckleberry, strawberry, mulberry; the melons, which are merely hard-rinded berries; and the *pomes*, the apple, pear and quince, which are formed from the permanent calyx and the seeds of which are not scattered throughout the pulp but are enclosed within membranous cells. The drupaceous fruits, including the cherry, plum, peach, nectarine, apricot, date, litchi, and mango, consist of a single-celled, stony nucleus containing the seed, which is surrounded by a succulent, fleshy coat. The principal edible nuts are the almond, brazil-nut, cocoa nut, walnut, chestnut, hazel-nut, filbert, beech-nut, acorn, pecan, and a few others. The peanut is simply the tough, leathery pod of a leguminous plant; the tamarind consists of the succulent pulpy pod of a leguminous tree; and the pineapple admits still less of classification, consisting as it does of the entire abortive flower spike, consolidated into a single head or fruit. The bread fruit, which is also tropical, is formed by the consolidation of the fleshy carpels of the pistillate flowers, which blossom in dense clusters, quite separate from the staminate flower spikes.

There has been much conjecture as to where the orange, the most important member of the citrus family, originated, although writers generally agree that it is indigenous to India. Galessio, in his "Traite du Citrus,"

Citron.

published in Paris in 1812, maintains that the Arabs, who penetrated further into India than former explorers, brought from that country both varieties, the bitter and the sweet. Part of the Arabs, coming to Italy through Persia and Syria, brought the sweet orange (*citrus aurantium*), while the remainder of the company, who came through to Seville by quite another route, brought the bitter (*citrus vulgaris*), commonly known to-day as the Seville orange. Both species have been greatly varied and multiplied since that time. They were not, however, introduced into other parts of Europe until some years later. In the sixteenth century Sir Walter Raleigh carried the orange into England, where the climate, it seems, has always been unfavorable to its growth. In Spain orange trees attain great size and bear fruit up to a good old age. It is said that there are trees still standing about Cordova which are six, possibly seven, hundred years old. Oranges are now extensively grown in California, Florida, and to a smaller extent in Mexico. Cultivators consider that size should not be secondary to color and flavor, other desired qualities being a smooth, thin skin, containing but a small quantity of oil, a light-colored, sweet pulp having but a small proportion of fiber. The varieties which have a thick coarse skin, with prominent oil glands, are usually inferior. The orange has always been more or less invested with romance, perhaps because the Crusaders, who first met with the fruit in their excursions to the Levant, so industriously fostered the theory that it belonged in reality among the golden apples of Hesperides.

The citron is a fruit of great antiquity and was held in high favor by the ancient Hebrews, who always, according to Josephus, carried branches of palm and citron trees to the tabernacles upon feast days. It is cultivated now in many of the Mediterranean countries, also largely in California, and the wild variety flourishes in portions of Asia Minor. The fruit is generally used as a sweetmeat or preserve. It is possible that the orange, lemon, lime, and grape-fruit have all been produced by culture from the original wild citron tree (*citrus medica*).

The lemon, like the orange, seems to have been unknown in Europe until brought to Spain by the Arabs in the thirteenth century. Since that time the culture of it has spread until it has become an important source of revenue in all the Mediterranean countries, and recently, also, in California. The trees, if well cared for, bear profusely and the fruit stands transportation well. Besides yielding a valuable essential oil, which is extracted from the rind, the lemon

Guava.

yields an acid juice which is wholesome, delicious as a flavoring agent, and an effectual preventive of scurvy. For this purpose it, or the juice of the lime, is always indispensable on shipboard. In England ships going to countries in which lemon or lime juice is not to be obtained are required by law to take with them a quantity large enough to furnish each of the crew with an ounce daily. The lime (*citrus limetta*), or wild lemon, is not extensively cultivated excepting in the island of Montserrat. The juice is valuable as an anti-scorbutic but is not ordinarily as highly valued for its flavor as lemon juice on account of the slightly musty odor, which invariably develops after it has been extracted for a few days.

The shaddock or grape-fruit, sometimes called sweet-ball, is another of the citron family. It is native to the Malaysian peninsula, possibly also to China, and derived its name from one Captain Shaddock, who first carried it from China into the West Indies. Both the tree and fruit are much larger than the orange, and the flavor, while delicate, is decidedly more acid. It is cultivated throughout the tropics, as well as in America and Europe. In the former country it is commonly known as grape-fruit, in England as shaddock.

According to an old Scandinavian legend the apple (*pyrus malus*) was early distinguished as the favorite food of the gods, who always ate of it whenever they found themselves growing infirm of either body or mind. When we remember that the apple so extraordinarily honored could have been nothing better than the little crab of northern Europe it seems appropriate to pay universal respect to the apple of to-day, with its glorious color, succulent texture, and truly delicious flavor. That it was one of the earliest fruits cultivated by the Romans, who seem to have attached great importance to all branches of horticulture, we know from the writings of Pliny, who mentions thirty varieties. Since that time nearly two thousand varieties have been produced, usually by means of grafting or cross fertilization.

The apple was early introduced into England, but the more delicate sorts, which were chiefly used for dessert apples, were little known until the reign of Henry VIII. By his gardeners large orchards were planted throughout all Kent, and pippins in particular became a frequent luxury at the royal table. Shakespeare frequently refers to the pippin, so called because raised from pips or seeds. Says Justice Shallow to Falstaff, "You shall see mine orchard, where, in an arbour, we will eat a last year's pippin of my own graffing."

Apples were brought to New England by the first settlers and were easily cultivated even on the barrenest land. To-day the fruit is cultivated all over our country, and the most insignificant farm is incomplete without its apple-orchard. The fruit may be had in excellent condition the year around as it does not lose flavor when transported or even after being stored for months. The tree bears fruit farther north than almost any other, although most prosperous in regions having long, hot summers. It may be roughly classified as of three varieties, dessert apples, cider apples, and those best adapted for cooking. The first kind, of which the pippin is a good example, must be fragrant, delicate of flavor, juicy, tender, and very digestible. Culinary apples are more acid, less digestible, and the flavor of which is developed only by the application of heat. Cider apples should be sweet and juicy, although inferior apples of all varieties are commonly used. As early as the reign of Charles I. large cider orchards were planted throughout England, and for a long time the manufacture of cider greatly interfered with the wine trade of France, a circumstance which in no measure displeased the English, who were for a century or so on none too friendly terms with their neighbors across the channel. Gerard describes a typical orchard, containing "so many trees of all sortes that the servants drink, for the most part, no other drink but that which is made of apples. The qualitie is such that, by the report of the gentleman himselfe, the parson hath for tythe many hogsheads of cyder."

The pear (*pyrus communis*) is closely related to the apple and, like it, is of ancient and distinguished lineage. Homer refers to the "pendent pear" in his description of the orchard and "squadron'd vineyards" of Laertes, father of Ulysses, and the fruit was in cultivation in Rome long before the time of Pliny. By the Romans the pear was carried to England, where it has always held high favor and the choicer varieties of which have customarily graced the royal tables. Pear cider or wine, called perry, has long been made in that land. Like the apple, the fruit is susceptible to great improvement under proper culture, although it is less hardy and does not stand transportation as well unless picked long before ripe. Our largest pears are grown in Washington and California, but lack

Fig.

the fine flavor of those grown in the middle and eastern states.

The quince is indigenous to Asia Minor, possibly to Greece, having been brought from the latter country to Rome. Both the Greeks and Romans cultivated it by grafting. Although related to the apple and pear, it is in many respects quite inferior, its toughness and astringency rendering it wholly unsuitable for a dessert fruit. But the fragrance and aromatic flavor, as well as the mucilaginous properties, are splendidly developed in cooking, while the toughness and indigestibility are greatly modified. It is principally used for marmalades, preserves and sauces, often in combination with apples. In recent years it has been greatly improved and a variety known as the orange quince is tender and of excellent flavor.

The grape (*vitis vinifera*) is the most important of all our berried fruits, owing both to its intrinsic value and to its great antiquity. Although native to some portion of Asia, its exact origin will probably never be traced. The Egyptians had a legend that Osiris taught men to cultivate the vine, a bit of divine helpfulness that among the early Greeks was attributed to Bacchus. Certain it is that the Greeks used wine long before Homer lived and sung, and since remotest of periods wine, pressed from grapes, has always been an appropriate offering to the deity among the Hebrews, and to the gods among all the polytheistic nations. From the scriptural statement that Noah planted a vineyard when he began to be a husbandman, it is evident that the grape was one of the earliest fruits cultivated.

In its dispersion throughout the various nations of the world the vine followed the same course as the other fruits, being first carried from Asia Minor into Greece, later into Rome, thence into the countries of northern Europe by the Roman conquerors, and later still to the new world. Vineyards were several times mentioned in the old Domesday Book, that record of all English estates, which was compiled under the direction of William the Conqueror. A wine trade which flourishes to-day was very early built up in France, as well as in Spain and Italy, where the finest vineyards were for a time cultivated by the monks. Within the last few years the wine industry of California has become important, although scarcely able to compete with the countries of Europe whose vineyards were first planted hundreds of years ago. Vineyards, once planted and well cultured, will last for centuries, as have many of those in France and along the Rhine, that river of legend, whose "clustering grapes hang about its temples as it reels onward in its triumphal march, like Bacchus, crowned and drunken."

There has been much speculation as to who first made wine, but the Germans have a legend which asserts it to have been of divine origin. "An angel, visiting the earth some time after the Deluge, found the patriarch Noah sitting at noon in the shadow of a fig-tree, very disconsolate. The angel inquired the cause of his grief. Noah replied that he was thirsty and had nothing to drink. 'Nothing to drink?' replied the angel. 'Look around. Do not the rains fall, and the rivers run, and is there not a spring of water bubbling up at the cottage door?' 'It is true,' replied Noah, smiting his breast, 'that there is an abundance of water in which thy servant can bathe; but, alas! when I think of the multitudes of strong men, of beautiful women, and of innocent children, and of the countless hosts of animals, that were drowned in the Flood, the idea of water becomes distasteful, and my lips refuse to drink.' 'There is reason in what thou sayest,' replied the angel, and spreading his wings, he flew up to heaven quick as the lightning-flash; and while the eyes of Noah were still dazzled with the brightness of his presence, he returned with stock of the vine, which he taught the grateful patriarch how to plant and tend, and how, when the fruit was ripe, to press it into wine."

The grape, while a favorite dessert fruit, is even more valuable in the raisin industry. Our best imported raisins are known as the Malaga, Valencia, and Muscatel, according to the locality in which produced. There are also the tiny

Pomegranate, Flower and Fruit. Sultana or seedless raisins and the Cor-inths or currants. Until the last twenty-five years the Mediterra-nean countries have had a monopoly of the raisin trade of both hemispheres, but since then have had a formidable rival in the growing industry in California. The same species of grape are grown as in Europe, the Malaga, Muscatel, known as the Muscat or Alexandria grape, the Sultana, Tokay, and many other varieties. Besides the use of intelligent and cleanly methods, the climate of California is a great factor in the production of raisins that are in no way inferior to the foreign product, for the grapes must always be dried in the sun, and there must be a minimum of dew at night that the drying process may not be checked. Experiments in dry-ing the grapes by artificial heat have always failed. The Sultana raisins of Europe are brought into the markets of Asia Minor on the backs of camels and are there repacked by the buyers before ship-ment. Raisins, like grapes, are considered to have a decidedly hygienic value, containing about one-half grape sugar besides potash and salts.

Our principal table berries are the currant and gooseberry, which belong to the saxifrages; the blackberry, mulberry, straw-

berry, and red and black raspberry, all of the rose family; the
elderberry, which is akin to the honeysuckle; and the cranberry
and huckleberry, which are heathworts. All are too familiar to
need an extended description. The currant, of which there are two
varieties, the red and black, is probably native to England. The
bush is nearly always to be found growing in the gardens of both
England and America, bearing fruit which is as luxurious as it is
cheap. Currants are chiefly used for jellies and pastries.

The gooseberry, like the currant, is native to moderately cold
climates and does not flourish well in countries much warmer than
England. Its numerous varieties have all been produced from two
main sorts, the prickly or hairy and the smooth skinned.

The blackberry, the fruit of the bramble, although very satisfactory in its wild state, is also extensively cultivated. It grows
abundantly in certain portions of England as well as America, in
fields and at the borders of woods, and its delicious fruit is each
year gathered by "berrying" parties.

The mulberry is the fruit of a tree which has been cultivated in
certain portions of Asia from time immemorial. It is several times
mentioned in the old Testament. In the sixteenth century it was
introduced into England and France. Although its aromatic fruits
are well worth cultivating, the tree is now generally utilized for
its leaves, which are necessary to the silk-worm industry.

The strawberry is primarily a plant of the temperate or colder
latitudes, and grows wild throughout northern Europe and portions
of North America. The fruit is peculiar in that it consists of the
fleshy torus or floral axis, greatly enlarged, and upon the surface of
which the tiny seeds lie imbedded. Cultivation has greatly enlarged
the succulent portion, at the same time improving the flavor, until
the strawberry has come to be considered one of our choicest dessert
fruits. It has long been grown in the gardens of England and is
mentioned by Holinshed in the "Chronicles," as well as by Shakespeare.

The raspberry, both the red and black varieties, is cultivated in
many gardens, although it is not a wholly satisfactory fruit as the
berries lose flavor so soon after ripening. The bush resembles that
of the currant in general size and appearance. According to one
writer the common name was given to it because of the roughness
of the fruit.

The elderberry is the deep purple fruit of a tall shrub which

grows wild in parts of America and Europe. It is never cultivated,
although the owners of land upon which the shrub flourishes, usually at the corners or edges of fields, prevent its destruction as far
as possible. Elderberry wine is occasionally used to adulterate the
more costly wines, such as port. The leaves and bark have a certain medicinal value, while the green fruit, preserved in brine, is
used for garnishing, like capers.

The cranberry has long been important commercially in parts
of North America, particularly in the Cape Cod region. It grows
upon low, moist soil, utilizing to great
profit hundreds of acres of marshy
land which would otherwise be almost
worthless. The berries ripen in the
autumn, and the picking continues until frosty weather. The berries, which
until cooked are tough, acid and
astringent, keep their flavor for weeks
if properly packed, and are shipped to
all portions of America, to the West
Indies, and to Europe.

The huckleberry, whortleberry or
blueberry, grows also at its best in and
about peat bogs and marshes in parts of
Scotland and America. It is but rarely
cultivated. Although hardy the fruit
does not stand transportation as well
as the cranberry.

Of the melons, which are immense,
hard-rinded berries, only two sorts are
commonly used as dessert fruits, the watermelon and the musk-
melon or cantaloupe. The latter is native to parts of central Asia
and was first introduced into Europe by the Romans. It is said
that the best melons in all the world grow in Persia, where they have
been cultivated for centuries. The fruit becomes in that climate
extremely succulent and sweet and some of our finest varieties have
been produced from seed brought directly from the Levant. The
best and most delicate variety is the canteloupe.

The watermelon is native to the warmer countries of the Orient,
to southern Europe, and to South America, although now cultivated
in all lands having long, hot summers, particularly our southern

Date Palm.

states. It is a specially cooling and gratifying fruit because of the quantities of deliciously flavored juice which it contains. The rhymer has well said of it:

> "The poet may sing of the Orient spices,
> Or Barbary's dates in their palmy array,
> But the huge, rosy melon in cold, juicy slices
> Is the Helicon font of a hot summer day."

What the cereals are to the inhabitants of the temperate regions the banana or plantain is to the natives of the tropics. Even the rudest of African tribes depend upon it so largely for food that they propagate it to the extent of cultivation. Although indigenous to Asia the banana is now nowhere to be found in a wholly wild state. It is an herbaceous plant (*musa sapientum*), related to the cinnamon, ginger and arrow-root, but which rises under favoring conditions to the dignity and height of a tree. After maturing its fruit, which it produces in immense clusters, the plant dies. The banana is enormously productive, more so to the acre than anything else in the entire range of food products. Humboldt has estimated that four thousand pounds of bananas may be produced from a space that could not be made to yield above thirty-three pounds of wheat or ninety-nine pounds of potatoes. Besides its productiveness, the fruit is so nourishing, being largely composed of starch and sugar, that its importance can hardly be overestimated. A patch of bananas only a few feet in extent will suffice to maintain a family in comfort. Bananas are commonly dried by the people of the tropics, when they somewhat resemble figs in both color and flavor, and are also preserved by immersion in a clear syrup. Banana meal, which is ground from the dried fruit, is even more valuable. It contains more than seventy per cent of starch.

The guava belongs to the myrtlebloom family, all the members of which are exotic trees or shrubs. It is now cultivated in nearly all of the lands to which it is indigenous, chiefly the East and West Indies, and Asia. The fruit of both the red and white varieties is sweet and aromatic, although, as it does not bear transportation, it is seldom seen upon our tables excepting in the form of a jelly or preserve.

The fig (*ficus carica*) is the fruit of a small tree native to the countries of Asia Minor and southern Europe, and is as remarkable in its nature as in its history. The pulpy fruit contains numberless seed-like pericarps, having developed directly from the tiny flower buds. These become fertile without putting forth petals after the

16

manner of other flowers, in fact, remaining almost wholly invisible.
The fig tree is mentioned in the sacred writings of the Hebrews as
well as in the earliest traditions of the Greeks. By the latter
people it was widely cultivated and later successfully transplanted
to their Italian colonies. We read in the statutes of Lycurgus
that flour, wine, figs, and cheese were to comprise the chief food
of all Spartan men who dined at the common tables. Equally with
the grape the fig was sacred to Bacchus, who was thought to have
derived from it alone his health and vigor.

The fig tree was planted in England early in the sixteenth century but, owing to the severity of the winters, it could never be depended upon to mature its fruit or even to remain in vigorous condition. Two, sometimes three, harvests of figs are gathered each
year in the Levant, the second crop or summer fig being dried for
export. It is now cultivated in the southern states and California.
The fruit, whether freshly plucked or dried, is very nutritious and
in parts of the Orient is often used as a substitute for bread. It
contains a large proportion of grape sugar.

Like the fig, the pomegranate was known to the early Hebrews
and was cultivated in the countries bordering on the Red Sea before any other fruit, excepting the grape, fig and olive. It was
used by the Jews in many of their religious ceremonies and also appears as an accessory in Greek mythology. You remember Persephone by eating half of the pomegranate which Pluto had given her
as an earnest of his love, condemned herself to spend half of each
year with him in his underground kingdom of Hades. The tree is
native to Persia, perhaps also to northern Africa, and is remarkable
alike for the stately beauty of its appearance, for its longevity, and
for its handsome flowers. The fruit is slightly acid, and is mild in
flavor.

The papaw (carica papaver) is native to tropical America. It
is curious in that the pistillate and staminate, or male and female,
flowers blossom on wholly different trees. The fruit, which is the
size of a small melon, is agreeable of flavor when at its best, but is
usually exported to foreign countries only after being pickled.

Of drupaceous or stony fruits the cherry, plum, peach, nectarine, and apricot are now grown in our temperate regions, although
not indigenous thereto, while the date, litchi, and mango are to be
found only in the tropics.

When Lucullus returned to Rome after his victory over Mithridates in the province of Pontus, he brought with him a cherry tree laden with fruit and with it adorned his triumph. "In less than one hundred and twenty years after," says Pliny, "other lands had cherries, even as far as Britain beyond the ocean." The small wild cherry, still to be seen in France, England, and the United States, is probably indigenous to those countries. In England, Henry VIII. was the first to cultivate the tree extensively and the fame of his Kentish cherry orchards spread all over Britain. There are now more than two hundred and fifty varieties. Certain sorts are mainly utilized for the manufacture of *liqueurs*, such as *kirschwasser*, *ratafia* and *maraschino*.

The plum is a native of Asia, and it is more than probable that the wild varieties which grow along the country lanes of England and America are simply degenerate specimens of the original, cultivated tree. It was introduced into England in the fifteenth century from France. The variety known as "green gage" takes its name from that of the English family that first cultivated it; the "damson," or damascene, is so called because, as the name would imply, it came originally from Damascus. Dried plums or prunes are almost as important an article of export from southern Europe as raisins. They are also exported from California.

The peach was first brought into Europe by the Romans, who found it growing wild in Persia. With characteristic zeal they soon transplanted it to most of the adjoining countries, where years of culture have

Mango.

developed it into an admirable fruit in every rsepect. Peach growing has within the last twenty years grown into an enormous industry in the United States, particularly in California, portions of Michigan, New Jersey, and Delaware. The two main sorts are the "cling-stone," in which the succulent portion clings to the stone, and the "free-stone," in which the parts readily separate. The nectarine is simply a smooth-skinned peach, very delicate in texture.

The apricot, while native to Armenia, has long grown wild in certain of the mountainous districts of Asia. It is an exceedingly choice fruit, ripening somewhat earlier than the peach, and is widely raised in China and Japan. In England it first found favor under the patronage of Henry VIII. This fruit, like the peach, pear, and plum, is especially adapted to the soil and climate of California and, canned or dried, is now to be found in all markets.

The date tree is the palm of the Hebrew scriptures, symbol of helpfulness and triumph, and, since times prehistoric, an object of peculiar veneration. Its habitat extends along the confines of the great, arid waste of the Sahara, from the Atlantic on the one hand to the boundaries of Persia on the other, utilizing that great intermediate region wherein no other vegetable foods will thrive. Here and in the oases no other vegetation greets the eye of the traveler excepting the unsympathetic cactus, and none better meets his requirements for food and for shelter from the sun. There is a South American legend that the entire human race sprang, like the soldiers from the dragon's teeth sowed by Kadmos, from the seeds of the date. Not a few of the Mohammedans of the Levant believe that the tree itself sprung spontaneously from the soil at the command of their prophet, and it is reverenced accordingly.

The date palm is slow of growth but lives to a great age, often two hundred years. The staminate and the pistillate, or fruiting, flowers are borne upon different trees and in the cultivated species the latter require to be fertilized artificially. This is accomplished by laborers who, after collecting the stamen-bearing flowers, climb the fruit-bearing trees and sprinkle the blossoms with pollen. In case this is not done the date crop is certain to fail.

Dates cannot be exported until dried, owing to their rapid fermentation when freshly plucked. Like raisins, they are dried in the sun. They are very nutritious, containing about six per cent of protein, twelve per cent of gum, and fifty per cent of sugar, and make an excellent substitute for bread. The fresh fruit, under pressure, yields a syrup; from the sap or juice of the tree a liquor is distilled, while the fibrous parts, as with all palms, are woven into mats, ropes, and cordage. Outside of the Orient, the tree is cultivated chiefly to supply branches or leaves for Palm Sunday and various church ceremonies. These, which are from five to twelve feet in length, are peculiarly graceful and lend themselves readily to decorative uses. Dates form the principal food of the people of Arabia and the date-raising countries of the East, and it is said that the first question asked by a Bedouin traveler is, "What is the price of dates at Mecca or Medina?"

The litchi tree is native to southern China, although occasionally to be seen in the hot houses of Europe. The fruit attains the size of a small peach and is sweet and mild in flavor. In drying, the tough, leathery coating separates from the pulp, at the center of which is a small stone. The dried fruit may be obtained at almost any large fruit store.

The mango is the fruit of a tall, tropical tree, native to Asia and Brazil. Although sour and acrid in the wild species, it becomes under culture sweet, succulent, and the size of a large plum. The ripe fruit is too perishable for export and is thus rarely seen in temperate regions excepting as a pickle or preserve. It is a valued ingredient of the sauce known as chutney.

> " The bread-tree, which, without the ploughshare, yields
> The unreap'd harvest of unfurrow'd fields,
> And bakes its unadulterated loaves
> Without a furnace in unpurchased groves,
> And flings off famine from its fertile breast,
> A priceless market for the gathering guest."

Thus wrote Byron, paying deserved tribute to what has been more than once styled "the most useful vegetable in the world." The tree is native to the islands of the southern Pacific and is even more indispensable to the inhabitants than is the date palm to the Mohammedan. The fruit, which is about the size of a melon, is most curiously formed from the pulpy carpels of the female flowers, and is composed almost wholly of starch. When slowly roasted it is a nourishing and delicious substitute for bread, whence its name. It is cut into slices and dried in the sun, and is also made into a flour. The tree, of which there are two main varieties, those bearing seeds and those in which the seeds are abortive, remains productive during eight months of the year. To tide themselves over the remaining four the natives make and store away a sort of paste from the fruit, called *mahe*, which is allowed to ferment before being eaten.

The value of the bread fruit was first made known to the western world by Captain Cook and his fellow explorers, many of whom were scientific men. They believed that the tree could be transplanted with success to certain of the British colonies, and at length a ship was fitted out under royal patronage for that purpose. Lieutenant Bligh (who had formerly accompanied Captain Cook) was placed in command, and the good ship *Bounty* sailed for Otaheite. After much delay, owing to contrary winds, they reached the island in October, 1788, closing a voyage of eleven months. The following spring they started for home with more than a thousand live plants. When three weeks out from land a mutiny occurred, and Lieutenant Bligh, with eighteen of his adherents, was sent adrift in a small boat. The plucky men had only a little food and a few instruments of navigation but they managed to reach one of the friendly Dutch islands, from which they at length returned to England. In 1792 a second expedition was fitted out under Bligh, the work was attempted with renewed courage, and, eighteen months later, several hundred bread fruit trees were left at St. Vincent and other of the West Indies. But, in spite of all care, the plants were not readily acclimatized, and it is not probable that the bread fruit will ever be seen in other than the tropical countries excepting as a hot-house curiosity.

The tamarind is the pod of a leguminous tree, grown in and probably native to both the East and West Indies. The fruit is hard-rinded but composed of a succulent, acid pulp, so grateful and refreshing that

" Whoso drank of the cooling draught,
He would not wish for wine."

In the pineapple the whole inflorescence becomes pulpy, continuous, and solidified into a single large fruit. The plant is indigenous to the tropics of the western hemisphere, and the fruit was first brought into England during the reign of Charles II., probably from Holland, where it was introduced somewhat earlier. It is now a common hot-house product in England, although it was not thus cultivated until the beginning of the eighteenth century. In America, hot-house culture is wholly unnecessary as the fruit is so abundantly grown in Florida as well as in the West Indies that its transportation is easy and inexpensive.

Bread Fruit.

Other and less important fruits are: the medlar, which is grown to a small extent in parts of England and Europe; the jaca or jak, a sort of inferior bread fruit; the prickly pear or Indian fig, the fruit of a species of cactus; the alligator pear, sweet sop, sour sop, custard apple, and mammee apple, all luscious, pulpy fruits native to the East and West Indies; the persimmon or date plum, common to the south of both America and Europe; monkey's bread, a fleshy, acid fruit found upon the western coast of Africa; and the durian of the Malayan peninsula and adjacent islands, a fruit the size of the shaddock and which contains a cream-like, nourishing pulp. That the number of tropical fruits is legion is proven by the fact that at the Columbian Exposition the little country of Siam exhibited something like one hundred and fifty varieties. Nearly all were preserved in a transparent syrup, many of them having been carved by the marvelously patient little Siamese women into intricate semblances of flowers. Our various and familiar fruits of the melon family, the pumpkin and squash, are universally prepared and eaten as vegetables. This is also the case with egg-plant, which belongs to the nightshade family and is closely allied to the common potato. The olive, so universally is it utilized as a condiment or for the oil contained, is mentioned as one of our fruits simply from a botanical standpoint.

Nuts differ from the other fruits both in appearance and in nutritive value. The succulent fruits contain quantities of water, very little protein, valuable salts, almost no fats, and varying quantities of starch and sugar. The nuts, on the other hand, contain quantities of nutriment in a highly concentrated form, and are composed chiefly of the oils and proteids, with very little of water or of the carbohydrates.

One of the commonest as well as one of the most ancient of nuts is the acorn. Both the oak and its unattractive fruit were ages ago utilized by the primitive Greeks, and were at a correspondingly early date sacred to the Druidical worship of Britain and Wales. Since the time of the early Britons acorns have been used for fattening swine and have rarely found favor as human food excepting in times of famine. Then, however, they have taken the place of bread and meat very satisfactorily. Froebel, the originator of the kindergarten system of education, was more than once compelled to send his little band of pupils into the woods to gather acorns with which to piece out the all too scanty dinner.

Chestnuts, both the large and small varieties, are considered quite a luxurious food by the peasants in the south of France and in the Mediterranean islands, particularly when freshly roasted. They are more farinaceous and less oily than nuts in general, and from them is made a cheap and nourishing flour. The tree is native to Europe, possibly also to America.

The walnut is a hard-shelled, drupaceous fruit, native to Asia Minor and Greece, but now cultivated in all temperate regions. The butternut, which is closely related, is somewhat more oleaginous. The hickory nut, also of the same family, is native to North America, from whence the nuts are exported to the European countries. The pecan is a species of hickory, to which it is much superior in flavor and texture. It is grown in the southern portion of the United States and in Texas. Beechnuts possess an agreeable flavor but are rarely, if ever, eaten as dessert nuts owing to their small size. They are not easily procurable excepting in country places.

The hazel grows wild in America, in England, northern Europe, and Asia. The filbert is a variety of hazel cultivated specially for the table and is much larger and richer of flavor. The word filbert is a corruption of the word "full-beard," the name first applied to distinguish the cultivated from the common wild species, although the poet Gower tells us that

> " Phillis
> Was shape into a nutte-tree,
> That all men it might see;
> And after Phillis, *Philberd*
> This tree was cleped."

The almond, a favorite table and pastry nut, belongs to the peach family. It is frequently referred to in the Bible and branches of almond blossoms are still used in certain Jewish religious ceremonies. Only the sweet almond is used as a dessert nut, although oil is extracted from both sweet and bitter. The sweet variety is now grown in California, as well as in the Mediterranean countries. The tree is indigenous to northern Africa, to portions of Europe, and to Asia Minor.

It has been said that "the most precious inheritance of the Singhalese is his ancestral garden of cocoanuts," the fruit of the cocoa palm and an important article of food in almost every portion of the tropics. The nuts, which grow in large clusters, are each enclosed in a thick coating of tough, elastic fibre, which, owing to its bulk, is usually taken off before the nuts are packed for shipment. The nucleus or kernel, which is white and meaty in consistency, is hollow, enclosing a quantity of delicate, milky liquid. When green the whole nucleus is soft, pulpy, and very digestible. During the ripening process the meat becomes toughened, owing to the development of the cellulose, and on that account the ripened meat is often cooked, with rice, by the people of the warmer countries. In Europe and America the nut is mainly used, after being grated or shredded, in the making of sweetmeats, puddings and cakes.

It is unnecessary to say that the meat, when dried and shredded, should contain the entire oil of the nut, but in not a few instances it is extracted and paraffine or glycerine is added to give it the proper "finish."

For many years the Dutch have carried on an immense trade with the Samoan Islands in the dried nut, called "copra." This is shipped to Holland, where the oil is expressed. In Ceylon, after the oil is extracted, the residue, called "poonac," is pressed into cakes. This poonac is similar to the oil cakes made in America from the oil of the linseed or cotton seed, and is equally valued as an animal food.

The Brazil nut is, as its name indicates, native to portions of South America, where it is commonly known as the "juvia." The tree, whose seeds form so important an article of commerce, grows from one hundred to one hundred and thirty feet in height, and its fruit consists of a hard shell, about the size of a child's head, enclosing from eighteen to twenty-four triangular seeds. These are particularly fine and creamy in texture and are rich in oil, but are liable to deteriorate in flavor if kept too long. The large nuts fall from the tree when ripe, but without releasing the seeds, and are then gathered by the natives, who break them open. Humboldt relates that the natives dare not go into the woods during the season when the nuts are ripe and falling without protecting the head and shoulders with a buckler of wood, owing to the great size of the nuts and the height from which they fall.

Tamarind.

The peanut has already been referred to in the chapter on vegetable oils. It furnishes nourishment in a concentrated and available form, and is no less valuable for the oil contained than for the flour or meal into which it may be converted.

Other nuts of less importance to the peoples of temperate regions are: the bread nut of Jamaica; the Pekea nut of tropical America; the kola nut of Africa, which possesses the properties of a stimulating food; the cashew nut, which is utilized mainly for its flavor; and the Souari nut of British Guiana. The latter is large, sweet and delicate, resembling an almond in flavor. The edible seeds of several species of pine are also eaten. The pistachio nut has already been mentioned as a flavoring agent. The sapucaya nut of Brazil resembles both the Brazil nut and the almond in its properties. The peculiarly shaped receptacles which contain the nuts are called by the natives "monkey pots" because the monkeys are known to be extravagantly fond of the seeds. The candle-nut of the South Sea islands is rarely used excepting as a condiment.

There has been so much discussion recently concerning a "natural food" system of diet and it has been so strenuously advocated by certain followers both in England and America, that it may be well to speak of it here. Its exponents lay great stress upon the assumption that it is, to quote their own words, "a natural diet or non-starch system." The following is quoted from the official statement of the principles of the Natural Food Society: "The Natural Food Society is founded in the belief that the food of primeval man consisted of the fruit and nuts of tropical climes, spontaneously produced; that on these foods man was (and may again become) at least as free from disease as the animals are in a state of nature. We urge that all fruits in their season, including figs, dates, bananas, prunes, raisins, and apples, fresh and dried, each of many varieties, be substituted for bread and other grain foods and starch vegetables; and experience convinces us that this course will be found by a brief experience highly beneficial, alike to to the meat eater and the vegetarian. . . . All persons about to experiment with the non-starch food system are at first urged not to use nuts, but to use instead whatever animal food they have been accustomed to. The central feature of this system consists in abstention from bread, cereals, and starchy vegetables, and the liberal use of food fruits." These theorists also claim that "the cereals and vegetables are unnatural and disease-producing foods, and the chief cause of nervous prostration and broken-down health," and assert, equally without any scientific proof, that a diet containing starchy foods "ruins the blood vessels [in what way they do not state], irritates and inflames the system, and makes men prematurely old."

The fruits most urgently advocated are figs, dates, raisins, prunes and bananas. Yet these very bananas are composed almost wholly of starch, and figs, dates and raisins of sugar, which is dietetically almost the same thing. In fact, all starch is converted into glucose, either within or without the system, before assimilation can take place. Banana meal and chestnut flour are constantly used in all their recipes, although, from a non-starch standpoint, why they are not just as unwholesome as wheaten flour it is difficult to understand.

In cases in which the fruitarians find it difficult or impossible to digest the required quantity of nuts, milk, eggs and meat are substituted, their principles in the latter regard differing from those of the vegetarians.

But, supposing the non-starch theory to be perfectly scientific; supposing that none of the fruits contained starch or sugar, such a dietary would be wholly inadequate to the needs of the system. The nuts furnish enough of the proteids to build up the tissues of the human system but without the starchy foods how can it do its work? A parallel case would be that of keeping an engine in perfect repair but furnishing it with too little fuel. A very useless machine would be the result. Fortunately for the health of the non-starch enthusiasts, their theory is not only unscientific but impractical. But it is worthy of attention because of the increasing numbers who follow it wholly or in part. I have in mind one family the members of which have continued this diet with almost absolute strictness for more than two years. All have maintained average or good health, which alone is sufficient proof that the diet meets the practical, working necessities of the human system, providing, of course, that the digestion is equal to the strain of assimilating quantities of nuts. The fruitarian doctrinists are doing good service in calling our attention to the value of nuts as a staple food, to be properly eaten, not as a dessert after a hearty meal but in the place of meats and other articles rich in protein. But the name "non-starch" system is entirely misleading, and the theory will never command respect until put, somehow, upon a scientific basis.

Filberts.

At the Columbian Exposition the tropical fruits, all of which were preserved in some manner owing to the difficulty of transporting them in a fresh state, were displayed in the Agricultural building, while fresh fruits of both the temperate and sub-tropical regions were placed in the state buildings and in the pomological section of the Horticultural building. Siam, Johore, the states of South America, the islands of both the East and West Indies, particularly Jamaica and Trinidad, exhibited among other fruits, preserved bananas and banana meal and flour. Algeria and Uruguay each sent preserved fruits, among the finest being preserved whole figs and bananas from the latter country. The French Colonies sent preserves and native nuts; the Orange Free State, jellies, dried fruits, and marmalades; guava jelly and various preserved fruits entered the lists from Porto Rico and our own Florida. Mexico was represented by dried and canned fruits but chiefly by *liqueurs*, some of which were distilled from the cherry, orange, quince and cocoanut. Costa Rica, Tunis and British Guiana each sent a large quota of their native nuts and fruits, among them the mammee apple, mango, guava, lime, pomegranate, banana, papaw, fig, date, pineapple, olive, and tamarind, the cocoanut, almond, pistache, Souari and cashew nuts.

A most remarkable exhibit of the entire citrus family of fruits was placed in the Horticultural building by southern California. There were the Malta, mandarin, navel and seedless varieties of oranges, Sicily and Lisbon lemons, the citron, and many varieties of grape fruits and limes. On the Midway Plaisance a large space was devoted to the exhibit of the growing fruits, among them another citrus exhibit from California. Apples, pears, quinces, and grapes were exhibited in abundance, not the least noteworthy being a display sent from Washington. The exhibit of apples was particularly large and represented nearly all of our states. To the visitor who believed that apples could be grown only in Michigan, Ohio, New York and a few of our northern states the splendid specimens sent from Arkansas, from Missouri and from the Northwest were a continual surprise. Nearly all countries exhibited preserves and marmalades while the finest of jellies, in most lavish array, were sent from the canning factories and home kitchens of our own states. Nothing is more delicate than a crystalline, quivering, fruit jelly, and nothing more surely tests the skill of the housewife. It is made possible through the existence of a vegetable jelly or pectin, which is one of the carbohydrates and an almost universal constituent of our fruits.

CHAPTER XXV.

SUGARS AND STARCHES.

U G A R S; starches, gums, and celluloses comprise the principal carbohydrates. Of these the only ones of special nutritive value are the sugars and starches, both closely allied chemically and having much the same effect upon the human system. They are the non-nitrogenous elements, furnishing heat for warming the body as well as potential energy for doing its daily work. If more of the carbohydrates are taken into the system than are required for its daily uses they are transformed into fat and are thus stored away to be drawn upon when necessity arises. This fat is accumulated in the liver as well as distributed throughout and upon the muscular tissues. The carbohydrates thus, either directly or indirectly, preserve the muscular tissues of the body from waste.

Scarcely any other food substance is more universal throughout the vegetable world than sugar. Like starch, it is composed of carbon atoms mingled with a varying proportion of hydrogen and oxygen atoms, hence the name, carbohydrates. But, unlike the starches, sugar is one of the most easily assimilated of foods, owing to its extreme solubility. From childhood to old age its use by man is universal, in spite of the "decayed teeth" bugaboo held up to children and the rheumatism threat that assails their elders. As a constituent of mother's milk it is consumed by the tiniest babe. A liking for sweets in some form extends even into the animal kingdom, although whether it is not often a cultivated taste in that realm is a mooted question. The bird loves it, the dog eats it greedily, the horse neighs and teases for it, even the little green chameleon accepts it in lieu of a spider; it is the nectar of our butterflies and the food of our bees, the latter rendering it back to us in doubly distilled sweetness and value. Sugar in some form is as wholly indispensable in the dietaries of this animate world as any other food substance could well become.

The word sugar refers in ordinary speech simply to cane sugar, or at least to some member of the sucroses or cane-sugar group. This is inaccurate, owing to the diverse sources of sugars, not all varieties of which are used as food, but which may still be roughly divided into the cane-sugar and the glucose groups.

The cane-sugar group comprises the sugar cane, the sugar maple, that which may be extracted from the root of the beet, carrot, turnip, and, in fact, of nearly all vegetables, of sorghum or Chinese cane, the young shoots of maize, chestnut buds, the melon and pumpkin, several species of palm, and the juices of tropical fruits, such as the papaw and banana. Melitose is a variety of cane sugar extracted from cotton seeds and from a species of Australian eucalyptus; glycyrrhizine, the sugar of the liquorice root; mycose, a saccharine constituent of the edible fungi; melizitose, a cane sugar found in the manna of the larch; lactose, sugar of milk; and maltose, a crystalline sugar produced from starch by the action of diastase of malt. This diastase is the ferment produced by the germination of the grain of the barley.

The principal glucose sugars are dextrose or grape sugar, and levulose or fruit sugar. Glucose is also largely manufactured from starch, when it is known also as starch sugar. Glucose may be divided into its constituent parts, when the granular portion is known commercially as grape sugar and the fluid or syrup as glucose. Honey, which contains both cane sugar and glucose, possesses characteristics peculiar to itself. Mannite is still another kind and is found in the manna ash, in celery, in onions, certain sea-weeds, and fungi, in the sap from apple and pear trees, and even in the nests and cocoons of a species of Syrian beetle (trehalose). The sugar extractable from the berries of the rowan or mountain ash tree is known chemically as sorbin; that from acorns as quercite; that from a species of pine, pinite. Muscle-sugar or inosite is present in the tissues of the human system, particularly in the muscles of the heart and lungs. Saccharine, a chemical constituent of one of the coal-tar products, is the only artificial sweet ever yet produced.

Only a small proportion of these sugars are used for food, a few being considered unfit or at least undesirable, owing to their origin, while others are not procurable because the extraction of them them would be unprofitable from a commercial point of view.

Those in common use are cane, maple, and beet root sugar, glucose or grape sugar, honey, palm sugar, and sorghum. Of all these honey is the most luxurious, the most precious, and of far the greatest antiquity. In fact, until the beginning of the sixteenth century it was almost the only sweet known and quite the only one generally used, perhaps due to the fact that it could be used for food without going through a more or less elaborate process of preparation. In the old Testament Palestine is referred to as "a land flowing with milk and honey," the greatest boon of richness and nourishment that could be desired. To this day the inhabitants of India, of Arabia, and other parts of Asia combine both honey and milk into a semi-liquid food, than which nothing more acceptable can be offered to either guest or traveler. The ancient Greeks immortalized in their literature the honey of Hymettus and Corinth, although the bees of classic lore, no wiser than those of to-day, occasionally selected their honey from the nectaries of poisonous flowers. Xenophon relates that once a number of soldiers who were encamped in a village near Trebezona, in which there were beehives, became violently ill after eating of the honey combs. "Not one of them could stand erect. Those who had swallowed but little looked very like drunken men; those who had eaten much were like mad men, and some lay as if they were dying. And thus they lay in such numbers as on a field of battle after defeat. And the consternation was great. Yet no one was found to have died; all recovered their senses about the same hour the following day, and on the third or fourth day they rose up as if they had suffered from the drinking of poison." The Romans used honey as an ingredient of their beverages, a custom which continued throughout most of Europe even beyond those fifteenth century days of "piment" and "mead." The national cake of Holland, called "deventer," is made from a mixture of honey, fruit, and flour.

Honey is the only sweet that comes to our tables in its pure and natural form, neither added to nor subtracted from by any chem-

ical process whatever. Whether the nectar itself, after being taken
from the flower, undergoes any change in the vital laboratory of the
bee is as yet an unsettled question. In composition it contains
both dextrose and levulose, mannite, small quantities of cane sugar,
wax, mucilage, mineral matter, and pollen. It varies in color and
flavor according to the sources from which gathered, the best of the
United States coming from the white clover and the flowers of the
bass-wood (the linden tree). That from buckwheat blossoms is
darker and less delicately flavored.
The honey from the vale of Chamou-
ni is noted for its good color and
fragrance; that from Hymettus,
Greece, gathered from the wild
thyme, has a somewhat coarse flavor,
by no means as ambrosial as the product of the average American honey
farm.

The sugar cane (*saccharum offici-
narum*) is a tall, strong-stemmed
grass, growing to a height of ten or
twelve feet and crowned with long,
feathery plumes of flowers. It has
been cultivated in both India and
China for probably two thousand
years, and the art of extracting and
boiling down the juice from the cane
was practiced in both countries as
early as the seventh century. Dios-
corides referred to it in the first century, and Alexander the Great mentioned a kind of honey made from a
sweet-stemmed Indian reed, undoubtedly meaning the cane. The Arabs

Sugar Cane.

brought the knowledge of this cane to the Spaniards who in their
turn carried it to the West Indies. From there it was introduced
into the United States and was first cultivated about 1751 by a band
of Jesuits, located near New Orléans. The first sugar mill, a crude
and inadequate affair in which all the power was supplied by cattle,
was erected in 1758. Sixty years later the production in Louisiana
alone reached twenty-five thousand hogsheads annually, an enor-

mous output considering the fact that steam was not used in the mills until 1822. While the sugar industry has since reached almost fabulous proportions, at no time has the supply appreciably exceeded the demand. From being considered a luxury, as was the case in Europe during the fifteenth and sixteenth centuries, sugar has come to be an indispensable and therefore common food.

Not more than four varieties of cane are now cultivated in the West Indies, the quality of each depending mainly upon soil, climate, and methods of culture. The Sandwich Islands also produce quantities of sugar. Cane juice contains, on an average, eighteen per cent of sugar, more than seventy per cent of water, small quantities of pectin or vegetable jelly, of albumin, and of mineral matters. Says Johnston, referring to the almost universal habit among the natives of eating the raw cane, "the nutritive property of the raw juice is due to the fact that it contains, besides the sugar, a considerable portion of gluten as well as mineral substances, which are present in all our staple forms of vegetable foods."

The process of making our granulated sugar is comparatively simple. The juice is first expressed from the cane by crushing the stalks between a series of heavy rollers, when it is clarified and boiled down to the required density in large copper pans. As the syrup granulates it is removed from the fire and, after cooling, the fluid part is drained away from the crystals. This raw sugar, called *muscovado* (from a Spanish word meaning "more finished") is then sent to the sugar refiners. It is scarcely ever found in the markets now, owing to the universal demand for a white, absolutely refined, granulated sugar. The process of refining sugar by claying was first used in Brazil. It is related that it was discovered by the agency of a hen which, with shockingly muddy feet, one day walked over a pot of sugar. The crystals that were touched by the clay were seen to be much whiter than the bulk of the sugar and a discovery of considerable importance was the result. The finest flavored cane sugar consists of the golden brown crystals that are manufactured in British Guiana and much used in England. The high tariff imposed on that quality has thus far effectually debarred it from America.

In 1747 Margraaf, a German, discovered in the course of his experiments that the sugar extracted from the root of the beet was identical with that of the sugar cane. He advised its cultivation for the extraction of sugar but no attempt in this direction was

17

made until nearly a half century afterward. Then, owing to the
crude methods used, a yield of only two or three per cent of sugar
was obtained and the attempt was abandoned. Finally, under
Napoleon I., the price of sugar advanced to six francs a pound. A
prize of a million francs was then offered to any one who should
successfully manufacture sugar from plants of home growth. After
many trials it was found possible to obtain from four to five per
cent of refined sugar from the beet, and success was assured. From
France the cultivation of the sugar beet extended into Germany,
Poland, and Russia, the latter country producing to-day vast quantities of our best sugar. The Marinski sugar manufactory on the
banks of the river Dnieper is one of the largest in the world.

Not long after the Civil War the industry was introduced into
the United States. The result, while in no way reaching the limit
of its possibilities, has more than justified every effort made by its
promoters. At present the area devoted to sugar beet raising in
the United States is claimed to be larger than that so utilized in
any other country. The crop is a profitable one, for, besides yielding an income of forty dollars per acre, the farmer may receive
back if he wishes, at a merely nominal price, fully fifty per cent of
his original amount of beets in the residuum pulp. This is what remains after the juice has been extracted and is valuable both as a
cattle food and as a fertilizer. To be sure, beets require skillful
cultivation and must be denied neither labor nor expense if a good
crop is to be secured. But, even at a cost of several dollars per
acre for cultivating, the crop is still more profitable than either
wheat or corn. The percentage of sugar in the beet of our western
prairies, particularly in Nebraska, has been as high as twelve per
cent, and fifteen, it is believed, will be yielded in the near future.
The largest factory is the Oxnard in Nebraska.

The extraction of beet sugar from the crude root is a much
more complicated process than the extraction of the juice from the
sugar cane, because the juice abounds in impurities. It contains
gummy matters, albumin, acids, and minerals. The juice is extracted both by pressure and by diffusion, and both lime and charcoal
filters are employed. The refining process, which is carried on in
large refineries, is identical with that used with the raw sugar of
the cane, the chemical properties of both being identical. Thus far
it has been impossible to produce a good syrup from beet juice.

The maple sugar industry is almost exclusively confined to the

United States and Canada. It is a cane sugar, produced by boiling down the sap from the maple tree (*acer saccharinum*), the sap being collected by tapping or boring the bark of the tree just before the buds start in the spring. The ideal sugar weather alternates warm days with frosty nights. The length of the season is always uncertain, for a few days of warmth will suffice to start the buds and foliage, after which the yield of sap is inferior in quality. The sap needs no purification and is prepared directly for the market by a simple boiling down process, conducted over large fires near the "camp" in the woods. The sap is reduced, either by boiling in kettles or evaporating in pans, to a thick molasses, delicious of flavor, or to a sugar which is solidified in cakes of various sizes. The principal states which manufacture maple sugar are Vermont, New Hampshire, Michigan, Ohio, and Pennsylvania.

Sorghum is a sweet extracted from the stem of the Guinea corn or great millet (*sorghum saccharatum*). It has long been cultivated in China and India, but the molasses is so inferior in flavor to the cane sugar of Europe and America that it has never found much favor in those lands. The process of extracting is similar to that used for the juice of the sugar cane, and generally the whole product is converted into a thick molasses. The plant yields about two and one-half per cent of flesh-forming and about eleven per cent of heat-producing material.

Sugar Beet.

Palm sugar is the inspissated juice of the palm tree, principally the wild date, although the cocoanut and several other varieties are also used. The sap or "toddy" is collected from the tree during the three winter months of November, December and January, and is boiled down by a crude native process into an unrefined sugar known as "jaggery." When refined it is equal to the best cane sugar. It is rarely met with even in the European markets, although occasionally imported into America by sugar refining companies.

The making of starch sugar, known commercially as glucose or grape sugar, is one of our most important and least appreciated industries. In Europe potato starch is generally employed, in America that from Indian corn or maize. The process of converting the starch into sugar is comparatively simple and open to no objections on the score of either cleanliness or health. It is first made soluble by the action of dilute sulphuric acid; the acid is neutralized by lime and is precipitated as sulphate of lime. This is separated from the liquid by filtration, the liquid is then filtered through a bed of charcoal and concentrated to the required density. This process gives us the glucose of the trade world. Although called grape sugar, this is not the purest form of grape sugar, the best example of which is found in the white, granular exudations of sugar from the surface of well dried grapes or raisins.

Starch sugar is produced much more cheaply than any other, for, while our sugar plants yield from four to fifteen per cent of their bulk in refined sugar, starch yields fifty per cent. Then, too, the sugar plants require a maximum of labor and expense if their cultivation is to be successful. But glucose has not found favor in our households because its sweetening properties are so inferior to those of our cane sugars and, since it has always posed as an adulterant, it has fallen into disrepute. Its good consistency and its non-committal flavor have caused it to be used extensively in adulterating honey, syrups, and candies. In some apiaries even the unsuspecting bees are fed upon it, as a cheap and convenient substitute for flowers. Besides this it is used in the manufacture of liquors.

The Japanese, who realize better than the western nations the value of glucose as a food, have long manufactured it from the starch of barley, and have given it the attractive name of barley honey. It forms part of the daily food in every Japanese household. Combined with rice flour it makes a sweetmeat far more healthful and delicious than most of our confectionery. Glucose itself is not only wholesome and nutritious but even more easily assimilated than the cane sugars, which are, in fact, themselves changed into glucose by the dilute acids of the human system before they are digested. It is to be regretted that glucose does not appear upon our tables, perhaps under the more attractive name of maize, wheat, or cassava honey, that its usefulness as an adulterant might be forgotten on account of its value as a food. There are two obstacles in the way of this use, one, the fact of its heavy, syrupy consistency, and the other, because of its low sweetening power. The chemist tells us that glucose contains one molecule more of water than cane sugar and, until that is extracted, which at present chemistry is unable to accomplish, it is impossible to convert it into sugar. The other objection may be more easily met because of the comparatively recent discovery of a substance known as saccharine. This was produced by a German chemist, Fahlberg, from coal-tar naphtha, and is the only artificial sweet ever yet produced. Its sweetening properties are remarkable. One part in one thousand parts of water will produce a distinctly sweet taste while one or two parts added to one thousand parts of glucose will render it as sweet as the cane sugars. Saccharine itself is two hundred and thirty times as sweet as cane sugar. Its use, however, is not to be advocated, as it is not assimilated, passing from the system unchanged. It thus in no way contributes to the building up or the maintaining of the tissues of the body, hence, it is a questionable article of food.

There were immense displays of cane sugar at the Columbian Exposition, the most important being from Russia, Italy, Mexico, and the United States. British Guiana sent quantities of pure, amber-colored crystals, guiltless of any bleaching process and unrobbed of their delicate and characteristic flavor. Hundreds of gallons of delicious maple syrup paid their tribute to Canada and to our own maple sugar producing states. Palm sugar was sent in a crude state from Ceylon. Florida exhibited glucose made from the root of the cassava, and Mexico sent a similar glucose from the agave or century plant. This, known as agave honey, was neither as delicate nor as clear as starch sugar, probably owing to the crude method of making it. Saccharine was exhibited in powders and in small tablets, particularly recommended for sweetening tea and coffee, as well as jams and jellies. This is, properly speaking, no more than an adulterant. Honey, tons of sweetness, was exhibited from our different states and from other countries as well. From Hymettus, Greece, was sent honey made from the flowers of the wild thyme, but not even its classic name could save it from criticism, for it was dark in color, strong in flavor, and not unlike our poorer grades of buckwheat honey. Holland sent quantities of their national honey cake.

Sago Mortar.

Starch is quite extensively distributed throughout the vegetable kingdom. It is present in nearly all tubers, in the cereals and legumes, in the trunks of various species of palm, and in many of the fruits and nuts, the bread fruit, banana, peanut, chestnut, and others. It exists in the form of minute granules and is always most abundant as the plant reaches maturity. These granules may be separated in most cases by a simple mechanical process.

The principal starches of our commerce are obtained from potatoes, wheat, corn, rice, the root of the cassava, the arrowroot, and from the stem or trunk of the sago palm. In Europe potatoes are most largely employed. After being thoroughly cleaned they are reduced to a pulp and the cellulose and albuminoids are separated by washing, leaving the starch granules to settle to the bottom of the vat, whence they are easily drawn off and dried. The extraction of the starch from wheat is a more difficult matter, owing to the presence of gluten, which serves to bind the constituents of the grain. It may be procured by a series of washings but is usually accomplished by a fermentative process which, through the action of the acids developed, destroys the tenacious properties of the gluten. Maize or Indian corn, mainly utilized for starch in America, contains so little gluten that the separation of the starch contained is a comparatively easy matter. That, combined with the low price of the grain, renders corn starch one of our cheapest cereal preparations. Rice starch is more commonly used in the Orient than among the western nations and is procured by both methods.

The various tubers, cereals, and starch-bearing fruits have already been described, as well as the cassava, from the root of which the tapioca of commerce is prepared. Of even greater importance, particularly in its native lands, is the starch of the sago palm, known to the trade world as sago. The entire trunk of this palm is filled with a nourishing starch which is in greatest abundance just before the palm puts forth its blossoms. In case it is not taken at this stage the sago is absorbed as nourishment for the fruit, and the trunk becomes almost empty and quite useless. The trees do not blossom until their growth, requiring twelve or fifteen years, is completed and are thus of considerable size when cut down. The center of the trunk is of a cheesy consistency and the starch or sago, after being scraped out in its crude form, is separated from its fibrous constituents by a crushing or grating process, followed by a series of washings. A section of the trunk of a sago palm containing the crude sago, and showing but a thin outer bark, was sent to the Columbian Exposition from Siam. There were also exhibited the crude metal rasps used for scraping it from the trunk and a mortar for crushing, fashioned from a hollowed section of the trunk itself.

Mr. Crawford, in his history of the Indian Archipelago, has estimated that a single acre of land, supporting four hundred and thirty-five palms, will produce 120,500 pounds of sago. This is not incredible when a single, thrifty, fully grown tree may yield six or seven hundred pounds. Excepting the banana, it is probably true that no other plant or vegetable is capable of yielding so great an amount of nourishment for man from a given extent of land. In certain parts of the East sago forms almost the exclusive food of the native peoples.

INDEX.

INDEX.

Wheat, 149-152.
Whelk, 75.
Whitebait, 64.
Whortleberry, 226.
Worcestershire sauce, 102.

YAM, 198.
Yarmouth bloater, 64.
Yeast, 113, 167.

ZEA MAYS, 152.